Opera as Dramatic Poetry

Opera as Dramatic Poetry

Wallace Dace

VANTAGE PRESS
New York

FIRST EDITION

Copyright © 1993 by Wallace Dace

Published by Vantage Press, Inc.
516 West 34th Street, New York, New York 10001

Manufactured in the United States of America
ISBN: 0-533-10413-0

Library of Congress Catalog Card No.: 92-93869

0 9 8 7 6 5 4 3 2 1

Contents

Acknowledgments

I am most grateful to Rodney Milnes, editor of *Opera*, for allowing me to reprint much of my article 'Toward a definition of opera' from Volume 40 (1989), pages 934–6.

Also, I am indebted to Lawrence Schoenberg, the composer's son, for permission to quote extensively from his father's unpublished play, *Der biblische Weg*.

Further, I am beholden to Barbara Hering, *Dramaturgin* at the Deutsche Oper Berlin, for many kindnesses and courtesies over the years.

Copyright ownership of quoted materials is acknowledged in the notes at the end of each chapter.

And I must acknowledge the patient and indulgent help afforded me by Carola Dietlmeier, Karen Steinmetz and Anneliese Snyder in the preparation of my translations from German-language sources.

Introduction

It is said that Brahms so admired Bizet's opera, *Carmen*, that he slept with a copy of the piano score under his pillow in the hope that nocturnal inspiration might enable him to write an opera himself someday. Alas, the inspiration never came. Nor did it to Gustav Mahler, who was asked once, after conducting many operas, both in Hamburg and Vienna, why he didn't write an opera himself, and replied that he left that kind of thing to his friend Richard Strauss. Mendelssohn, too, was attracted to the art of the opera and even signed a contract with a British publisher to set a piece by J. F. Planché, author of the text of Weber's *Oberon,* but nothing came of it. So, it would appear that creating an opera calls for more than musical talent, however great. The opera composer must also possess that rare attribute, histrionic imagination, which is required of all artists who dream of expressing themselves on the stage, whether playwright, opera composer or ballet choreographer. It is this special talent that sets off Mozart, Verdi and Bizet from those composers whose music is intended for the concert hall or the church.

This talent also manifests itself, especially in modern opera, in the practice many opera composers have of writing their own librettos, a practice that owes much to the ideas of the nineteenth-century dramatic poet (as he liked to style himself), Richard Wagner. In his book *Oper und Drama* (1851), Wagner postulates the ideal opera of the future as a *Gesamtkunstwerk,* a creation of a single musical and histrionic imagination capable of conceiving and creating every element of a work of dramatic poetry.

Perhaps the most controversial aspect of this theory is Wagner's belief that the composer must write his own libretto. After reviewing the historical separateness of dramatic poet and composer and commenting on the pervasive egoism of people in the society of his time, he argues:

> Today, two different people cannot entertain the possibility of achieving a finished drama because, as they candidly discuss—in view of the circumstances of modern life—the obstacles to such a collaboration, their enterprise will be nipped in the bud. Only the lonely one, in the grip of inspiration, can

transmute this melancholy situation into the joy of creativity and, as though drunk, urge himself on to render the impossible possible. For he alone is driven by two artistic forces, against which he cannot struggle, and to which he must voluntarily sacrifice himself.[1]

This is contrary, of course, to almost all prior thinking on the subject of opera, and it would be hard to take seriously the audacity of Wagner's intellectual leap toward the future were it not for the enormous success of his own works for the lyric theater, for which he prepared the texts in prose, versified them, then set them to distinguished, unforgettable music.

The present study is an investigation of the response of four modern composers to Wagner's injunction. Is there a trend toward the practice of the composer as his own librettist? Is our perception of opera turning away from the idea of "opera as a form of music" toward "opera as a form of dramatic poetry"? Is the opera libretto becoming better understood as the vital underpinning of the finished work, without which opera can turn into oratorio or scenic cantata? And is this perception leading more and more composers to the belief that they are obligated to control all the variables of the text themselves, in order to create an opera that truly expresses their own most deeply felt ideas and beliefs?

The answer to all these questions seems to be "Yes". Even a cursory glance at the opera scene since Wagner discloses a large number of prominent and successful opera composers who have followed his advice.

Russian opera in the nineteenth and twentieth centuries offers examples of both sides of the coin. Modest Musorgsky (1839–1881) wrote all his librettos himself and achieved a masterpiece of the form with his *Boris Godunov,* the text of which he developed from Pushkin's play of the same name.

Nikolay Rimsky-Korsakov (1844–1908), too, either wrote his own librettos or made substantial contributions to them. In the case of his finest work for the lyric theater, *Sadko,* he had help from the writer V. I. Bielsky in shaping a libretto drawn on an eleventh-century legend about the adventures of the daughter of the King of the Sea. He also devised the libretto for his more popular extravaganza, *The Golden Cockerel.*

Two other important, modern Russian composers, however, took the traditional path to operatic creation. Igor Stravinsky (1882–1971) composed *The Rake's Progress* to a libretto in English by W. H. Auden and Chester Kallman and Dmitry Shostakovich (1906–1975), in composing his *Lady*

Macbeth of Mtsensk, made use of a libretto by Alexander Preis, who derived his material from a short story by Nikolai Leskov.

But Sergey Prokofiev (1891–1953) followed Wagner's example and devised his own librettos for all his significant operas, *The Gambler, The Love for Three Oranges* (after Gozzi), *The Fiery Angel, Semyon Kotko, The Betrothal in a Monastery,* and—his finest achievement—*War and Peace* (after Tolstoy).

In Czechoslovakia, the prominent composer Leoš Janáček (1854–1928) also wrote his own texts for the theater. His first important opera, *Jenůfa,* is based on his adaptation of the play by Gabriela Preissová. He derived the text of his next work *Kát' a Kabanová*—one of the masterpieces of modern opera—on the play *The Thunderstorm* by the Russian playwright Aleksandr Ostrovsky and used a novel by another Russian author, Dostoyevsky, *From the House of the Dead,* as his source for a compelling opera on life in a tsarist prison camp in Siberia. His text for *The Cunning Little Vixen* is derived from a Moravian folk tale about a clever fox and a forester, and *The Makropulos Secret* is based on a play by his countryman, Karel Čapek. It is hard not to ascribe some of the stature of Janáček in the opera world of today to the fact that he himself shaped for musical expression all the texts of his extraordinary dramatic poems.

Elsewhere in Middle Europe, the Hungarian Béla Bartók (1881–1945) composed his finest opera, *Duke Bluebeard's Castle,* to a libretto by the film author and theoretician Béla Balász, who made use of a version of the tale by Maurice Maeterlinck. On the other hand, the Polish composer Krzysztof Penderecki (1933–1992) wrote his own libretto on the German translation by Erich Fried of John Whiting's play *The Devils of Loudun,* in turn derived from the novel of the same name by Aldous Huxley. Since its first performance by the Staatsoper Hamburg in 1969, this has been one of the most influential operas of modern times.

For more than two centuries, French operatic tradition evolved from the classic duology of librettist and composer, reaching a very high plateau of popularity with *Carmen,* composed by Georges Bizet (1838–1875) to a text by the experienced theatrical writers Henri Meilhac and Ludovic Halévy who, in turn, drew their work from a short novel by Prosper Mérimée. But between 1892 and 1902, Claude Debussy (1862–1918) pointed the way toward the new tradition of the composer as librettist by making his own adaptation of Maurice Maeterlinck's play *Pelléas et*

Mélisande for the lyric theater and then conceiving one of the most evocative musical settings of a transformed play in our time.

The success of this great opera had its effect on subsequent French composers. The most prolific of all, Darius Milhaud (1892–1974) adapted his own librettos from such diverse sources as Jean Cocteau's play *Le pauvre matelot* [*The Poor Sailor*], Paul Claudel's translation of the *Oresteia* trilogy of Aeschylus, the same writer's epic drama *Christophe Colomb* and Franz Werfel's play *Juarez und Maximilian*. On the other hand, his contemporary, Francis Poulenc (1899–1963), composed one of the most popular operas of the modern French repertory, *Dialogues des Carmélites*, to a text by the poet Georges Bernanos, who drew his material from the novella by Gertrude von Le Fort.

In Italy, a similar condition developed. After Verdi and Puccini, who always worked with librettists, the tide began to turn with the appearance, in 1892, of the *verismo* opera *I pagliacci* [*The Clowns*], by Ruggiero Leoncavallo (1858–1919). The composer fashioned his own libretto from an actual episode and wrote the librettos for all the rest of his operas. He even worked on the text of *Manon Lescaut* for Puccini. This tendency was taken up by two more Italian opera composers of the twentieth century, Luigi Dallapiccola (1904–1975) and Gian Carlo Menotti (born, 1911). Dallapiccola's *Il prigionero* is composed in Schoenberg's twelve-tone system to an original text on the subject of a political prisoner who is subtly tortured by the hope that he may one day be released. Menotti wrote all of his librettos (except *Amelia al ballo*) in English and achieved substantial success with such pieces as *The Consul* and *The Saint of Bleecker Street,* in spite of a tendency to set English words and phrases to false musical accents. Even so, if his literary talent (in English) was limited, he nevertheless possessed a genuine histrionic imagination; he even wrote a libretto, *Vanessa,* for his close friend, the American composer Samuel Barber, whose setting of this text turned out to be the most popular of the latter's operas.

But the most remarkable of all modern Italian musicians was the composer, concert pianist and essayist Ferruccio Busoni (1866–1924), who was born with extensive literary and histrionic talents. He wrote his own librettos for his principal operas, *Die Brautwahl* [*Bride of Choice*], *Arlecchino, Turandot* and *Doktor Faust* and even, like Menotti, wrote librettos for his friends. He wrote prolifically and influentially in the field of musical aesthetics. His text for *Doktor Faust* is based on the old German puppet plays and achieves an originality of dramatic structure that marks it off definitively from the important earlier treatments of the subject by Marlowe and Goethe.

Since the time of Purcell, opera in England has been slow to mature, but the development of the art form since 1900 has more than made up for the barren years of the eighteenth and nineteenth centuries. The most popular of modern British composers, Benjamin Britten (1913–1976), depended on several writers to provide librettos for his operas. For *Peter Grimes,* the appearance of which in London in 1945 marked a new and fruitful era in the course of British opera, Montagu Slater fashioned the libretto from George Crabbe's poem, *The Borough.* For his next opera, *Billy Budd,* E. M. Forster and Eric Crozier devised the libretto from Herman Melville's novel, *Billy Budd, Foretopman.* The text for *Albert Herring* was written by Eric Crozier after a short story by Guy de Maupassant, and Myfanwy Piper provided texts for both *The Turn of the Screw* (after Henry James) and *Death in Venice* (after Thomas Mann).

Other British composers, however, took the other path. The first opera of the present century to be composed under the influence of Wagner's prescription was *Romeo und Julia auf dem Dorfe* [*A Village Romeo and Juliet*], which Frederick Delius (1862–1934) worked on from 1900 to 1902, making his own adaptation for music of a short story of the same title by Gottfried Keller. And for his last opera, *Fennimore und Gerda,* Delius prepared a version in German of the Danish novel *Niels Lyhne* by Jens Peter Jacobsen, only part of which he set to music.

More recently, Michael Tippett (born, 1905) has attracted international attention with several operas for which he wrote his own texts, among them *The Midsummer Marriage, The Knot Garden* and *The Ice Break.* Equally adept at preparing his own texts for musical expression has been Peter Maxwell Davies (born, 1934), whose *Taverner* is derived from the life of the English church composer of the sixteenth century, John Taverner. And Stephen Oliver (1950–1992) wrote most of the texts for his nearly fifty operas.

Wagner's idea about the advantage to the composer of writing his own libretto has found, not unexpectedly, more adherents in Germany and Austria than in other countries. The Munich composer, Richard Strauss (1864–1949), under the influence of Wagner's writings and stage works, wrote the text for his first opera, *Guntram,* himself, but for his second, *Feuersnot* [*Fire-Famine*], perhaps due to the failure of his initial work for the stage, he accepted the services of the cabaret writer, Ernst von Wolzogen, who provided a clever libretto that contributed substantially to the modest success of the piece. But his most spectacular early success in the theater was the exotic psychological melodrama, *Salome,* the text of which he adapted himself from Hedwig Lachmann's German translation of the play by Oscar Wilde. In spite of this portent, however, Richard Strauss wrote only one more libretto of his own, *Intermezzo* and, in composing the rest of his operas, he set texts written for him by Hugo von Hofmannsthal, Stefan Zweig, Josef Gregor and Clemens Krauss.

Another inheritor of the Wagnerian tradition was the Austrian composer Hans Pfitzner (1869–1949), who spent several years developing and writing the libretto for his masterpiece, *Palestrina.* He derived his text from a popular Italian legend that Palestrina rescued polyphonic church music during the deliberations of the Council of Trent by composing his *"Pope Marcellus" Mass.*

The opera *Palestrina* is a good example of the advantage that accrues to the composer when he has total control over both text and music. Pfitzner wanted a subject that would enable him to make an artistic statement regarding the tendencies of certain musical experimenters of his time. He was able to use the Palestrina story to expound his own belief in the superiority of the great classical traditions over the new, atonal music beginning to appear, especially in Vienna. The figure of Palestrina stands for the richness of tradition in music, much as Hans Sachs speaks for traditional values in the art of song in Wagner's *Die Meistersinger.*

Many of the musical theories and ideas to which Pfitzner objected were first advanced by the Viennese composer, teacher and theoretician Arnold Schoenberg (1874–1951), inventor of the twelve-tone method of musical composition. His earliest opera, *Erwartung [Expectation],* is an Expressionistic work in monodrama form for solo soprano and large orchestra. Schoenberg devised the plot structure himself but entrusted the writing of the lines to the Viennese poet Marie Pappenheim. He wrote his own libretto for his next short opera, *Die glückliche Hand [The Favored Hand],* and then worked with his wife, Gertrud (whose name appears on the score as "Max Blonda"), on the text for what became the first twelve-tone opera, *Von Heute auf Morgen [All in a Moment].* For his only full-length opera, *Moses und Aron,* Schoenberg shaped his own libretto from Biblical sources on the theme of the unbridgeable chasm between Idea and its Representation.

A Viennese contemporary of Schoenberg's was Franz Schreker (1878–1934) who also wrote the turbulent librettos for his operas, such as *Der ferne*

Klang [*The Distant Sound*], *Die Gezeichneten* [*The Stigmatized Ones*] and *Der Schatzgräber* [*The Treasure Digger*]. There has been a marked revival of interest in Schreker's operas recently, at least in the German and Austrian theaters.

Perhaps the greatest composer of twentieth-century opera is Schoenberg's distinguished pupil, Alban Berg (1885–1935), whose operas *Wozzeck* and *Lulu* have entered the repertories of all the world's major opera houses to ever-increasing admiration and critical acclaim. Not a little of the success of *Wozzeck* in the modern theater is due to the playwriting skill Alban Berg displayed in condensing the twenty-six scenes of Georg Büchner's early nineteenth-century play, *Woyzeck*, into a gripping fifteen-scene libretto in three acts. His histrionic gift is also manifest in the way he was able to combine the elements of two plays by Franz Wedekind, *Erdgeist* [*Earth-Spirit*] and *Die Büchse der Pandora* [*Pandora's Box*] into a superb play for musical expression, *Lulu*, which, since its first complete performance by the Paris Opéra in 1979, has emerged as one of the towering achievements of modern dramatic poetry.

A composer strongly influenced by the classical theater of Greece was Carl Orff (1895–1982), whose major operas (as did those of Aeschylus) occupy a border area between dramatic poetry and oratorio. His scenic cantatas, *Carmina burana, Catulli carmina*, and *Trionfo di Afrodite*, are played in the concert hall as orchestral tone poems and, now and then, staged in the opera house in elaborate stage settings with costumed chorus, soloists and dancers. He also devised his own texts for several folk plays with music such as *Die Bernauerin* (after Hebbel's *Agnes Bernauer*), *Der Mond* [*The Moon*] and *Die Kluge* [*The Wise Woman*]. But his most remarkable works for the theater are his musical settings of two translations by Friedrich Hölderlin from Greek tragedy, *Antigonae* and *Oedipus der Tyrann*. In these operas, Orff achieves a union of music and language punctuated by a huge battery of percussion instruments that evokes the very heart of Greek tragedy in a convincing and original dramatic style.

A contemporary of Carl Orff's, born in the same year, was Paul Hindemith (1895–1963), who began his operatic compositions with short satirical pieces in the mood of Berlin in the twenties. Like Schoenberg, he created his first work for the stage with the help of a librettist, Marcellus Schiffer, who supplied him with a clever text, *Hin und Zurück* [*There and Back*] in 1927. But when he began work on his finest opera, *Mathis der Maler* [*Mathis the Painter*], he devised his own libretto on the subject of the sympathy the painter, Matthias Grünewald, develops for the common people during the Peasants' War of 1525, who demand justice from the unfeeling nobility. The hero of the opera speculates on the question of whether art can possibly have any real meaning when it can bring no succor to those dying on the battlefield, a theme brought poignantly home to Hindemith himself, when he was forced into exile from his homeland by Hitler and his Nazi Party.

A talented pupil of Franz Schreker's was the Viennese composer Ernst Krenek (1900–1992), who followed the tradition, by this time becoming well established, of writing his own librettos. His most sensational early success was his jazz opera *Jonny spielt auf* [*Johnny Strikes Up*], which attracted attention in America when the Metropolitan Opera staged it with Lawrence Tibbett in the title role. Krenek's most enduring achievement, however, is his historical opera *Karl V,* in which he levels criticism at the repressive political situation of the time (1938) in his native country through the medium of opera, and for which he was forced by the Nazis to emigrate to the United States.

A contemporary of Krenek's was the Bavarian composer Werner Egk (1901–1983), who also wrote his own librettos, composed the music and then, often, conducted the first performances of his works. His best known opera, *Peer Gynt,* was adapted from the play by Ibsen and, from a short novel by Heinrich von Kleist, *Die Verlobung in San Domingo* [*The Betrothal in San Domingo*], about the slave uprising in the French section of the island in 1803. Egk drew a text the musical expression of which gave him an opportunity to explore relationships between black and white people during a time of calamity for both.

Perhaps the most difficult of all modern operas is the work, *Die Soldaten,* by the avant-garde composer Bernd Alois Zimmermann (1918–1970). For his libretto, Zimmermann made his own adaptation of the play of the same title by Jacob Michael Lenz, the eighteenth-century *Sturm und Drang* playwright who influenced both Büchner and Brecht with his ideas about abolishing the three unities and playing several scenes simultaneously on the stage. The text gave the composer ample opportunity to employ a wide variety of theater and cinema techniques, among them, *Sprechstimme,* electronic music played not only on the stage but through speakers surrounding the audience in the auditorium, rhythmic noises made by groups of people on the stage and light-projected scenery.

One of the more prolific modern German opera composers, however,

Hans Werner Henze (born, 1926), depended on various librettists in devising his major works for the lyric theater. The text for his opera, *Elegy for Young Lovers,* was prepared by W. H. Auden and Chester Kallman and the same team adapted the text of his opera *The Bassarids* from *The Bacchae* of Euripides. And for Henze's elaborate, leftist political statement, *We Come to the River,* the English playwright Edward Bond created the libretto.

And Aribert Reimann (born, 1936), one of the most successful and influential of contemporary German opera composers, also set librettos written by others. His finest opera, *Lear,* one of the significant achievements of the modern theater, is set to a text by Claus H. Henneberg that he adapted from Shakespeare, and the same writer prepared the text for an earlier Reimann opera, *Melusine.*

Although there are important exceptions, since Wagner, the majority of composers who struggle with that most demanding of all forms of art—the opera—have opted to fashion their own librettos, come what may. The reason seems clear enough. If a composer accepts a libretto from another person, that person establishes the dramatic tone (either comic or tragic), the theme, the plot structure, the characters, the scenic background, and all the dialogue of their opera. The composer becomes subservient to the ideas of the librettist, as did Richard Strauss during his twenty-year collaboration with Hugo von Hofmannsthal.

Even Metastasio (1698–1782), the greatest of all opera librettists, voiced feelings of reservation about the duality of opera composition when he remarked to Charles Burney that "no music drama would be perfect or interesting till the poet and musician were one, as in ancient times, and that when Rousseau's *Devin du village* came out, and so delighted every hearer, the literary patriarch Fontenelle attributed its success to that union of poet and musician."[2] Later on, Verdi's librettist, Salvatore Cammarano, remarked, "If I were not afraid of being thought Utopian, I would be tempted to say that to achieve the peak of perfection in an opera the same mind should be responsible for both the words and the music."[3]

Metastasio's reference to "ancient times" reminds one again that the Greek tragic poets composed music for their plays and that, as Aristotle noted, part of the superiority of dramatic poetry over epic poetry resided in the fact that the former has "as no trifling components, music and spectacle,[*]

---

[*] Meaning, probably, the dance movement of the chorus.

in which the pleasure of tragedy to a great extent consists."[4] Metastasio, thus, looks back to Greek tragedy and forward to modern opera with equal perspicacity.

The following study of four composers of opera who wrote their own librettos endeavors to assess their literary talents and seeks to determine how significant these talents were in the creation of their masterworks of dramatic poetry.

Notes

1. Richard Wagner, *Oper und Drama* in *Gesammelte Schriften und Dichtungen* (Leipzig: Fritsch, 1888), IV, 209: "Nicht Zweien kann gegenwärtig der Gedanke zur gemeinschaftlichen Ermöglichung des vollendeten Drama's kommen, weil Zweie im Austausche dieses Gedankens der Öffentlichkeit gegenüber die Unmöglichkeit der Verwirklichung mit nothwendiger Aufrichtigkeit sich eingestehen müßten, und diese Geständnis ihr Unternehmen daher im Keime ersticken würde. Nur der Einsame vermag in seinem Drange die Bitterkeit dieses Geständnisses in sich zu einem berauschenden Genusse umzuwandeln, der ihn mit trunkenen Muthes zu dem Unternehmen treibt, das Unmögliche zu ermöglichen; denn er allein ist von zwei künstlerischen Gewalten gedrängt, denen er nicht widerstehen kann, und von denen er sich willig zum Selbstopfer treiben lässt."

2. Quoted by Herbert Lindenberger, *Opera, the Extravagant Art* (Ithaca: Cornell University Press, 1984), 115.

3. Quoted by Andrew Porter, "*Stiffelio*—an Introduction," *Opera* 44 (1993), 15.

4. Aristotle, *Poetics*, ed. and trans. Allan H. Gilbert in *Literary Criticism: Plato to Dryden* (New York: American, 1940), 114 (1462a14).

Opera as Dramatic Poetry

CHAPTER ONE
Summer Night on the River: Frederick Delius

An early believer in Wagner's theory that the composer of opera should write his own libretto was Frederick Delius, who was born in Bradford, England in 1862. His parents were members of an industrial family centered in Bielefeld, Germany and had come to Bradford to manage one of the family's interests. Delius received his primary and secondary education in England and then was sent to Florida in 1884 to manage a family estate. He completed his musical education in Leipzig from 1886 to 1888 and, after some travelling about, settled in Paris where he met his future wife, Jelka Rosen. A painter who was descended from an old Schleswig-Holstein family, she owned a house with a large garden in Grez-sur-Loing, about forty miles from Paris, that Delius found to be an agreeable place in which to live and compose his music. It was here, from 1900 to 1902, that he constructed a very effective libretto in six scenes from the novella *Romeo und Julia auf dem Dorfe* by the Swiss poet and novelist Gottfried Keller. He then set this text to music of such intense, rhapsodic conviction that the love story of Sali and Vrenchen, in the imaginary town of Seldwyla, lives on the stage today just as vividly as it does in the pages of Keller's fiction.

Why was Delius attracted to this story? What does a composer seek when reading a possible source for an opera? What is "musical" about a prose work intended for the reading public?

First, the story itself is dreamlike, suggestive and filled with musical episodes reminiscent of the story of Tristan and Isolde that so appealed to Wagner many years earlier. Sir Thomas Beecham comments on the "frail and intimate nature" of the lovers, who "wander on and off the stage as in a fairy tale."[1] The town of Seldwyla is set in an idyllic section of Switzerland, near a river, with hills and mountains in the distance. The entire atmosphere must have inspired musical ideas in the composer's imagination as he read through the story because, like Wagner, Delius was fundamentally a mystic. As John Klein has observed:

For no twentieth-century composer succeeds in capturing an otherworldly atmosphere with quite so sensuous a fervour. Elgar may have slightly exaggerated, but he was surely justified in saying to his great contemporary, "You are too much of a poet for a workman like me." For a real and true poet Delius undoubtedly was: has any musician expressed his attitude to his art in quite such a rapturous spirit? "Music is a cry from the soul," he exclaimed, in a moment of self-revelation.[2]

As Delius read through Keller's story he must have sensed, many times, that he was in touch with a kindred spirit. The poet describes Sali and Vrenchen beginning their day and night of love by walking together across the open country on a fine Sunday morning in September:

> ... there was not a cloud in the sky, but the hills and forests were clothed with a delicate haze that conveyed everywhere a mysterious, solemn atmosphere. And from every side they heard church bells. Here, a deep, harmonious clanging from a rich town and there, the gossipy tinkle of two small bells from a poor village. The lovers forgot what would happen at the end of their day and gave themselves up to deep-breathed, wordless joy as they ventured forth, dressed in their Sunday best, a free, happy, mutually promised couple. Every distant cry and fading tone that they heard in the Sunday morning stillness vibrated through their souls, because love is like a bell that transmutes the sounds of the remote and the ordinary into a special music of its own.[3]

Delius may also have been attracted by Keller's compression of the last part of his story into a single day of love and death, thus employing a unity familiar in both the classical drama and in various musical forms:

> For the poor young people had been granted only one day in which to recapture the tenderness of their courtship and to experience all the further joys and moods of love as they eagerly anticipated the passionate climax of their union in the surrender of their lives.[4]

In shaping his play for music, Delius paid closer attention to the demands of the theater than to those of the novel. He cut the scenes in which the farmers nurse their hatred of each other, including the psychologically significant scene of the fight on the bridge between Manz and Marti in the presence of their children. He cut out the two wives of the farmers and eliminated the transformation of Manz into a tavern keeper. He removed

2

smaller touches, too, such as the way Sali measures Vrenchen's foot with a string in which he ties knots so he can buy her a new pair of shoes in town, and the way he gets a little money for their visit to the fair by selling his last belongings.

By cutting so much realistic detail, Delius was able to bring the underlying symbolic elements of Keller's story to the surface, and it is this symbolic substructure that became the foundation of his opera. He turns the wild land into an image of "unspoiled nature, gnawed away by the ploughs of a rapacious, sterile, and self-destructive civilization. The Black Fiddler—in Keller's story an unwashed, half-crazed wastrel—becomes a poetic figure: a homeless wanderer, the bitter spokesman of 'natural man' dispossessed by civilization of his birthright."[5] Delius also added symbolic value to the individualized country sweethearts of Keller's story.

> They have become (as Debussy said of Wagner's Tristan and Isolde) simply "he and she"—universal tragic symbols of all ideal youthful love and erotic passion which cannot find lasting fulfillment in civilized life. As in *Tristan,* this love occupies most of the action, and finds consummation only in death—here regarded as absorption back into the world of nature.[6]

Delius organized his dramatic poem into six scenes, to be performed without intermission. His first scene establishes the basic situation: two farmers are seen plowing; each one slices a furrow off the wild land; the two children bring their fathers' midday meal in a little wagon; they play in the wild land and meet the Black Fiddler; and we learn the circumstances of the bastard grandson of the old Trumpeter who originally owned the wild land. At the end of the scene, the farmers quarrel and forbid their children to see one another again, suggesting the traditional obstacle to the fulfillment of the love of Romeo for Juliet.

The second scene takes place six years later in front of Marti's house. The grounds have run wild with neglect and many windows in the house have been broken. Sali and Vrenchen speak of the dire results the lawsuits have had on their families. At the end of the scene, they agree to meet later in the wild land.

In the third scene, Delius develops the erotic awakenings in Sali and Vrenchen in which the unspoiled nature of their surroundings becomes a symbol for the ecstatic love that is growing between them. They encounter the Black Fiddler, who encourages them to let their love blossom and flourish, and says they will meet him again. Vrenchen then weaves herself

3

a wreath of red poppies which she puts in her hair. This symbol of sleep, dreaming and death seems to have appealed to Delius and he takes care to specify the flowers in his description of the scenery for the scene: "The wild land overgrown with red poppies in full bloom, surrounded by cornfields; in the background fields and small villages perched here and there in the hills. Snow-mountains in the distance."[7]

The lovers kiss for the first time and sit down together amid the poppies. But their happiness does not last long for Marti, who has been searching for his daughter, discovers them in each other's arms and tries to drag Vrenchen away, whereupon Sali strikes him on the head with a stone. The scene ends on a poignant note, with the simplest kind of language Delius could find:

Vrenchen.
　My God! You have killed him!
Sali.
　Vrenchen!
Vrenchen.
　Sali, Sali—oh, what have you done?[8]

Between the third and fourth scenes, Vrenchen takes her father to a mental institution, then sells all she has left. As she waits hopefully for Sali to come to her, she sings of spending her last night in her old home. For the first and last time in his opera text, Delius employs a naive little rhyme scheme:

Vrenchen.
　Ach, die Nacht bricht herein,
　ja die letzte Nacht im alten Heim.
　Ach, bald ist das Feuer verbrannt
　und ich bin ganz allein,
　nun bin ich ganz allein.

　[Ah, the night is approaching,
　The last night in my old home.
　Soon the fire will burn out,
　And I am all alone,
　Now, I am all alone.][9]

Delius cuts the episode in the novella of the woman who buys the bed

4

and takes the bundle of Vrenchen's clothing, but the audience senses anyway that the two lovers now have only each other. Sali comes, and they sleep side by side, dreaming. In Keller's story, they have two separate dreams but Delius condenses them into a single dream—their marriage in the church in Seldwyla. He paints an elaborate musical picture of their wedding using a large orchestra, chorus, many percussion instruments, harps, organ and bells, the last possibly suggested by Keller's description noted above. The text sung by the chorus consists of the simplest kind of prayers for the happiness of the young couple:

Chorus.
Lord God, before thy marriage altar
Humbly kneels an engaged couple.
Let thy blessing rest on them.
Pure be their hearts and devout their deeds.
Take them, Lord, under thy devoted protection.
Amen.
Bless thou this young couple!
Praise be to God in the highest![10]

The musical and dramatic power of this sequence is difficult to convey in words. With the barest minimum of literary material, Delius builds a rhapsodic marriage ceremony that takes place only in the dream of the lovers and the imagination of the audience. It is an aspect of Delius's literary talent that he sensed how much he could achieve musically with such modest textual resources.

Sali and Vrenchen elect to spend one last day together attending a fair nearby and in dining and dancing before she must leave him to go into domestic service. The fifth scene takes place at the fair, which allows Delius to add some small roles and to write more choral music for the townsfolk. He establishes separate vocal lines for a gingerbread woman, a wheel-of-fortune woman, a cheap-jewellery woman, a showman, a carousel man and a shooting-gallery man, all of whom sing over a chorus in four parts. Delius also calls for a circus orchestra on stage.

As in the novella, the lovers are recognized by people from Seldwyla, and they confront the dawning realization that they can never simply get jobs, save their money and get married. Sali describes to Vrenchen the Paradise Garden, a tavern where they can dine and dance together in blissful anonymity, and the lovers set forth on their last walk together. Between the fifth and sixth scenes, Delius inserts a musical interlude for orchestra which, under the title "The Walk to the Paradise Garden", is often played in the concert hall. Toward the end, the lovers appear walking hand in hand in silent, joyous expectation.

The entire Paradise Garden sequence as described in Keller seems made for music. The tavern sits amid overgrown foliage on a hill overlooking the nearby river. Formerly the pleasure house of a rich, eccentric family, it even has musical figures worked into the structure. "On the cornices of the roof, small sandstone angels with fat faces and bellies sat playing once-gilded musical instruments—triangle, violin, flute, cymbal and tambourine."[11] Gathered in and about the tavern are the Black Fiddler and his free-spirit companions. He tells them about the loss of his land, the feud of the two farmers and the subsequent ruin of them both. They invite Sali and Vrenchen to join them in a life of free love and idle wandering, but this prospect is as unappealing to them as living in Seldwyla, and the lovers turn their steps toward the river.

In his novella, Keller describes Sali and Vrenchen hearing a strange sound as they approach the river:

> The stillness of the world sang through their souls while, below them, they heard the sweet, soft murmur of the slowly flowing river. . . . They listened for a time to these sounds, real or imaginary, that arose from the deep stillness, or that seemed to mingle with the magic of the moonlight that, far and near, permeated the ground-clinging autumn fog.[12]

It was one of Delius's happiest inspirations to turn this brief hint of "music in the air" into actual music, that of the bargemen sailing slowly down the river in the distance. They sing of wandering through the world, of "passing by" and hint at the transitory, fleeting nature of life.

Delius condenses Keller's description of the final events on the boat. In the novella, the boat drifts downstream all night and becomes stuck under a bridge as the lovers slip over the side into the water. Since this sequence defies theater technology, Delius found a better solution to the problem. Sali pulls the drain plug from the bottom of the boat so it will sink as he and his Vrenchen at last consummate their love.

The final moments of the opera reach a musical and dramatic apotheosis of intense beauty. Delius writes stage directions and dialogue as follows:

(*While Sali kisses Vrenchen, a miraculous glow spreads over the Paradise Garden. The rising yellow moon floods the distant valley with a soft and mellow light. It seems as though a beautiful, enchanting and mysterious magic has utterly transformed the scene.*)

Bargemen (*in the distance and slowly approaching*).

Halleo! Halleo! The wind is sighing in the leaves.

Halleo! Halleo! We glide downstream in our boat.

Heigh-ho, wind sing softly. Sing softly, sing softly.

Vrenchen.

Oh listen! Now I understand. This is the Garden of

Paradise! Listen, the angels are singing.

Bargemen.

Quiet homesteads lie on the shoreline where people live and peacefully die. We are at home on the river, strangers, drifting by.

Sali.

They are bargemen on the river, drifting by. Shall we also drift down the river?

Vrenchen.

Yes, let's drift away forever! Oh Sali, how I love you! I've wished this a long time but didn't dare to ask you. I can never belong to you, and I can't live without you. Let us die together![13]

The lovers go to the riverbank and climb in the hay boat. Vrenchen throws her bouquet of flowers into the water ahead of the boat as Sali casts it loose and pulls out the drain plug.

Vrenchen.

See, my flowers go on before us!

Sali.

And our lives follow after them!

Bargemen.

Ho, strangers drifting by. Ho, Heigh-ho,

Heigh-ho![14]

The boat sinks in the distance as the music, dominated by strings, harps and the organ, fills the air in a crescendo of passion and love fulfilled.

The final bars of the music remind one of the last scene in Richard Wagner's *Tristan und Isolde*. Although the effects of the two musical scores are similar, the dramatic atmospheres are somewhat different. Tristan and Isolde die in each other's arms, totally cut off from the world of reality.

7

Delius suggests, however, that there is a relationship between the transitory nature of love and the idea of life as a journey in which the same things happen over and over; that people come together, love, then pass on, unknown and forgotten. The English composer Peter Warlock has commented on this:

> The whole work is charged with an atmosphere of mystery: through it all there blows a wind as from a far country . . . The keynote of the work lies in those words of the boatmen: "Heigh-ho, strangers we, a-passing by". What lies beyond is shrouded in mystery, but there is no staying the journey onwards toward the setting sun.[15]

In the case of the last opera Delius composed, however, *Fennimore und Gerda* (first performed by the Opernhaus Frankfurt, 1919), his histrionic imagination failed him. His choice of subject, *Niels Lyhne,* a psychological novel by the Danish writer and poet Jens Peter Jacobsen (1847–1885), was just as filled with possibilities for subtle musical expression as was Gottfried Keller's novella about village life in Switzerland during the same period.

The story explores various emotional crises in the life of Niels Lyhne, a daydreamer, atheist and failed poet who experiences erotic involvements with two interesting women, Fennimore and Gerda, then—in a bitter final episode—dies of wounds he received in battle. Delius fashioned his own libretto in German from the Danish original in nine "pictures" (scenes). The first seven depict the early, naive feelings of love that Niels has for his friend, the painter, Erik Refstrup; the situation of both young men being in love with the same woman, Fennimore Claudi; the unhappy marriage of Fennimore and Erik; the passionate affair between Niels and Fennimore; the accidental death of Erik; and Fennimore's decision, under the influence of guilt, to terminate her relationship with Niels and never to see him again.

This action constitutes the first act of the opera that Delius titled, during the composition stage, *Niels Lyhne.* He then composed two more "pictures", the first part of the second important experience in the life of his hero, the affair with Gerda Skinnerup. For some reason, no longer determinable, Delius decided not to set what would have been Act II, scene 2 of his opera—the conversion to Christianity of Gerda, followed by her death. Nor did he set what would have been Act III—the agonizing death of Niels, the atheist romantic, defeated by reality in the brutal environment of a military

8

hospital. This decision also cost him the obvious title for his dramatic poem, *Niels Lyhne.*

Some surviving musical sketches indicate that Delius had every intention of setting the entire story, but he broke it off in the middle. Perhaps his own atheism blocked work on the scene of Gerda's conversion to Christianity, and perhaps Niels's struggle to find a convivial philosophy of life failed to evoke a satisfactory musical response in Delius's creative imagination. Whatever the cause, *Fennimore und Gerda* remains a fragment, albeit one of the most evocative creations from the years of his musical maturity.

Whether or not *Romeo und Julia auf dem Dorfe* or *Fennimore und Gerda* would have profited from the literary services of a Lorenzo da Ponte or an Arrigio Boito is impossible to say. But new ideas about opera were in the air. By the beginning of the present century, more and more composers had come to the same conclusion about the Lonely One creating the opera of the future. That Delius succeeded as well as he did bears testimony to the prescience of Wagner's revolutionary proclamation.

Notes

1. Sir Thomas Beecham, *Frederick Delius* (New York: Knopf, 1960), 89.

2. John W. Klein, "Delius as a Musical Dramatist," *The Music Review* 22 (1961), 297.

3. Gottfried Keller, *Sämtliche Werke*, ed. Jonas Fränkel (Zurich: Rentsch, 1927), VII, 158: " . . . keine Wolke stand am Himmel, die Höhen und die Wälder waren mit einem zarten Duftgewebe bekleidet, welches die Gegend geheimnisvoller und feierlicher machte, und von allen Seiten tönten die Kirchenglocken herüber, hier das harmonische tiefe Geläute einer reichen Ortschaft, dort die geschwätzigen zwei Bimmelglöcklein eines kleinen armen Dörfchens. Das liebende Paar vergaß, was am Ende dieses Tages werden sollte, und gab sich einzig der hoch aufatmenden wortlosen Freude hin, sauber gekleidet und frei, wie zwei Glückliche, die sich von Rechts wegen angehören, in den Sonntag hineinzuwandeln. Jeder in der Sonntagsstille verhallende Ton oder ferne Ruf klang ihnen erschütternd durch die Seele; denn die Liebe ist eine Glocke, welche das Entlegenste und Gleichgültigste wiedertönen läßt und in eine besondere Musik verwandelt."

4. Keller, 162: Denn die armen Leutchen mußten an diesem einen Tage, der ihnen vergönnt war, alle Manieren und Stimmungen der Liebe durchleben und sowohl die verlorenen Tage der zarteren Zeit nachholen als das leidenschaftliche Ende vorausnehmen mit der Hingabe ihres Lebens.

9

5. Deryck Cooke, "Delius's Operatic Masterpiece," *Opera* 13 (1962), 230.

6. Cooke, 230-1.

7. Frederick Delius, *Romeo und Julia auf dem Dorfe,* lyric drama in six scenes after Gottfried Keller, text, Frederick Delius, piano reduction, Otto Lindemann (Vienna: Universal, 1910), 60: (*Das Brachland üppig mit blühenden roten Mohn überwuchert, umgeben von Kornfeldern, weiter hinten Wiesen und kleine Dörfer, hügeliges Land, in weiter Ferne Schneeberge.*)

8. Delius, 85–6:

Vrenchen.
　Mein Gott! Du hast ihn erschlagen!
Sali.
　Vrenchen!
Vrenchen.
　Sali, Sali, was hast du getan?

9. Delius, 88–9.

10. Delius, 114–18:

Chor.
　Herr Gott, vor deinem Traualtar
　kniet demutsvoll ein liebend Paar.
　Laß deinen Segen auf ihnen ruhn!
　Rein sei ihr Herz und fromm ihr Tun!
　Nimm du sie, Herr, in deinen treuen Schutz!
　Amen.
　Segne dieses junge Paar!
　(Ehre sei Gott in der Höh!

11. Keller (see n. 3), 170–1: "Auf dem Gesimse des Daches saßen ringsherum kleine musizierende Engel mit dicken Köpfen und Bäuchen, den Triangel, die Geige, die Flöte, Zimbel und Tambourin spielend, ebenfalls aus Sandstein, und die Instrumente waren ursprünglich vergoldet gewesen."

12. Keller, 182: "Die Stille der Welt sang und musizierte ihnen durch die Seelen, man hörte nur den Fluß unten sacht und lieblich rauschen in langsamen Ziehen ... Sie horchten ein Weilchen auf diese eingebildeten oder wirklichen Töne, welche von der großen Stille herrührten oder welche sie mit den magischen Wirkungen des Mondlichtes verwechselten, welches nah und fern über die weißen Herbstnebel wallte, welche tief auf den Gründen lagen."

13. Delius (see n. 7), 229–45:

(Während Vrenchen Sali küßt, breitet sich ein wunderbarer Schimmer über den Paradiesgarten aus. Der aufgehende gelbe Mond überflutet das ferne Tal mit seinem warmen, weichen Lichte. Es scheint, als ob ein geheimnisvoller, entzückend schöner Zauber den Garten so verändert habe.)

Schiffer (*in der Ferne und langsam näher kommend*).

Halleo! Halleo! In den Blättern weht der Wind. Halleo! Halleo! Abwärts gleiten wir im Kahn. Heiho! Wind leise sing! Leise sing, leise sing.

Vrenchen.

O lausch! Nun verstehe ich! Dies ist der Garten vom Paradies! Lausch nur! Die Engelein singen.

Schiffer.

Hütten still am Ufer liegen, wo man lebt und friedlich stirbt. Wir sind auf dem Fluß zuhause, gleiten ungekannt vorbei.

Sali.

Es sind Schiffer auf dem Fluß. Gleiten ungekannt vorbei. Sollen wir auch stromabwärts gleiten?

Vrenchen.

Ja, niedergleiten auf ewig! Oh Sali, wie ich dich liebe! Das hab ich mir ja längst gewünscht und war zu bang dich drum zu bitten. Niemals kann ich dir gehören, ohne dich kann ich nicht leben, laß uns zusammen sterben.

14. Delius, 242–5:

Vrenchen.

Sieh, mein Sträußchen geht uns voran!

Sali.

Unser beiden Leben folgt ihm!

Schiffer.

Ho, gleiten unbekannt vorbei. Ho, Hei Ho, Hei Ho.

15. Peter Warlock, *Frederick Delius* (New York: Oxford University Press, 1952), 88.

CHAPTER TWO
The Musician as Littérateur: Ferruccio Busoni

A musician whose ideas about opera were largely contrary to those of Richard Wagner and Frederick Delius was the Italian composer, pianist and theorist Ferruccio Dante Michelangiolo Benvenuto Busoni, who was born in Empoli, Italy on April 1, 1866 (both April Fool's Day and—in that year—Easter Sunday), was named by his father in the expectation that he would follow in the footsteps of various famous sons of Tuscany, and who died in Berlin on July 27, 1924. During the course of his distinguished creative life he composed four operas on verse librettos that he wrote himself: *Die Brautwahl* [*Bride of Choice*] (1912), *Arlecchino,* in one act (1917), *Turandot,* in two acts (1917) and the work for which he is best remembered today, *Doktor Faust,* which was completed after his death by his student and colleague, the Catalan composer Philipp Jarnach and first performed at the Opernhaus Dresden in 1925 under the musical direction of Fritz Busch.

Like the Polish novelist, Joseph Conrad, who found his spiritual home in England, Busoni came to prefer living in Germany rather than in his native Italy. And, although he is remembered today as a major composer in all the musical and dramatic forms, while alive he supported himself by giving piano recitals as one of the great keyboard virtuosos of the time, his only serious rival being the Polish pianist and political figure, Ignace Jan Paderewski.

Busoni's concert career required him to travel widely, and he had to seize what time he could between engagements for his composing and for the writing of his letters, his newspaper articles and his aesthetical essays. An early concert engagement took him to Helsinki where, in 1888, he met and later married Gerda Sjöstrand, the daughter of a Swedish sculptor. He spent some months teaching piano in Moscow then taught at the New England Conservatory of Music, in Boston, for two years. In 1894 he returned to Europe and settled in Berlin where, despite his strong emotional feelings for Italy, he found his psychological home. He tried once to settle himself in Italy, in 1913, by accepting the directorship of the Liceo Musicale in Bologna, but things didn't work out well for him and, after a year, he returned to Berlin. He spent much of the First World War in America and Switzerland then, in 1920, he returned to Berlin where he lived until his death of heart and kidney disease in 1924. By the time of his return to Berlin he was a famous man as pianist, writer and composer. Ernst Krenek has described the almost daily after-lunch social gatherings held in Busoni's penthouse apartment in Berlin's Victoria-Luisenplatz:

> At his afternoon meetings, musicians were in a minority. Painters, writers, poets, architects, scientists and a large number of miscellaneous intellectuals were all attracted by the fireworks of his fascinating soliloquy which would go on for an hour or more before he retired ceremoniously to the inner sanctum, obviously to attend to his creative work proper.[1]

It is not by accident that Busoni gathered around him people interested in subjects other than music. Although not as dominant as his musical talent, his literary instincts went well beyond what one generally encounters among composers, orchestra musicians, and conductors. An interviewer from an Italian newspaper, in describing Busoni's Berlin apartment, noted that "all around the large room were handsome bookshelves with an extensive collection of literary works: Italian and German authors, French and English, all in the original, of course, since Ferruccio Busoni speaks and writes with absolute mastery in those four languages."[2]

Antony Beaumont, one of Busoni's major biographers, has also commented on the composer's penchant for literature:

> Busoni's literary instincts have been of particular significance to me. By referring to the books mentioned in his letters and diaries, or to the source material of his several libretti, one gradually came to realize how predominant a part the world of literature actually played in his work as a composer: one discovered that many of his works, even instrumental compositions, were directly inspired by what he read.[3]

And, in his edition of some of Busoni's correspondence, Beaumont estimates that, over a fifty-year period, the composer wrote about 50,000 letters![4]

As a young man, Busoni displayed an interest in prose writing that paralleled his interest in music. While he was living in Vienna, from 1882 to 1886, he sent reviews of musical events to the Trieste newspaper *L'Indipendente* under the anagram Bruno Fioresucci, and an article of his on the musical scene in Italy appeared in a newspaper in Graz. In 1887, he wrote a "very detailed treatise for the jubilee anniversary of Mozart's *Don Juan,* which was published in the *Neue Zeitschrift für Musik.*"[5]

Busoni also wrote detailed prefaces to the editions of his transcriptions for modern piano of Bach's keyboard music, as well as a study of the editions of Liszt's piano music, both of which suggest a latent penchant for musical scholarship. "I know you are a philologist," the Italian poet and playwright Gabriele d'Annunzio said when he met Busoni in Paris in 1912.[6]

Early in his life, Busoni found himself attracted to the theater—opera, spoken drama, even puppet plays—and he soon became aware of his substantial histrionic gifts. In 1884, he exchanged correspondence with the librettist J. V. Widman about a possible operatic version of the Swiss novella that so appealed to his friend of later years, Frederick Delius, *Romeo und Julia auf dem Dorfe* by Gottfried Keller.[7] The libretto was never delivered, however, and the following year Busoni turned to a new opera project that he worked on in Leipzig with the writers Frida Schanz and Ludwig Soyaux. Their title was *Sigune, oder das vergessene Dorf* [*Sigune, or the Forgotten Village*] which they adapted from a short story, by Rudolf Baumbach, about a mysterious village which, together with a beautiful maiden (in the mood of Lerner and Loewe's *Brigadoon*), magically appears and then disappears from time to time.[8] Busoni composed some of the music, but the opera remains unfinished.

After approaching several literary personages, including d'Annunzio, about writing an opera libretto for him, Busoni ultimately decided that he would have to write his own texts, in verse, that "he alone could find the words to express the inexpressible, which he was constantly seeking in his music for the theatre,"[9] thus acknowledging Wagner's conviction that only the Lonely One can achieve a convincing amalgam of word and music in the opera house.

Busoni discovered that he could write fluently in verse. He possessed a good command of German vocabulary and rhyme possibilities, a sense of rhythmic structure and a graceful style of expression that often disclosed his innate sense of humor. He once bewailed the fate of the travelling concert artist in some clever verses that have been preserved and translated by Edward J. Dent:

Vorerst das Kursbuch. Sich zurechtzufinden!
Doch schließlich lernt man's—Seite 103.
Kein Anschluß. Läßt es sich denn nicht verbinden?
Und auch kein Wagon-lit? Nun einerlei!

Verschlafen, fröstelnd, komm ich elf Uhr an.
Da steht ein Mann: "Die Probe wartet schon!"
"Ich hab' noch nicht gefrühstückt." Sagt der Mann:
"Mir leid, doch öffentlich ist die Repetition."

Nun hin denn! Das Hôtel wird übersprungen,
Der Stadtrath, der empfängt mich sauer-süss:
"Sie sind ein bißchen spät! Schon längst gesungen
Hat ihre Nummern die betreffende Miss."

Ich stürze an's Clavier. Der Reisekleider
Sind nicht gewechselt. Und die Hände kalt.
Nun ist's vorbei. Der Kritiker war leider
Schon da. Zum Spät-ausgeh'n ist er zu alt.

Was hilft es, daß es Abends glänzend geht?
Die Recension bespricht das Probespiel.
Nur keine Zugabe, sonst wird's zu spät,
Und bis zum Bahnhof ist's ein weites Ziel.

Noch "naß" erreich' ich richtig mein Coupé—
"Abfahren!" und der Zug ist schon im Gehn.
Und wieder mußt' ich fort ohne Souper,
Und morgen früh die Probe ist um Zehn.

[Where is my Bradshaw? How do I get there?
Ah! Page a hundred: here's the only train.
Change—can I risk it? Three minutes to spare.
No sleeping-car? Well, useless to complain.

15

Next morning, at eleven, half awake
And shivering, I arrive. A man comes up.
"Make haste! Rehearsal's waiting! You must take
A cab at once!" No time for bite or sup.

No time to change or wash. "You're rather late,"
Says the presiding magnate. "You must know
The rehearsal's public. We have had to wait;
The songs were all sung half an hour ago."

Straight to the platform—play as best I can—
Hungry and dirty, fingers frozen quite—
That's done! Why, there's the critic! Poor old man,
You can't expect him to go out at night.

The concert's a success—but what of that?
The critic writes on how *he* heard me play.
Encore? No time. I seize my coat and hat,
For to the station, it's a goodish way.

Into the train just as the whistle blows—
On to the next place, supperless again,
Clammy with sweating, still in evening clothes—
Tomorrow the rehearsal is at ten.][10]

Busoni composed his first verse libretto in 1907, an adaptation of a
novella by Comte Joseph Arthur de Gobineau, *Der mächtige Zauberer* [*The
Mighty Magician*] which, however, he did not set to music. This libretto,
which was published by Schmidl Verlag of Trieste in 1907, reflects Busoni's
lifelong fascination with the theatrical possibilities of magic and the supernatural, dramatic elements that make it unnecessary to account for every
twist and turn of the plot structure by means of rational cause and effect, so
popular in the *verismo* theater of his day. The text of this early libretto
contains some lines that perhaps express Busoni's own personal aspirations
regarding knowledge and language:

"What do you search for? Speak! What do you expect?"
"I don't know. I am longing for the unknown!
What I already know is limitless.
But I want to go farther.
The final word still eludes me."[11]

16

The quest for the "final word", the ultimate meaning of human existence, is a popular theme in German dramatic poetry. Busoni may have remembered some lines from Scene 3 of Goethe's *Faust I.* The hero considers translating the New Testament from Greek into German but is stopped short by the very first line:

It is written, "In the beginning was the word!"
Here I am baffled. Who will help me now?
It is impossible to value "the word" so highly,
I will have to try another translation.
If I am truly enlightened by the spirit,
It is written, "In the beginning was the idea."[12]

The "ultimate word" also occupies the thoughts of Moses at the end of the second act (and the last one set to music) of Arnold Schoenberg's opera *Moses und Aron.* Moses senses defeat. Everything that he has believed in has proved to be a false image of the truth and, in despair, he cries out, "Oh word, thou word, that I lack!"[13]

The first of his opera librettos that Busoni actually set to music was *Die Brautwahl,* which he wrote between 1906 and 1908. Based on a story of the same name by E. T. A. Hoffmann who, along with Edgar Allan Poe, had become one of Busoni's favorite authors, *Die Brautwahl* relates the story of Leonhard, a goldsmith who cannot die and a patron of the arts for three centuries. He enables a painter, Edmund Lehsen, to win Albertine, the girl of his choice during a scene, borrowed from *The Merchant of Venice,* in which three suitors choose for her hand in marriage from among three jewelled caskets, one of which has her picture inside. Leonhard sees to it that Edmund chooses the right casket. The opera plays on two levels, the realistic and the supernatural, a characteristic, also, of Busoni's finest work for the theater, *Doktor Faust.*

Busoni worked on the musical setting of *Die Brautwahl,* through innumerable interruptions, for the next five years and finally saw it performed at the Hamburg Staatsoper on April 12, 1912 under the musical direction of Gustav Brecher. Audience response was good but the critics were not impressed. This early opera, in the style of Offenbach's *Tales of Hoffmann,* has not achieved a place in the repertories of the world's opera houses.[*]

---

[*] It is scheduled for the 1992–93 season by the Deutsche Staatsoper Berlin.

In a preface Busoni wrote for the 1914 edition of the *Phantastische Geschichten* of E. T. A. Hoffmann, he makes some observations about Hoffmann that apply equally well to himself:

> In actual fact, Hoffmann very rarely abandons reality; and although we sometimes have the feeling that something improbable, illegal and supernatural is going on, it is almost impossible to put one's finger on a passage and say exactly when we first had this feeling . . . But in most cases, it is someone who is either dreaming, drunk, delirious or mad, who thinks he has seen or is seeing the apparitions and tricks that are being described; and next morning, by the sober light of day, everything is back to normal, in a middle-class and commonplace environment, totally devoid of any element of fantasy or grandeur.[14]

For this first of his completed operas, Busoni developed the musical means of expression that would distinguish all his subsequent creations for the lyric theater. Rejecting Wagner's by-then popular technique of through-composition based on the statement and symphonic development of musical leitmotifs, Busoni divided his operas into short sections, each of which could be unified musically by a particular musical form. In *Die Brautwahl,* he makes use of an overture, a waltz of spirits, various solos for instruments of the orchestra in standard symphonic manner, intermezzos, a passacaglia, all kinds of dances—waltzes, minuets, a polka, a galop—and several purely vocal forms—duets, quintets and, at the end, a four-part scherzo reminiscent of the fugue that ends Verdi's *Falstaff.* In later works for the stage, he makes use of folk tunes and dances, religious chants and plainsong, classical forms such as the theme and variations, the fugue, the suite, the canon and the sarabande. These venerable musical forms imbue the scenes of his dramatic poems with a certain feeling of timelessness and demonstrated to other composers of this period that there was a viable alternative to Wagner and his dramatic recitative built on repeated leitmotifs, an alternative that came to be known as the neoclassic style, a style adopted and further developed by Alban Berg and Igor Stravinsky, among others.

In 1913, Busoni wrote a verse libretto for his piano and composition student Louis Gruenberg, *Die Götterbraut [Bride of the Gods]*, based on the Indian epic poem *Mahabharata,* about the love of Prince Nala for the beautiful princess Damajanti, somewhat reminiscent of the style of Gustav Holst's later opera, *Savatri,* taken from the same source. The libretto was published in 1921 in a special issue of *Blätter der Staatsoper Unter den*

Linden, Berlin. Gruenberg completed the musical setting of *Die Götterbraut*, but the opera remains unperformed. (He had better luck with his setting of Eugene O'Neill's *Emperor Jones*, which was produced by the Metropolitan Opera in New York in 1933 with Lawrence Tibbett singing the title role.)

Busoni completed the libretto for his greatest stage work, *Doktor Faust*, in December of 1914 but, due to the tension and foreboding brought on by the war that had broken out in August, he felt unable to work on the musical setting and went to America for a concert tour. In 1915, in Switzerland, he wrote his best short libretto, *Arlecchino*, which he set to music in 1916. An effort to bridge the chasm between the artistic worlds of Italian and German opera, *Arlecchino* is based on the style and structure of the Italian *commedia dell'arte*, but the text is written in German. The first performance of the opera took place on May 13, 1917 at the Opernhaus Zurich, and the title role, a speaking part, was played by Alexander Moissi, an actor of Italian extraction who spent much of his professional career on the German stage playing leading roles in the productions of Max Reinhardt.

Arlecchino is a charming, light-hearted, satirical piece with a strong anti-militarist element, expressed by an inventive musical setting that often parodies such venerable conventions of Italian opera as the revenge aria, the aria in praise of wine, and others. Busoni describes the inspiration for his opera as follows:

> The idea for *Arlecchino* came to me from the masterful performance of an Italian actor . . . who attempted to capture the old *commedia dell'arte* and played and spoke the role of my hero exceptionally well. At the same time, I became acquainted with the Roman marionette theater . . . From these two experiences, the first of which influenced the poetry and the second the composition, I developed my "theatrical caprice" . . . *Arlecchino* is a dramatized confession . . . a light satire on life and the theater, intended sincerely . . . and undertaken with loving care for artistic form.[15]

It was probably Busoni's belief in the superiority of the older operatic forms over the newer that led him to compose his librettos in verse rather than in prose, and much of his literary production for the theater is reminiscent of the elegant style of Lorenzo da Ponte. The Prologue to *Arlecchino*, spoken by the hero, affords a good example:

Ein Schauspiel ist's für Kinder nicht, noch Götter,
Es wendet sich an menschlichen Verstand;
Deute es drum nicht völlig *à la lettre,*
Nur scheinbar liegt der Sinn offen zur Hand.
Der Szenen-Horizont zeigt heitres Wetter,
Die Handlung spielt in heitren Wetters Land,
Sprichwörtlich abgefaßt, wie sie erscheinen
Von alters her auf aller Länder Bühnen.

Betrogner Ehemann, fremd dem eignen Lose,
Rivalen, um ein zweites Weib in Streit;
Blutiger Zweikampf folgt, daran sich lose
Landläufge Weisheit und Betrachtung reiht;
Ein grader Mann in buntgeflickter Hose
Greift hurtig-keck in die Begebenheit;
So spiegelt sich die kleine Welt im kleinen,
Was lebend wahr, *will* nachgeahmt erscheinen.
(*zum Kapellmeister:*) Maestro? . . .

['Tis not for children, nor for gods, this play;
For understanding people 'tis design'd.
The sense of what the characters may say
May well escape an all too literal mind.
The curtain rises on a sunny day
In that fair land where Nature's always kind.
The story is an old one; every age
And every land has put it on the stage.

A husband, absent-minded and betray'd,
Two rivals fighting for another bride,
A sanguinary duel, with first aid
By Physick and Divinity supplied,
An honest man in chequer'd suit array'd
Invites you all their folly to deride.
The little world in miniature is treated,
And truth in masquerade is counterfeited.
(*To the conductor*) Maestro? . . .][16]

The acceptance for production of the one-act opera *Arlecchino* by Alfred Reucker, *Intendant* of the Opernhaus Zurich, led to the question of a companion piece to fill out the evening, and Busoni decided to utilize some

20

incidental music he had composed for Max Reinhardt's 1911 Berlin production of Carlo Gozzi's play *Turandot,* in a new translation by Karl Volmoeller. In an effort to devise something stylistically compatible with *Arlecchino*, Busoni composed a verse libretto in German that emphasized the lighter, *commedia dell' arte* aspects of Gozzi's play. He made the eunuch, Truffaldino, a major character and expanded the roles of the buffoons, Pantalone and Tartaglia, while cutting the role of Brighella. As in the play, Prince Kalaf has travelled through the kingdom of Keikobad to Peking where he is reunited with his old servant, Barak. Busoni cuts the figure of Barak's wife and he also replaces Gozzi's Ismael with his own invention, the Queen Mother of Samarkand, whose son has lost his head trying to guess Turandot's riddles. It is she who, with a curse, hurls to the ground Turandot's portrait, which ignites the fires of love in the bosom of Prince Kalaf. And, among other changes, Busoni invented a new set of riddles on themes quite different from those of Gozzi.[17] Text and music were both composed with dispatch and *Turandot* was first performed, with *Arlecchino*, at the Opernhaus Zurich on May 11, 1917, under the musical direction of the composer himself.

Busoni's *Turandot* has not prospered on the stage partly, of course, because of the enormous success of the opera on the same subject by Giacomo Puccini, whose interest in Gozzi's play had been aroused by the 1911 Reinhardt production in Berlin with Busoni's incidental music. Busoni thought of the play as modernized *commedia dell' arte* and preserved this atmosphere in his musical version. Puccini took everything quite seriously, however. He and his librettists, in the *verismo* trend of the times, invented a long tale of bygone treachery to explain Turandot's bloodthirsty attitude toward men and added a new character, the faithful servant Liu, to whom they could give a good death scene in the third act. Puccini composed a great *verismo*-romantic opera, perhaps his finest work for the lyric theater, while Busoni took only another step toward his final statement on the subject of opera, fable, magic and man—*Doktor Faust.*

About this same time Busoni wrote another short libretto in verse that he described as a "scene and pantomime" entitled *Das Wandbild* [*The Picture on the Wall*]. He adapted his text from a collection of Chinese ghost stories edited by Martin Buber, and it was published in July, 1918, in a Zurich magazine, *Die weißen Blätter.* Although he dedicated his libretto to Philipp Jarnach, it was the Swiss composer Othmar Schoeck who set it to music. The story concerns a young man named Novalis, who enters a

Parisian antique shop and falls in love with a picture hanging on the wall of a girl in a Chinese dress. In a scene reminiscent of Offenbach's *Tales of Hoffmann,* the picture comes to life and the magical kingdom of Chinese fable overwhelms the student's mundane world of books and solitude. Schoeck's opera was first performed in Halle in 1921, but it has languished in the shadow of his later, powerful musical setting of Heinrich von Kleist's psychological study of depraved femininity, *Penthesilea.*

One of Busoni's intentions, in working on his version of the Faust legend, was to avoid comparison with Goethe. To do this, he turned to the eighteenth-century puppet plays that had replaced the many versions of Christopher Marlowe's play *Dr. Faustus* that had been performed all over Germany in the previous century, and to Marlowe's own source, the *Spies Faustbuch,* first published in Frankfurt in 1587.

He begins his text with an introduction in verse, spoken before the curtain, in which he describes the literary sources that led him to his Faust opera. There follows a prologue, in Wittenberg, Germany, in two scenes. In the first, three mysterious students from Cracow present Faust with a book, *Clavis Astartis Magica,* that enables him, in the second scene, to call forth Mephistopheles and conclude the traditional contract.

The following scene is an intermezzo inside a cathedral. The "girl's brother", a soldier in armor, kneels before a crucifix. Busoni evidently wanted to pay his respects to Goethe's immortal story of Faust, Gretchen and her brother, Valentine, but decided to use the soldier merely as an abstract figure of vengeance and, as such, drops his name. Gretchen has died long ago and her brother lives only to find and punish her satanic seducer. At Faust's command, Mephistopheles contrives the death of "the brother".

Busoni considered that his own, personal treatment of the Faust legend begins with the next scene, which transpires at the court of the Duke and Duchess of Parma on their wedding day. Mephistopheles, in the guise of a herald, introduces the renowned magician, Doktor Faust, who will conjure up famous scenes from history for the entertainment of the guests. Faust beguiles the courtiers with three visions—that of Solomon and the Queen of Sheba, then Samson and Delilah and, finally, Salome and John the Baptist. In each vision, the figures bear an uncanny resemblance to Faust himself and the enchanted Duchess of Parma, who soon rides away with her magician lover. Mephistopheles suggests to her husband that, since the

Duke of Ferrara is planning an attack on Parma, why not prevent it by marrying his sister?

The next scene takes place in a tavern back in Wittenberg some months later. Students are drinking, laughing and quoting Plato. They draw Faust into their discussion, and he offers an observation thought by Busoni's English biographer, Edward J. Dent, to be one of the major themes of the drama, "Nothing is proven and nothing is provable."[18] Dent states that Busoni wrote these lines on the title page of the proof copy he gave him in London, "Niente è provato e niente è provabile."[19]

The students quarrel briefly over religion, then one of them asks Faust about his love affairs, deliberately recalling the similar scene in Offenbach's *Tales of Hoffmann.* Faust begins the story of his affair with the Duchess of Parma when Mephistopheles, dressed as a messenger, arrives to inform Faust that the Duchess is dead and has sent him their son. But Mephisto turns the child's body to straw and sets it afire, causing the students to withdraw in alarm. From the smoke emerges the dancing figure of Helen of Troy, wearing only a transparent veil. Faust tries to embrace her, but she vanishes. Suddenly, in the background, the three students from Cracow appear and demand the return of their book, but Faust has destroyed it. As the students vanish, they announce the end of his life at midnight.

The last scene of the opera takes place in a street in Wittenberg. A beggar woman sits on a doorstep. Faust offers her a coin in the hope that a last good deed will influence his fate after death, clearly reminiscent of the draining of the swamp for the good of the people by Goethe's hero.

The beggar woman turns into the Duchess of Parma, who gives Faust their son a second time with the exhortation to complete his work before midnight. He takes the child as she vanishes and turns to enter a nearby church, but the girl's brother, in armor, bars his way. He attempts to pray before a crucifix on the wall of the church, but it turns into a vision of Helena. Finally, he lays the dead child on the ground and covers it with his cloak. He draws a magic circle around the child and conjures his last feat of magic. The child will receive Faust's own being and essence, and he will carry Faust's existence on into the future. He will make straight what Faust has built crooked and will pass on to generations yet to come the Faustian passion for universal knowledge.

From the magic circle arises a naked young man who carries a flowering branch in his right hand, recalling the miracle of the flowering staff in the hand of the Pope in Wagner's *Tannhäuser.* He strides through the snow into the night, arms upraised, as Faust dies, his work completed. His last line is "I, Faust, an eternal will!"[20]

This line embodies another basic theme of Busoni's opera—that the past, present and future are linked by the ideals of the human race, ideals of morality, beauty and wisdom, ideals that become more and more firmly established as the human race matures.

Mephistopheles, as night watchman, takes no pleasure in finding the dead body of Faust. He knows he has been defeated and merely inquires, rhetorically, if the man in his lantern light has met with an accident.

With this unique resolution to the story of the famous magician, Dr. Faust, Busoni achieves an entirely original solution to the hero as symbol of both good and evil. In the puppet plays and in Marlowe's *Dr. Faustus*, the hero goes down to hell at the end of the bargain period. In Goethe's play, Faust performs a symbolic good deed and, like Everyman, who is accompanied only by Good Deeds when he faces Judgment, goes to his reward— reunion with Gretchen in heaven. But in Busoni's version of the great story, Faust is neither winner nor loser but rather—in a state beyond good and evil—he becomes an immortal being, a personage who achieves the transference of his essential self to his son and, in this form, embodies forever the universal human desire for knowledge.

Busoni added an Epilogue, in a charming verse, intended to be recited at the conclusion of the opera:

> Von Menschensehnsucht ward vor Euren Blicken
> den Abend durch ein tönend Bild entrollt;
> Von Fausts Verhängnissen und Un-Geschicken
> Bericht zu geben hat das Stück gewollt.
> Der ungeheuere Stoff, durft' er mir glücken?
> Enthält die Mischung auch genügend Gold?
> Wär's so, *Euch* fiele zu, es auszuscheiden:
> des Dichters Anteil bleibt sein selig Leiden.
> Noch unerschöpft beharren die Symbole,
> die dieser reichste Keim in sich begreift;
> es wird das Werk fortzeugen eine Schule,
> die durch Jahrzehnte fruchtbar weiter reift;
> daß jeder sich heraus das Eigne hole,
> so, daß im Schreiten Geist auf Geist sich häufft:
> das gibt den Sinn dem fortgesetzten Steigen—
> zum vollen Kreise schließt sich dann der Reigen.
> 23. Juli 1922   F.B.

[A legendary tale of Man's desire
    This night to sound of music has been told;
The tragedy of Faustus did inspire
    The scenes of doom before your eyes unroll'd.
Strange were the ingredients cast into the fire;
    Does my alloy contain sufficient gold?
If so, then seek it out for your own hoard;
    The poet's travail is his sole reward.

Still unexhausted all the symbols wait,
    That in this work are hidden and conceal'd;
Their germs a later school shall procreate
    Whose fruits to those unborn shall be reveal'd.
Let each take what he finds appropriate;
    The seed is sown, others may reap the field.
So, rising on the shoulders of the past,
    The soul of man shall reach his heaven at last.][21]

His libretto for *Doktor Faust* is, without question, Busoni's finest literary achievement. Hugo Leichtentritt observes, "I do not hesitate to call Busoni's libretto [for *Doktor Faust*] an outstanding achievement of modern German literature, a dramatic poem of great power, abundant in poetic beauty, in profound thoughts, and strong in the delineation of dramatic characters."[22] The libretto was published, before the music was completed, by Gustav Kiepenheuer Verlag, Potsdam, in 1920.

All of Busoni's librettos disclose a substantial literary talent—a feeling for the theater, a fluent command of German prose and verse and a number of thematic ideas that he is able to render sensuous with style and conviction. His librettos abound in scenes of magic, fantasy and the dramatically interesting contrast of the supernatural with the routine of everyday existence. Like E. T. A. Hoffmann, he grounds his flights of imagination in a solid, realistic plot structure with a recognizable beginning, middle and end in the style of the classical drama. In this way, he manages to create dramatic texts that are exceptionally efficacious for musical expression in the opera house.

In addition to his journalistic activity, his correspondence and his opera librettos, Busoni wrote a number of short aesthetical essays that were published in four collections. The first, *Entwurf einer neuen Aesthetik der Tonkunst* [*Outline of a New Aesthetic of Music*], appeared in 1907 and was followed, in 1916, by a second edition, containing some new essays. In 1922, he included some more new material in a volume entitled *Von der Einheit der Musik* [*On the Unity of Music*] and, after his death, two excerpts from this collection, *Über die Möglichkeiten der Oper* and *Über die Partitur des "Doktor Faust"* [*On the Possibilities of Opera* and *On the Score of "Doktor Faust"*] were published in 1926. Finally, his best essays were gathered into the collection, *Wesen und Einheit der Musik* [*Essence and Unity of Music*] and published in 1956.

Toward the beginning of his *Entwurf,* Busoni defines the aim of all the arts, in the classical terminology of Aristotle, as "the imitation of nature and the representation of human feelings."[23] Further, he defines the task of the creative artist as "making laws and not obeying them",[24] reflecting Aristotle's belief that the inevitability of an art work is established by the artist and not by nature. Busoni explains that the true creator achieves this because he "strives basically for perfection, and when he is able to bring this into harmony with his own individuality, a new law appears without premeditation."[25]

In discussing the opera practices of his own time, Busoni observes:

> The greater part of recent theater music suffers from the error of repeating the stage action instead of fulfilling its real task of depicting the soul-states of the characters involved. If the illusion of a thunderstorm is presented on the stage, the eye exhaustively absorbs it. But almost all composers try to capture the storm in music, not only an unnecessary and feeble repetition, but also a failure of the true function of music. The character on the stage is either intensely moved by the storm or, if his thoughts are occupied with more compelling matters, he remains detached. The storm can be seen and heard without help from the music. It is what transpires in the soul of the character, invisible and inaudible, that music must make manifest.[26]

From this, Busoni draws the conclusion that the older, classical opera form is preferable to the newer, because "emotions aroused by a dramatic scene were concentrated and rounded out in a closed set-piece (the aria)"[27] while recitative was used to underline exposition and plot development. He points out that,

> The sung word will always be a convention on the stage and a hindrance to truth. This conflict could be successfully overcome only by a plot in which the characters, from the beginning, sing of the unbelievable, the untrue and

the unlikely. Thus, one impossibility supports the other, rendering both possible and acceptable.

> For this reason, I consider the so-called Italian *verismo* unacceptable on the musical stage because, from the beginning, it has ignored this vital principle.[28]

His conviction that supernatural action is especially suited to musical expression probably explains his absorption in the Faust legend, with its evocations of magic, spirits from the netherworld and uncanny visions from history. In this belief, he may have been more under the influence of Richard Wagner than he realized.

Continuing his discussion of opera, he asks, "At which moments on the stage is music indispensable?"[29] and replies, "During dances, marches, songs and at the appearance in the action of the supernatural."[30] He elaborates his theory of the supernatural by holding that opera should create "an illusionary world in which life is reflected in either a magic mirror (for serious opera), or a comic mirror (for light opera), which consciously exemplifies that which cannot be found in real life."[31] In creating this special kind of opera, the composer should "make use of dance, mask-play and apparitions, so that the spectator remains continuously aware of the charm of pretense and never mistakes it for actual experience."[32]

These aesthetic beliefs are plainly manifested in Busoni's oriental opera *Turandot* and in his *commedia dell' arte* piece, *Arlecchino*. In fact, a taste for the exotic and the supernatural seems to have determined his choice of subject not only for his operas but also for some of his abstract musical compositions, such as his *Sonatina seconda* (1912), with its evocations of mystery and the occult.

In his second major collection of essays, *Von der Einheit der Musik,* Busoni develops a theory of opera that is diametrically opposed to the "Bayreuth style". He begins by defending opera music against the vague but popular charge of inferiority: "I believe not only that opera is not an inferior form of music . . . but in the future it will become the highest, the universal form of musical expression and content."[33] He goes on to argue that only in opera can music further develop its capability of making the unspoken understandable, lift human suffering to the level of imagination and find satisfactory room for its further development. But it will not merely describe visible actions on the stage. The outer action appeals to our eyes, but the inner being of the characters we hear through our ears. Opera holds within itself all the forms that appear only singly in concert music. "The realm of the opera extends from simple song, march and dance tune clear up to the most involved counterpoint, from song to orchestra, from the 'worldly' to the 'spiritual,' and—further—since it commands an unlimited space, it is able to absorb every form and style of music and to reflect every mood thereof."[34]

Obviously, theatrical presentation increases musical difficulty. The most complex musical material must be constantly adapted to the needs of the stage:

> For . . . an opera score should provide a complete musical picture that follows but can be detached from the stage action, something like a suit of armor, that is designed to envelop a human body but which displays in itself a valuable creation in material, form and artistic execution. Finally—and this may sound paradoxical—opera composition leads us back to purer and more absolute music. It does this by eliminating everything illustrative. Only those elements that are organically capable of musical expression will attain their rightful place—the content, the feeling and the form, that correspond to spirit, heart and knowledge.[35]

Busoni continues his thinking on the subject by declaring that there is a final, unbridgeable gap between the spoken drama and the opera:

> Above all, opera should not be identified with spoken drama. They should be distinguished from one another, like man and wife. Opera is a *musical* combined work of art as distinguished from the Bayreuth idea of a "combined work of art." . . . I think the most important act is the choice of text. While there are almost unlimited possibilities of subject matter in the spoken drama, for opera there are only subjects that cannot be satisfactorily expressed except by music, subjects that demand music, and can only be fulfilled by music.[36]

Busoni calls on members of the opera public to free themselves from their desire for cheap amusements and sensational scenes on the stage. Thinking perhaps of the second act of Wagner's *Tristan und Isolde,* he inveighs against sexual music in the theater and calls for a kind of half-religious opera, elevated and stimulating, and adds that the Catholic Church achieves homage to God with help from music, costume, choreography and mysticism. The ideal opera in this lofty style is Mozart's *The Magic Flute.* It provides entertainment, spectacle and instruction, all held together by musical form, an "absolute opera" (*die Oper "schlechtweg"*), which ought to be held up as a model for all subsequent opera composition.

After noting that Goethe wrote a second part to *The Magic Flute,* Busoni describes *Faust II* as being in itself a play for music which, if it had been set by an artist of equal rank, might have achieved the status of what he is here describing. "For, in *Faust II,* music is called for throughout; it is indispensable . . . and it will aid the performance of the play as light enhances the observation of a painting."[37]

He then denounces the practice, using as examples *La dame aux camélias* and *La Tosca,* of setting to music plays that need no music for satisfying performance in the theater. He admits that Verdi, with his genius for big scenes, pathos and abrupt changes in tempo, sometimes overcomes this barrier and, in his *Otello,* in which he inserts "a drinking song, a mandoline solo with chorus, a bedtime prayer and a romance (that of the Willow)"[38] as distinct musical numbers, he succeeds in making this unmusical play "almost an opera."[39]

He condemns love duets as shameful, untrue and laughable. "Above all, the erotic is no subject for art but for life."[40] He discovers no love duets in the older operas,* citing the good taste of the earlier composers as the reason. He then explains how condensation in an opera text replaces the tirade in spoken drama and contrives an example of his own showing that excess verbiage in a play can be eliminated in an opera text. "The opera is a theater piece, a poem and music all in one."[41]

He then repeats his view that an opera score must establish itself as a musical entity, independent of the text, and that the text must contribute to this condition. For this reason, the composer has much to say to the librettist, but the librettist very little to the composer. "Ultimately, the ideal solution to the problem is found when the composer becomes his own librettist. In this capacity, he will have the uncontested right during the course of the composition to shorten, to lengthen or to reorganize the words and the scenes, always with regard to the demands of the music."[42]

With this statement, he arrives—by means of his own train of reasoning—at the same conclusion expressed by Richard Wagner many years earlier. In fact, it may be said that, despite his protests against the "Bayreuth style" in his essays and his letters, Busoni was to Wagner a true kindred spirit. Although he observes that opera as a musical composition "always

---

* He overlooks Monteverdi's *L'incoronazione di Poppea.*

consisted of a series of short, closed pieces"[43] he is able to find such pieces in Wagner: "It is no accident that one can take from the 'endless chain' of the *Ring* separate numbers to be played in the concert hall—'Forest Murmurs', 'Ride of the Valkyries', 'Magic Fire Music' and so forth."[44]

Busoni concludes his thoughts on the art of the opera with the observation that, if one takes his work seriously, he must not make any compromises with the demands and conventions of the stage because "the opera, which is made of the improbable, the unbelievable and the impossible has the right to claim these attributes on the best and most convincing of grounds."[45]

These ideas about opera, expressed by Busoni over a period of many years and finally collected in his last volume of essays, reveal a reasonably consistent theory of opera that is usually summed up by the idea of the "neoclassic" in modern music. As Leichtentritt notes,

> Neo-classicism is nowadays generally attributed to Stravinsky. But in fact, Busoni was the first to formulate the maxim of neo-classicism, which in his own words means "the mastery, study and exploiting of all achievements of former experiments carried over into firm and beautiful forms" . . . Busoni was in quest of an art that "would be old and new at the same time."[46]

The old, in opera, was the division of the work into numbers, and the new became those twentieth-century experiments in harmony and orchestration that Busoni found compatible with his own ideas and developed in his own way. All about him, he was confronted by new and surprising trends in music—atonality, the theory of numbers, numerical relationships in composition, mathematical concepts, formulastic construction of musical materials, hyperorganization and—ultimately—in reaction, the aleatory essence of totally open form. Against all this, Busoni employed a polyphonic style of composition that he described as "a free, contrapuntal process, linked to no traditional form, and yet formed through the laws of equilibrium, proportion, deployment, intensification and termination."[47]

In the midst of all these trends and influences, Busoni struggled with his Faust project and his ultimate achievement crowns a lifetime of intense devotion to art. He calls his work neither opera nor music drama, but "a *Dichtung für Musik*—a poem for music,"[48] a decidedly autobiographical poem, in the spiritual sense. As Humphrey Searle noted, on the occasion of the first performance of *Doktor Faust* in England in 1937, Busoni was himself a Faust, "a tortured soul struggling with the deepest problems of humanity, and rarely finding a solution; a tragic figure, but many-sided, one who had *durchausgelebt* the things of this world and tasted their full flavor."[49]

Busoni described the genesis and gestation period of his last opera in some reminiscences entitled, *Über die Partitur des "Doktor Faust"*:

> I intended, on principle, to center my opera on an exciting, historical and proverbial figure who was associated with magic and unsolved riddles. These figures, from Zoroaster to Cagliostro, made up a row of columns through the course of time.[50]

Busoni searched for a figure who would not be so far back in history or legend as to make it difficult for the modern spectator to empathize with his struggles, nor so recent as to violate the need for aesthetic distance in the theater. In 1911, he talked over with Gabriele d'Annunzio a possible libretto on the figure of Leonardo da Vinci—the "Italian Faust"—as the poet called him, but nothing came of this. For a time, Busoni says, he considered Merlin, then Don Juan in a version much different from Mozart's, one that would feature monks, the Holy Inquisition, Moors, Believers and Jews. But these figures, too, were discarded. The figure of Faust dominated his thoughts and, to avoid Goethe, he began a study of the eighteenth-century Faust puppet plays. When he had completed his research, he was able to compose his libretto with despatch:

> As in a fever, and in six days, I wrote down the first sketch of *Doktor Faust*, toward the end of 1914, between the outbreak of the War and my preparations for an ocean voyage.

> My own drama begins with the scene at the Court of Parma where the story steps from the mystical into reality.[51]

He goes on to state that Faust's union with the Duchess is instinctive, since he does not know what the final aim of his life is. Only in his last vision of the Duchess does Faust realize the significance of their child and, moments before his death, fulfill the ordained destiny of his exhausted life.

He comments on the episodic form of his libretto, saying that he purposely left gaps in the narrative to be filled out by music. In making his adaptation of the puppet plays he discarded almost all traces of Goethe's treatment except for Gretchen's brother, who fulfills only symbolic func-

31

tions in Busoni's text. He mentions that he had made some earlier musical studies for his Faust project, his *Nocturne Symphonique* (1914) and his *Sonatina seconda* (1912). He used both the theme and the style of these compositions in his opera, along with the *Sarabande und Cortège* (1920).

After the libretto was finished, he says of his task, "before everything else, I had to develop musically independent forms that expressed both words and stage actions, but which, when detached from the words and the stage actions, retained their own autonomous existence."[52] It is in this use of absolute musical forms to encompass scenes and actions on the stage that Busoni demonstrates his originality. In his essay he states that as melody is the soul of composition, so the human voice remains the richest of all instruments of expression. The voice depends on words for emphasis, however, and on text for train of thought; thus, words lend life to musical intervals.

In *Doktor Faust*, Busoni adhered to polyphonic forms and cut down on harmonic formations. Hence, the picture of the notes is more horizontal than vertical—another aspect of his opera that may be described as neoclassic rather than modern.

After discussing ways in which music can make clear to an audience events that are transpiring off-stage, Busoni comments that "Inspiration is a gift and opinion is an aspect of character, but it is form that transmutes the possessor of these qualities into an artist."[53]

He then provides some examples of how he utilized forms from absolute music while composing *Doktor Faust*. In the second prologue, he arranged the scene between Faust and the six spirit voices as a theme and variations and, further, the range of voices goes from very deep to very high so that Mephistopheles, the last voice to be heard, must be performed by a tenor capable of singing a very high tessitura. The scene in the church is composed in the form of a rondo, and the garden festival at the Court of Parma in the form of a ballet suite. These observations on the importance of form in opera composition conclude his essay on the score of *Doktor Faust*.

The Faust *Puppenspiele,* to which Busoni turned for inspiration in preparing his Faust libretto, have a curious origin. The earliest play for human actors on the subject is Christopher Marlowe's *The Tragicall History of Dr. Faustus,* written in 1592 or early in 1593, and based on an English translation of the *Spies Faustbuch* of 1587. Many versions of Marlowe's play were performed in Germany by groups of *Englische Komödianten* during the seventeenth and early eighteenth centuries, the earliest record of one being a performance in Graz in 1608. An important feature of these Faust plays was the addition of a clown, Harlekin, or Hans Wurst (also called Kasperle, or Pickelhäring) who, as Faust's servant, told jokes, danced and sang, learned a little magic himself and, in the end, avoided his master's fate by convincing the devil that he had no soul to sell.

His antics on the stage began to get out of hand, however, and in the 1730s, Johann Christoph Gottsched, the critic, and Karoline Neuber, an actress who headed a prominent theatrical troupe, banished Hans Wurst from the German stage. As the character of the comic servant disappeared, so did that of his master, the magician Doktor Faust, and soon they could be seen only in puppet plays that shortly took over the popularity of the old story. The first recorded performance of a puppet play on the Faust subject took place in 1746,[54] and its popularity continued, in many countries besides Germany, up to the present day.[*]

By the time Busoni began work on his libretto, all the manuscripts of the old German Faust plays, based on Marlowe, had been lost and he had only the texts of the puppet plays to read. He soon discovered various ideas about Faust's adventures that appear only in these plays. For example, Faust's choice of a devil based on his speed appears in neither Marlowe's play nor the *Faustbuch*. And, of special appeal to Busoni, only the puppet plays contain the scenes at the court of an Italian prince, the Duke of Parma. He also found in these sources the scene of the crucified Christ turning into an image of Helen of Troy.

At first, Busoni planned to use the Kasperle figure to lighten the atmosphere of his opera by telling stories between scenes in front of the curtain while scenery was being changed behind, but he finally separated Faust and Kasperle, using the latter figure as the model for his hero in his one-act opera *Arlecchino*.

Busoni begins his opera with a symphonia, subtitled *"Oster-Vesper und Frühlings-Keimen"* ["Easter Vesper and Augurs of Spring"], built on an imitation of church bells heard in the distance, recalling a similar scene in Delius's *Romeo und Julia auf dem Dorfe*. Soon, an off-stage chorus is heard singing the single word "Pax", suggesting both the atmosphere of

---

[*] The first experience with the legitimate theater that the author had, as a child, was a performance of *Faust* by the Tony Sarg Marionette Theater in Harlingen, Texas.

Easter and Busoni's own private cry of protest against the war raging in Europe at the time he composed the music, in 1917.

The off-stage chorus helps set the atmosphere of mystery and magic that is to dominate the opera in much the same way as do the off-stage choruses in Weber's *Der Freischütz,* Act II and Verdi's *Rigoletto*, Act IV. In fact, Busoni makes use of the convention of the invisible chorus several times in *Doktor Faust.*

When the curtain rises at the end of the orchestral and choral prelude, a *Dichter* appears who recites a ten-verse introductory poem to the audience. The poet plainly speaks for Busoni himself and the verses are wholly autobiographical. He says in the early verses that, as a child, he once watched, enthralled, a play in which the devil took a role, that as he matured he realized that the theater, though only a mirror of life, offers possibilities for serious thought.

Plays of unreality require music because music stands remote from the commonplace and wakes desire in the spectator as it floats toward him. Three figures could make good subjects for music—Merlin, Don Giovanni and Faust. The poet chose the third for his intellect, his feeling for magic and his desire to solve life's final riddle. He mentions Goethe's *Faust* and asks how he could hope to measure himself against such an achievement. He replies, in the last verse, by evoking the Faust *Puppenspiele* of old:

> Its quaint old figures tenderly I scann'd;
> age to them gave a beauty rare and strange.
> Their colours I renew'd with loving hand;
> time does not ruin all that he may change.
> Some sharper outlines, some more vague I plann'd,
> new stitches in the old web sought to range.
> The half-forgotten tale may yet surprise,
> and from the chrysalis a night-moth rise.
>
> Yet though I seek to tell the tale anew,
> its puppet parentage is plain to view.[55]

The poet departs, the inner curtain rises and the scene with the students from Cracow begins. Busoni modelled this episode on the *Ulmer Puppenspiel,* possibly the oldest of the puppet-play texts to survive. A comparison of the central sequence of the source with Busoni's version may throw some light on the composer's dramatic technique.

34

ULMER PUPPENSPIEL,
Actus V

(*Faust—Zwei Studenten—Wagner*)

Wagner.

Herr Doctor, es sind zwei Studenten draußen, sie begehren mit Ihro Excellenz zu reden.

Faust.

Studenten, sagst du? Es werden vielleicht Politici von einem guten Freund seyn; lasse sie hereinkommen.

Wagner.

Es soll verrichtet werden.

Faust.

Alles was hier in Wittenberg lebt, ehret Fausten. Wünschen wollte ich, daß mir die zwei Herren bei meinem Fürnehmen behülflich seyn könnten.

1. Student.

Mit Erlaubniß, wenn wir den Herren Doctor etwa beunruhigen sollten.

2. Student.

Ich wünsche Ihro Excellenz alle Wohlfahrt, bitte es nicht übel zu nehmen, wofern wir dieselbe molestiren.

Faust.

Habt Dank, meine Herrn; die Ankunft Ihrer Personen ist mir lieb und angenehm; darum bitte ich, Sie wollen vernehmen lassen, was Ihnen beliebt. Jung, Stühle her!

1. Student.

Es sey ohne Bemühung. Die Ur-

BUSONI'S *DOKTOR FAUST*,
Vorspiel I

(*Wittenberg.   Vormittags. Studierzimmer.*)

Wagner.

Euer Magnifizenz Verzeihung . . . Euer Magnifizenz Verzeihung: allein, es melden sich drei Studenten.

Faust.

Ihr Wunsch?

Wagner.

Sie wollen ein Buch überreichen.

Faust.

Wagner! Wagner, wahrhaftig! Ich mag so nicht weiter; das Leben rollt rascher—und nicht mehr aufwärts; nicht darf ich so breite Zeit an Andre wenden; und dem hilft doch kein Rat, der sich nicht selber besinnt! Macht mich bei ihnen entschuldigt.

Wagner.

Euer Magnifizenz Verzeihung; es ist keine Arbeit, diesmal, die man von Ihnen heischt; das Buch mag sein eine seltene Handschrift, denn es trägt einen sonderlichen Titel: "Clavis Astartis Magica."

Faust.

Clavis Astartis! Irrt Ihr Euch nicht? Wollt Ihr mich gar nasführen! Fangt Ihr Grillen? Seht Ihr Geister?

Wagner.

Nein, nein, nein, ich kann Magnifizenz versichern.

35

sache, daß wir Ihro Excellenz besuchen, ist, weilen wir vernommen, daß Ihro Excellenz jetziger Zeit dem Studio magico nachhängen. Hier aber habe ich ein Buch wunderlicher Weise bekommen, welches *propter magicam artem* etwas Sonderliches in sich enthält, wie man die Sonne verfinstern, die Sterne stillstehend machen und dem Mond seinen Lauf benehmen könne. Wofern es dem Herrn Doctor beliebt, stehts zu Diensten.

2. Student.

Mit Erlaubniß, Herr Doctor; meiner Schuldigkeit nach habe ich Ihro Excellenz hiemit aufwarten wollen. Hier habe ich unter meines Vaters Bibliothek einen sonderlichen Autoren gefunden, welcher dem Herrn Doctor in seinem neuen angefangenen Studio sehr dienlich. Ihro Excellenz kann nach Dero Gefallen selbigen gebrauchen, jedoch so, daß für keine Seele Gefahr daraus entstehen möge.

Faust.

Edle Herren, Sie machen mir mehr Freud, als jemals ein Cäsar gehabt. Ihr Herren machet mich gegen Euch höchst verpflichtet. Jetzt will ich meine bishero geübte Theologie auf die Seite setzen und mich mit diesen und dergleichen Büchern ergötzen.

Faust.

Also laßt die Studenten ein.

(*Wagner ab.*)

Faust, Faust, nun erfüllt sich dein Augenblick! Die Zaubermacht in meine Hand gegeben, die ungeheueren Zeichen mir erschlossen, heimliche Gewalten mir geknechtet, und ich kann—ja, ich kann—O, ihr Menschen, die ihr mich gepeinigt, hütet euch vor Faust! In seine Hand die Macht gegeben, heimliche Gewalt ihm zu Gebot, er wird euch zwingen, euch bezwingen. Wehe, wehe, über Euch! Wenn Wagner dennoch irrte . . . vielleicht zum Heile?

Wagner (*tritt ein*).

Eure Magnifizenz, die Studenten sind hier.

Faust.

Sie sollen kommen.

(*Es treten auf drei schwarzgekleidete Studenten.*)

Wer seid Ihr?

Alle.

Studenten aus Krakau.

Faust.

O, mein altes, mein teueres Krakau! Eure Gestalten rufen die Jugend mir zurück. Träume! Pläne! Wieviel hatt' ich gehofft! Seid willkomen. Und was führt Euch zu mir?

1. Student.

Dieses Buch leg' ich in Eure Hand.

36

1. Student.

Wohl, Herr Doctor; es sollte mir lieb seyn, daß ich Ihnen ferner dienen könnte; bitte aber noch, der Herr Doctor wolle sich nicht darinnen vertiefen, denn es möchte Schaden bringen.

2. Student.

Dergleichen bitte ich auch Ihro Excellenz; denn der Teufel ist ein Tausendkünstler, die Menschen zu fangen und zu fällen.

Faust.

Meine Herren, ich bedanke mich des guten Erinnerns; ich bitte, leben Sie ohne Sorg. Beliebt den Herren, ein wenig zu verziehen, auf ein Gläschen Wein? Ich werde es für die größte Ehre halten.

1. Student.

Wir bedanken uns gegen den Herrn Doctor und nehmen hiemit unsren Abschied.

2. Student.

Und ich deßgleichen bitte unterthänig um Vergebung; nehmen also hiemit unsren Abschied.

Faust.

Leben die Herren wohl! Ihr Gedächtniß soll stets bei mir verbleiben. Jetzt kann ich Alles das sagen, was einem gefällt, das des Menschen Herz erfreut. Diese zwei Bücher will ich mit Fleiß durchlesen, und sollte gleich mein Leben darauf

2. Student.

Von mir erhaltet Ihr den Schlüssel.

3. Student.

Diese Briefschaft macht es zu Eurem Eigentum.

Faust.

Wie kommt ein solches Geschenk mir zu?

Alle.

Du bist der Meister!

Faust.

Also darf ich es eignen?

Alle.

Es ist Deines.

Faust.

Und wie soll ich Euch dieses vergelten?

Alle.

Später, später. Leb' wohl, Faust.

Faust.

Verweilet, bleibet meine Gäste!

Alle.

Leb' wohl, Faust.

Faust.

So saget, daß ich Euch wiederseh!

1. Student.

Vielleicht.

2. Student.

Vielleicht.

3. Student.

Vielleicht.

Alle.

Leb' wohl, Faust.

(Sie gehen ab.)

Faust *(sieht ihnen kopfschüttelnd nach).*

Sonderlinge!

(Wagner tritt wieder ein.)

stehen. Dieses ist beschrieben
von dem spanischen Runzifar
und dieses von dem spanischen
Varth: zwei große Meister dieser
Kunst. Die Bücher zu verstehen,
will ich mich hin verfügen, ich
will ein Sieger seyn und mag
nicht unten liegen.[56]

Habt Ihr den Studenten begeg-
net? Und wollt Ihr nicht sie
geleiten?
Wagner.
Eure Magnifizenz, Ich begeg-
nete Keinem.
Faust.
Soeben gingen sie.
Wagner.
Ich sah Niemanden.
Faust.
Ihr habt sie versäumt . . . Ach!
Nun weiß ich, WER sie ge-
wesen!
(*Der Metallbrei auf dem Herd
überkocht mit lautem Geprassel.
Wagner eilt geschäftig hinzu.*)[57]

[ULMER PUPPENSPIEL, V
(*Faust, Two Students, Wagner*)
Wagner.
Sir, there are two students out-
side who wish to speak to your
Excellency.
Faust.
Students? Perhaps they are
protégés of a good friend. Let
them in.
Wagner.
It will be done.
Faust.
Everyone living here in Witten-
berg honors Faust. Perhaps these
gentlemen may be able to help
me with my plans.
1st Student.
Excuse us if we disturb you, sir.
2nd Student.
I wish you prosperity, sir, and

**[BUSONI'S *DOKTOR FAUST*,
First Prologue**
(*Wittenberg. Morning. Faust's
study.*)
Wagner.
Sir, if you will give me leave one
moment . . . Sir, if you will give
me leave one moment. Outside
three students are waiting to see
you.
Faust.
Their wish?
Wagner.
To give you a book they have
brought you.
Faust.
Wagner! Wagner—nay truly,
can I thus continue? With life
rolling faster, and ever down-
ward, I dare not devote my time
to helping others; and what help

38

hope you do not take it ill if we interrupt your work.

Faust.

I thank you, gentlemen. Your arrival is a pleasant diversion, and I will be glad to hear what you have to say. Bring chairs, Wagner!

1st Student.

Please, don't trouble. We have come because we heard that you are now studying magic. I have come into possession of a remarkable book on the magical arts. In it are amazing things: how to darken the sun, make the stars stand still and change the course of the moon. If you would like this book, it is yours.

2nd Student.

With permission, sir, I too have the duty to offer you an unusual book. In my father's library, I found the work of a special author which should be useful to you in your new studies. You are welcome to use this book as you wish, always with the proviso that you do not put your soul at risk.

Faust.

Honorable gentlemen, you bring me more joy than Caesar ever knew. I am much in your debt. I will set aside my studies in theology and take pleasure in these and similar books.

1st Student.

It is my pleasure to be able to can I bring if men will not help themselves? Go and make my excuses.

Wagner.

Sir, if you will bear with me one moment. It is not your counsel this time, that they have come to seek. It seems the book is a rare and precious volume, for it bears a strange and curious title: "Clavis Astartis Magica."

Faust.

Clavis Astartis! You must be wrong! You want to make a fool of me. Are you crazy? Seeing visions?

Wagner.

No, no! Not so, I do assure your worship.

Faust.

Then be it so; let the students in. (*Wagner exits.*)

Faust, Faust, now your moment is come at last. To my own hands the magic pow'r is given, to me revealed is the whole black world of sorcery, dark and secret forces are my servants. I have power. I have power. Yes, oh mankind, you who oft have plagued me, stand in fear of Faust! Into his hands the power is given, dark and secret forces are his slaves, he shall compel you, he shall rule you. Woe, woe to you, to you all. Yet, should Wagner be mistaken . . . perchance to save my soul?

serve you. I do hope that your studies are not so intense as to bring you harm.

2nd Student.

And may I say the same thing, sir? For the devil is a great conjurer for tricking and catching a man.

Faust.

Gentlemen, I thank you for this reminder. Do not worry about me. Will you tarry a bit and join me in a glass of wine? I would be deeply honored.

1st Student.

We thank you, sir, but we must take our leave.

2nd Student.

Apologies again for disturbing you, sir. We will now take our leave.

Faust.

Goodbye, gentlemen! You will remain always in my memory. At last, I will be able to speak of those things that fill my heart with joy. I will read these two books with great care, as though my life depended on it. This one was written by the Spanish author Runzifar, and this one by another Spaniard, Varth. Two masters of the art of magic. I shall devote myself to understanding these books. I shall triumph over magic! I shall never accept defeat!]

Wagner (*enters*).

Please, your worshipful grace, the students are here.

Faust.

Then let them enter.

(*Three students, dressed in black, enter.*)

Who are you?

All.

Three students from Cracow.

Faust.

Oh, my old, my dearly loved Cracow! Seeing you here before me I once again feel young. Daydreams! Visions! The hopes I once had cherished. Sirs, be welcome. And what brings you to me?

1st Student.

This book I must deliver to you.

2nd Student.

And here is the key that will unlock it.

3rd Student.

You are now the rightful owner by virtue of this deed of gift.

Faust.

How comes a gift of such price to me?

All.

You are the master!

Faust.

I may take it and own it?

All.

It is yours alone.

Faust.

And for recompense, what can I give you?

All.

Later, later. Farewell, Faust.

Faust.

Nay, go not. I would entertain you.

All.

Farewell, Faust.

Faust.

Then tell me . . . are we to meet again?

1st Student.

Perhaps.

2nd Student.

Perhaps.

3rd Student.

Perhaps.

All.

Farewell, Faust. (*They exit.*)

Faust (*watching them, shaking his head*).

Strange fellows!

(*Wagner re-enters.*)

Why, man, did you not see the students? Did you not open the door for them?

Wagner.

I beg pardon of your Grace, but nobody passed me.

Faust.

Just now, they went away.

Wagner.

I saw nobody.

Faust.

How could you have missed them? Ah! Now I know *who* these men were!

(*The crucible boils over. Wagner hurries to it.*)]

Busoni's histrionic imagination led him to make a number of changes when composing the text of this key scene. He changes two students to the more mystical number of three and has them sing "Farewell, Faust" three times at the end. And for the sake of unity he reduces two books to one, then adds a key and a deed of gift, so each student will have something to present to Faust.

In both scenes, the plot structure allows some character development for the hero while Wagner is off-stage. In the puppet play, the author paints Faust as a rather vain man, unduly concerned over whether these students will show him proper respect. Busoni, however, uses this stage-time to establish quite a bit more. We learn that Faust has been thinking of giving up the study of theology for that of magic. He knows what is in the book—the "Key to the Magic of Astartis" no less—and exults in the power about to be placed in his hands. His intended use of the power is somewhat disturbing, however. He will exact revenge on all those who have plagued him in the past; he will compel, he will rule; his enemies will experience woe. Only at the end of his soliloquy does he pause for a moment with the thought that he may have to pay dearly for his new-found power. This last idea is also developed in the puppet play, in which the two students warn Faust not to risk his soul to achieve supernatural power. Faust scoffs at their concern but we know, in the audience, that he is ripe for plucking by the devil.

Busoni's most original idea comes at the end of the scene. He suggests that Faust will meet the three students once more, giving his plot structure a feeling of unity by bringing the ending back to the beginning, just as Wagner unifies his epic tale, *Der Ring des Niebelungen,* when Brünhilde returns the stolen ring to the Rhine Maidens at the end of *Götterdämmerung.* Busoni also reinforces the supernatural quality of the students in a short scene with Wagner, who has not seen them leave. Faust suddenly realizes *who* they are.

As to the language, Busoni sharpens and refines the dialogue, cutting what is not essential and using as few words as possible. The language of the puppet play displays a stilted, literary quality, whereas Busoni renders the content of the scene into lines that are more vivid, more succinct and, hence, easier to set to expressive music. Throughout his text, he reveals a talent for dramatic dialogue, whether in verse or in prose.

For the next *Vorspiel,* the scene with the devils, Busoni used a different source—Lessing's fragmentary scene from his projected Faust play, that was published in the 17th *Literaturbrief* of February 16, 1759. In the scene, Lessing calls for seven spirits, a number that Busoni reduces to six:

LESSING'S *FAUST*

(Faust und sieben Geister)

Faust.
Ihr? Ihr seid die schnellesten Geister der Hölle?

Alle.
Wir.

Faust.
Seid ihr alle sieben gleich schnell?

Alle.
Nein.

Faust.
Und welcher von euch ist der schnelleste?

Alle.
Der bin ich!

Faust.
Ein Wunder! Daß unter sieben Teufeln nur sechs Lügner sind. Ich muß euch näher kennen lernen.

1. Geist.
Das wirst du! Einst!

Faust.
Einst! Wie meinst du das? Predigen die Teufel auch Buße?

1. Geist.
Jawohl, den Verstockten. Aber halte uns nicht auf.

Faust.
Wie heißest du? Und wie schnell bist du?

1. Geist.
Du könntest eher eine Probe, als eine Antwort haben.

BUSONI'S *DOKTOR FAUST*

(Der nämliche Raum, um die Mitternacht)

Faust.
Die Sanduhr zeigt die Mitternacht: ich darf beginnen. Rätselvolles Geschenk, nun sollst du dich bewähren.

(Faust entschließt sich und schlägt das Buch des Astartis auf.)

So wäre dies die erste Handlung!

(Er löst seinen Gürtel und bildet mit ihm einen Kreis auf dem Boden; tritt in den Kreis, den Schlüssel in der Hand.)

Lucifer! Lucifer! Gefallner Engel, du der Stolzeste, herbei!

(Er hebt den Schlüssel, der erstrahlt. Fahlgrünes Leuchten durchtanzt den Raum.)

Lucifer! Hierher! Zu mir!

(Der Schlüssel erstrahlt mehr und mehr. Eine sichtliche Erregung uberfällt Faust).

Chor. *(unter der Bühne, unsichtbar.)*
Dein Begehr?

Faust.
Entsende mir deine Diener.

Chor.
Du willst?

Faust.
Ich will.

Chor.
Du beharrst? Du beharrst?

Faust.

Nun wohl. Sieh her; was mache ich?

1. Geist.

Du fährst mit deinem Finger schnell durch die Flamme des Lichts—

Faust.

Und verbrenne mich nicht. So geh auch du, und fahre sieben-mal ebenso schnell durch die Flammen der Hölle, und verbrenne dich nicht. Du verstummst? Du bleibst? So prahlen auch die Teufel? Ja, ja; keine Sünde ist so klein, daß ihr sie euch nehmen ließet. Zweiter, wie heißest du?

2. Geist.

Chil; das ist in eurer lang-weiligen Sprache: Pfeil der Pest.

Faust.

Und wie schnell bist du?

2. Geist.

Denkest du, daß ich meinen Namen vergebens führe? Wie die Pfeile der Pest.

Faust.

Nun so geh, und diene einem Arzte! Für mich bist du viel zu langsam. Du, dritter, wie heißest du?

3. Geist.

Ich heiße Dilla; denn mich tragen die Flügel der Winde.

Faust.

Und du vierter?

4. Geist.

Mein Name ist Jutta, denn ich

Faust.

Ja, ich will!

Chor.

Sie kommen! Sie kommen!

(*Die Studierlampe und der Schlüssel erlöschen. Sechs Zun-genflammen schweben im Raume.*) *
* *
* * *

Faust.

Was tat ich! Wie konnt' es al-sobald gelingen? Darf ich mich weiter wagen? Ich sollte sie befragen, doch es ekelt mich davor; schon ihre Stimmen könnten mich töten!

Chor.

Frage immerhin!

Faust.

Wohlan! So sprich, du Erster, du tiefster, gib deinen Namen.

1. Stimme.

Gravis.

Faust.

Sag' an, wie sehr du geschwind bist.

1. Stimme.

Wie der Sand in dem Uhrglas.

Faust.

Wie der Sand . . . wie der Sand in dem Uhrglas?! Hinweg! Hin-weg, kriechendes Wesen, verlösche!

(*Die erste Flamme erlischt. Für sich*).

Sie gehorchen.

(*Laut*)

Der Zweite! Welcher bist du?

44

fahre auf den Strahlen des Lichts.

Faust.

O ihr, deren Schnelligkeit in endlichen Zahlen auszudrücken, ihr Elenden—

5. Geist.

Wurdige sie deines Unwillens nicht. Sie sind nur Satans Boten in der Körperwelt. Wir sind es in der Welt der Geister; uns wirst du schneller finden.

Faust.

Und wie schnell bist du?

5. Geist.

So schnell als die Gedanken des Menschen.

Faust.

Das ist etwas! Aber nicht immer sind die Gedanken des Menschen schnell. Nicht da, wenn Wahrheit und Tugend sie auffordern. Wie träge sind sie alsdann! Du kannst schnell sein, wenn du schnell sein willst; aber wer steht mir dafür, daß du es allezeit willst? Nein, dir werde ich so wenig trauen, als ich mir selbst hätte trauen sollen. Ach!

(*Zum sechsten Geiste.*)

Sage du, wie schnell bist du?

6. Geist.

So schnell als die Rache des Rächers.

Faust.

Des Rächers? Welches Rächers?

6. Geist.

Des Gewaltigen, des Schrecklichen, der sich allein die Rache

2. Stimme.

Levis. Ich bin geschwind wie das fallende Laub. Levis. Levis.

Faust.

Der Mensch fällt hurtiger als du: verschwinde, verschwinde.

(*Die zweite Flamme erlischt.*)

Gib Rede, Dritte, gleich den Andren.

3. Stimme.

Ich bin Asmodus. Ich eile, eile wie der Bach, der sich vom Felsen stürzt: über Bergeskämme, durch die Felder Sprudelnd, hin bis zum Ozean!

Faust.

Ein Prahler bist du. Dich zieht es nur abwärts: Fort mit dir! Fort!

(*Die dritte Flamme erlischt.*)

(*Für sich.*)

Mein Hoffen sinkt, ob auch mein Mut sich hebet.

(*Laut.*)

Offenbare dich, Vierter!

4. Stimme.

Ich bin Fürst Belzebuth.

Chor.

Belzebuth!

4. Stimme.

Ich schnelle wie die Kugel aus dem Rohre; genügt's dir?

Chor.

Genügt's dir?

Faust.

Nein, nein, nein! Ein Spottfürst! Ist die Flinte nicht etwa Menschenwerk? Ist des Menschen Wunsch, ist denn nicht sein Traum höher zielend,

vorbehielt, weil ihn die Rache
vergnügte.

Faust.

Teufel! Du lästerst, denn ich
sehe, du zitterst. Schnell, sagst
du, wie die Rache des—Bald
hätte ich ihn genennt! Nein, er
werde nicht unter uns genennt!
Schnell wäre seine Rache?
Schnell? Und ich lebe noch?
Und ich sündige noch?

6. Geist.

Daß er dich noch sündigen läßt,
ist schon Rache!

Faust.

Und daß ein Teufel mich dieses
lehren muß! Aber doch erst
heute! Nein, seine Rache ist
nicht schnell, und wenn du nicht
schneller bist, als seine Rache,
so geh nur.

(*Zum siebente Geiste.*)
Wie schnell bist du?

7. Geist.

Unzuvergnügender Sterbliche,
wo auch ich dir nicht schnell
genug bin—

Faust.

So sage; wie schnell?

7. Geist.

Nicht mehr und nicht weniger
als der Übergang vom Guten
zum Bösen.

Faust.

Ha! Du bist mein Teufel! So
schnell als der Übergang vom
Guten zum Bösen! Ja, der ist
schnell; schneller ist nichts als
der! Weg von hier ihr Schnecken

weiter tragend? Wie könntest
du mir, Faust, genügen?
Entweiche!

(*Die vierte Flamme erlischt.*)
Und du, und du, Zweitletzter,
nenn' dich, bezeichne dich,
Fünfter!

5. Stimme.

Schaue hier, Megäros.

Chor.

Schaue hier, Megäros.

5. Stimme.

Wie der Sturm behende.

Chor.

Hier schaue Megäros, Megäros.

Faust.

Das klingt nach Etwas, doch es
erschöpft nicht.

Chor.

Als wie der Sturm behende.

Faust.

Ich blase, Sturm, dich aus: Verwehe, verwehe, verwehe!

(*Die fünfte Flamme erlischt.*)

Chor.

Üh!

Faust.

Schweiget! Schweiget!

(*Er tritt aus dem Kreise.*)
Ein einzelner blieb. Ich zögre,
die letzte Hoffnung zu zerstören.
Mir bangt vor der ek'len Leere,
die folgen muß. So wäre dies der
ganze Höllenprunk! Wie steht
doch eines Menschen Geist
darüber! In ihm ist des Gottes
Hauch. Wie ich euch verachte,
die ihr hier gedämmert, und nun
dunkelt, ihr Dünkelhaften! Ich

des Orkus! Weg! Als der Übergang vom Guten zum Bösen! Ich habe es erfahren, wie schnell er ist! Ich habe es erfahren! usw.—[58]

kehre mich ab von euch. Welchem Wahn gab ich mich hin! Arbeit, heilende Welle, in dir bade ich mich rein!

6. Stimme.

Faust!

Faust.

Wie hell flackert das Licht! Das Licht! Ist es von ihm aus, daß die Stimme ruft? Wie hoch züngelt es auf! Wirst auch nicht mehr vermögen als die And'ren, o du lichtere Flamme. Ich mag nichts erfahren von dir.

6. Stimme.

Faust! Faust! Faust!

Faust.

Noch einmal, noch einmal, und dringender? So magst du reden! So magst du reden!

6. Stimme.

Faust, ich bin geschwind als wie des Menschen Gedanke.

Faust.

Als wie des Menschen Gedanke? Was will ich mehr? . . . Dein Name?

6. Stimme.

Mephistopheles.

Faust.

Mephistopheles?

6. Stimme.

Mephistopheles.

Chor.

Mephistopheles,   Mephistopheles.

Faust.

So zeige dich in greifbarer Gestalt.[59]

47

[LESSING'S *FAUST*

(*Faust and Seven Spirits.*)

Faust.

You? You are the swiftest spirits of hell?

All.

We.

Faust.

Are all seven of you equally swift?

All.

No.

Faust.

And which of you is the swiftest?

All.

I am he.

Faust.

Wonderful! Among seven devils, only six liars. I must get to know you better.

1st Spirit.

You will, one day.

Faust.

One day? What do you mean? Do devils preach about atonement?

1st Spirit.

Yes. It will come. But don't keep us waiting.

Faust.

What is your name? And how swift are you?

1st Spirit.

You might prefer a test to an answer.

Faust.

Well then, what should I do?

1st Spirit.

Run your finger quickly through the flame—

[BUSONI'S *DOKTOR FAUST*

(*The same room at midnight.*)

Faust.

The hourglass marks the midnight hour. I may begin now. Now, mysterious gift, let thy power be proven!

(*He opens the book.*)

Thus I perform the initial process.

(*He takes off his girdle and makes a circle on the ground with it. He then enters the circle, the key in his hand.*)

Lucifer! Lucifer! Thou fallen angel, thou the proudest one, appear.

(*He raises the key, which glows. A pale green light dances about the room*

Lucifer! Appear to me!

(*The key shines more and more brightly. Faust is visibly excited.*)

Chorus (*behind the scene; invisible*).

What's thy will?

Faust.

First send me those who will serve me.

Chorus.

Thy will?

Faust.

It is my will.

Chorus.

Thy resolve? Thy resolve?

Faust.

Yes, 'tis my will.

Faust.

—without burning myself. Why don't you go and run seven times as fast through the flames of hell without getting burned? No comment? Still here? Do all devils boast like this? Yes, yes. You don't let even the smallest sin slip through your fingers. Second! What is your name?

2nd Spirit.

Chil. In your dull language, Arrow of the Plague.

Faust.

And how swift are you?

2nd Spirit.

Do I carry my name in vain? As the arrows of the plague.

Faust.

Then go and serve a doctor! You are much too slow for me. You, third. What is your name?

3nd Spirit.

I am Dilla. I am carried by the wings of the wind.

Faust.

And you, fourth?

4th Spirit.

My name is Jutta. I ride on the rays of light.

Faust.

Oh you, who express your speed in so many numbers. You wretches—

5th Spirit.

Do not waste your indignation on them. They are Satan's messengers only in the corporeal world. We are messengers in the

Chorus.

They come now. They come now.

(*The lamp goes out and the key stops shining. Six tongues of flame float in the room.*) *
                                    * *
Faust.   * * *

'Tis begun now. How could it be successful so soon? I ought to question them. Yet, the very thought disgusts me. Well might it be their voices could kill me!

Chorus.

Fear not, question us!

Faust.

I will! So speak, thou first one and deepest. Say what thy name is.

1st Voice.

Gravis.

Faust.

Then say, how swift is thy motion?

1st Voice.

As the sand in the hourglass.

Faust.

As the sand, as the sand in the hourglass? Begone! Begone! I want no sluggards. Be extinguished!

(*The first flame goes out. To himself.*)

They obey me.

(*Aloud.*)

Thou second, what is thy name?

2nd Voice.

Levis. I am as swift as the falling leaf. Levis. Levis.

world of the mind. You will find us much swifter.

Faust.

And how swift are you?

5th Spirit.

I am as swift as the thoughts of man.

Faust.

That is something. But the thoughts of man are not always swift. Not when they are challenged by truth and virtue. How languid they are then! Yes, you can be swift if you want to be, but how do I know you will always deliver? No, I won't trust you any further than I would trust myself. Ah!

(*To the sixth spirit.*)

Tell me, how swift are you?

6th Spirit.

As swift as the vengeance of the avenger.

Faust.

The avenger. Which avenger?

6th Spirit.

The mighty one, the terrible one, who reserves vengeance to himself, because he enjoys wreaking vengeance.

Faust.

Devil, that is blasphemy. You are shivering. Swift, you said, as the vengeance of the—I almost said his name! No, he won't be named among us! Swift is his vengeance? Swift? And I live still? Sin still?

Faust.

A man falls quicker far than thou. Vanish! Vanish!

(*The second flame goes out.*)

Make answer, third one, like the others.

3rd Voice.

I am Asmodus. I hasten, hasten like the brook that spurts from rock and crag. Over mountain ranges, through the valleys gushing, on till I reach the sea.

Faust.

Vain boaster art thou: thy path ever downwards. Hence, begone! Begone!

(*The third flame goes out. To himself.*)

My hopes fall down, although my courage rises.

(*Aloud.*)

Show thyself, thou fourth one.

4th Voice.

I am Prince Beelzebub.

Chorus.

Beelzebub!

4th Voice.

I fly as fast as bullets from the barrel. Will that suffice?

Faust.

No, no, no! Thou mock Prince! Is the rifle not the work of man? Is it not man's wish, his dream to aim higher, to cast his thoughts farther? How could thou satisfy me, Faust? Away from me!

(*The fourth flame goes out.*)

And thou, thou the last but one.

6th Spirit.

The fact that he lets you sin is his vengeance.

Faust.

And I must learn this from a devil? And only just today? No, his vengeance is not swift and since you are not swifter than his vengeance, then leave me.

(*To the seventh spirit.*)

How swift are you?

7th Spirit.

You are a mortal hard to please. I am probably not swift enough for you.

Faust.

Tell me anyway. How swift?

7th Spirit.

No more and no less, than the transition from good to evil.

Faust.

Ha! You are my devil! As swift as the transition from good to evil! Yes, that is swift—nothing is swifter than that. Away from here, you snails of Hades! As the transition from good to evil! I have experienced how swift it is. I have had experience.

Etc.]

Fifth one, declare thyself. Answer!

5th Voice.

Look on me, Megäros.

Chorus.

Look on him, Megäros.

5th Voice.

Swift am I as tempest.

Chorus.

Look on him, Megäros. Megäros.

Faust.

These words ring truer, yet they suffice not.

Chorus.

He is swift as tempest.

Faust.

Tempest, I blow thee out! Abate!

(*The fifth flame goes out.*)

Chorus.

Ugh!

Faust.

Silence! Silence!

(*He steps out of the circle.*)

A single light remains. I hesitate to destroy the last hope. I fear the loathsome emptiness that is sure to follow. So this is the splendor of hell! In the spirit of mankind dwells the breath of God. How I despise you, whose light dies out. Prisoners of darkness! I turn my back on you. I cast away such madness. In the healing power of work, I wash myself clean!

6th Voice.

Faust!

Faust.

How bright flickers the light! The light! Is it from there then

51

that the voice did call? How high
flares up the flame. No more success will thou have than the
others, though more brightly
thou burnest. I could not learn
aught from thee.
6th Voice.
Faust! Faust! Faust!
Faust.
It calls me, it calls me insistently.
I will hear thee. I will hear thee.
6th Voice.
Faust, I am as swift as are the
thoughts of man!
Faust.
As are the thoughts of man.
What more do I want?

. . .

Your name?
6th Voice.
Mephistopheles.
Faust.
Mephistopheles?
6th Voice.
Mephistopheles.
Chorus.
Mephistopheles. Mephistoph-
eles.
Faust.
So show yourself in form I may
grasp.]

Lessing divides the speed of his devils into two categories, that of the
physical world and that of the human mind. The speed of four of the devils
can be measured in centimeters per second, the one who travels on rays of
light plainly being faster than anybody else. But Lessing's Faust is more
interested in swiftness of thought, which travels faster, perhaps, than the
speed of light, and chooses the devil who moves with the speed of man's
impulse from good to evil, an impulse Faust has experienced himself.

52

Busoni must have concluded that man's thoughts travel with equal speed regardless of destination, and his Faust, after rejecting five devils whose speed is finite, chooses Mephistopheles to serve him.

Busoni also adds an idea to the dramatic structure. If Faust can simply choose a devil to serve him indefinitely, where is the bargain? What does the devil get? So Busoni's Faust inadvertently steps out of the magic circle formed by his girdle and, when Mephisto appears, they stand in each other's presence as equals. The devil will serve Faust for a certain period but, when the time is up, Faust must serve the devil.

Busoni heightens the tension and mystery of the scene by employing an off-stage chorus to accent and reiterate the lines of the later devils and establishes a special kind of musical unity by starting the first devil at the bottom of the bass clef and continuing in five steps to a very high tenor tessitura, making the role of Mephistopheles one of the most demanding in the modern repertory.

A key scene in all Faust plays is the nature of the pact the hero signs with the devil. Busoni again avoids comparison with Goethe by eliminating the idea that Faust becomes a young man again before embarking on his adventures. Instead, he continued to draw ideas from the puppet plays, using some, discarding others. In the puppet play performed in the 1820s and 1830s, by the Schütz und Dreher Kasperletheater of Berlin, Faust demands that Mephistopheles agree to serve him for forty-eight years and that, during this period, Faust will taste of all the earthly joys—of beauty and fame—and will receive true answers to all his questions. Mephisto must submit this request to Pluto for approval, but he soon returns to tell Faust that the arrangement is satisfactory except that it can be for only twenty-four years—that's as long as these things are allowed to run. (Later, Mephistopheles halves this time period to twelve years by arguing that twelve years of days plus twelve years of nights obviously equal twenty-four years. He then cautions Faust about doing business with the devil!)

The contract also requires that Faust renounce Christianity, give up washing, shaving, combing his hair and trimming his nails, and will forswear marriage. Faust thinks these conditions may be the hardest to abide, but he agrees to sign the pact in his own blood. As he takes the quill pen from his new servant, Faust reflects for a moment in lines, translated by David Nutt,[60] as follows:

Faust (*aside*).

Freely my blood shall flow upon this day
When to thy Lord my soul I sign away.
Behold the ruddy stream, which seems to brand
In scarlet letters, flaming on my hand.
Great H and F that all too plainly say
From the impending doom "Homo Fuge!"
Yet! F might stand for Faust and H for Honour great,
But whether fickle Chance it be or fixèd Fate,
I may no longer stand in doubt and hesitate.
The deed is signed, is sealed, repentance were too late.
Yet I would clasp the parchment, but that o'er me creep
Strange langours of a faint and death-like sleep.[61]

From this poignant scene in the puppet play, Busoni develops a much more complicated, more musical interpretation of the primal image of the man who sells his soul to the devil. His Faust, following Busoni's own lifelong desires, makes unusual demands:

Faust.

Say, will you serve me?

Mephistopheles.

Serve, you say. In what fashion?

Faust.

Ensure for me through all my earthly life
that all my wishes are granted absolutely.
Let me embrace the world, both the East and the South,
for they call me too. O grant me, grant me
to know the works of all men
and past belief enhance them.
Give me genius, and give me too
its sorrows.

    . . .

Mephistopheles.

Well, what more?

Faust.

Make me free! Make me free![62]

In addition to universal knowledge, Faust demands genius together with its sorrows and, further, he must be made free. Genius and freedom: twin pillars of the artist's ideal, the pillars on which Busoni supported his entire creative life. In genius, Faust demands the highest of all human creative power, the power to establish the laws of art. And in freedom, Faust will reach a state beyond good and evil, beyond the powers of God and the devil, a state of immortality achieved by transmutation of the essence of himself to posterity, in the physical manifestation of the son he has fathered by the Duchess of Parma.

At the moment when he must sign the contract, Busoni's Faust, like his forebear in the puppet play, hesitates. Mephisto reminds him that outside his door his creditors stand, demanding payment for past wrongs; that he got a poor girl in trouble and left her to die; that her brother is looking for him to exact revenge; and that the clergy are closing in on him because they suspect him of having had prior dealings with the devil—in fact, they are preparing to burn him at the stake. Faust hears the sounds of many people pounding on his door. Mephisto offers to dispose of the lot. Faust accepts. "Töte sie" ["Kill them"], he commands, and the devil obliges with alacrity. Faust has agreed to the contract, but now he must sign it in his own blood. As he goes through with the signing, Busoni again employs an off-stage chorus, signing the *Credo* and *Gloria* to enhance the atmosphere of magic that he established at the beginning of his opera.

Chorus.
I believe in one God the Father Almighty, Creator of heaven and earth, and of all things visible and invisible.
Faust.
What more do you want of me?
Mephistopheles.
A few words written and signed with your own blood.
Faust.
Let me have it.
Mephistopheles.
Good.
Faust.
Where is my willpower, where the pride I once had? O wretched Faust, the work of Hell's begun.
(*Goes to the window.*)
How will it be with me?
(*Dawn is breaking. Easter Chorus. Peal of bells.*)

Chorus.

And the third day he rose again according to the scriptures and ascended into heaven and sitteth on the right hand of the Father.

Faust.

Easter Day! And there go all good folk to the minster. Day of my childhood!

Mephistopheles.

Stop this everlasting mumbling.

Chorus.

And he shall come again with glory to judge both the quick and the dead.

Faust.

You, Faust, are now a dead man. I wait for the judgment. Who will help me? Who will help me?

(*A raven flies in with a pen in its beak. Mephistopheles takes the pen from it.*)

Mephistopheles.

Be a man, Faust. You gave your word, now keep it. Fulfill it! Fulfill it! Fulfill it!

Faust.

There is still time—there is no compassion, there is neither blessedness nor hope of reward, no bliss of Heav'n, no awful power of Hell: I defy the future.

Mephistopheles.

Bravo, bravo. That's what I call good progress, and now you're moving in the right direction.

Faust (*signs the paper and hands it to Mephistopheles, shuddering*).

There then, when my term is up we shall know for certain—perchance 'twill be you that fall. Am I not thy lord?

(*He falls to the floor, unconscious.*)

Chorus.

Glory be to God on high and on earth, peace.

(*Mephistopheles gloats for a time over his victim, then tears the paper from his hand.*)

Mephistopheles.

My victim!

Chorus.

Hallelujah!⁶³

After the scene in the church in which Faust orders the death of the "Brother", Busoni turns to the *Hauptspiel* of his opera, the encounter of

Faust with the Duchess of Parma. In the puppet play, Kasperle enacts a scene with Don Carlos, Master of Ceremonies at the Court of Parma, in which the irritated courtier pursues the clown about the stage. They are shortly joined by the Duke of Parma, who places his crown on a bench and joins in the merry chase. Meanwhile, his Duchess receives Faust and Mephistopheles:

Mephistopheles (*as herald*).

You're playing hide and seek. Our coming is intrusion.

Duchess.

Ah no, if you would speak, say on to the conclusion.

Mephistopheles.

My master, Dr. Faust, far-famed for Necromancy.

Duchess.

I've heard of him.

Faust.

                    Fame here exceeds my hope and fancy.

Mephistopheles.

Soon all the round world o'er, men will say and sing his praises.

Duchess.

Sure! He's the master who the spirit calls and raises.

Faust.

The ring of Solomon ensures me their obedience.

Duchess.

Pray show us of your art, though black are its ingredients.

Faust.

Fairest of women, fain would I obey,

if such things could but be in light of day.

Mephistopheles.

What matter where the sun, since day and night obey you?

Faust.

Ah, true, it shall be done.

Duchess.

                    One moment, Sirs, I pray you.

Now cease that jackanapes to chase thus faster and faster.

For while you seek the man, see! I have found the master,

Great Dr. Faust himself, Duke over all the Spirits!

Faust (*aside*).

She ranks me with herself according to my merits.

Duchess.

He'll crown our wedding feast with honour and renown.

Mephistopheles.

And his Grace's crownèd head will freshly now recrown.

Duke (*resuming his crown*).

Herr Doctor, pray come in. I'm still quite overheated.

Duchess.

The play will now begin; so please let all be seated.[64]

Busoni builds on this naive but effective sequence in his own way. Since he doesn't have to bother with Kasperle, he devises a very grand entrance for Faust, after he is announced by Mephistopheles, in the role of Herald:

> (*Faust approaches slowly at a great distance, from above. He is followed by a fantastic suite of Negro boys or apes who carry his train. His appearance should be very startling, but not that of a charlatan. The Master of Ceremonies trips in front of the group, half leading, half inviting.*)[65]

Busoni uses the chorus to describe the mysterious entrance of Faust. With him comes the world of the unseen. Night things invade the day and turn true to false. Faust moves with grace and dignity; the unnatural is, to him, natural. He is fearsome and strange, yet he must be looked on. The scene continues:

Duchess (*aside*).

He is a prince in manner and in bearing.

No man has ever yet so charmed my heart.

Duke (*aside*).

Methinks that hell, that hell itself has sent him here.

Mephistopheles (*aside*).

The watch dog barks. The sheep are bleating.

Chorus.

Strange is this man, strange is his guest. What shall we see?

Faust (*aside*).

This night will I possess you, proudest of women.

Duke.

Good doctor, to our court we would bid you welcome and thank you for the art you will display. We hope our gracious lady will be pleased. Will you begin, sir?

Duchess (*aside, softly*).

What shall I see?

Faust (*half aside*).

Fear not, my lord, I will.

(*He lifts his hands and makes a few conjuring gestures. A swarm of faun-like little devils rushes in from all sides and disappears in the bushes.*)

Chorus.

Ah! Ha ha ha ha ha!

Faust.

Pardon me if I go my own way.

Wonders are not conjured up by day.

Light be extinguished and turn to night.

Stars come forth. Adorn the sky.

(*The day is changed to a starlit night.*)[66]

In the puppet play, Faust also begins his magical demonstrations by turning day into night. He then conjures up a scene in which Solomon appears, kneeling before the Queen of Sheba. The Duke of Parma quickly notes the resemblance of the Queen to his wife while the Duchess sees Faust in every feature of King Solomon.

The Duchess asks Faust if he can read her wishes in her eyes. He replies by producing the lovers Samson and Delilah. Again, all observe the resemblance of the conjured lovers to the magician and his hostess.

A scene follows showing Judith beheading Holofernes but, this time, although the Duchess resembles Judith, Holofernes appears to be an image of the Duke. Faust conjures up David and Goliath but seems unable to produce Lucretia for the Duchess. She asks to touch the figures, but Faust refuses this. Don Carlos announces dinner. Faust would follow the others but Mephistopheles warns him that the Duke is suspicious, and the food to be offered Faust is poisoned. Further, because he has been known to contradict Holy Writ, the Inquisition is preparing to boil him in oil. Faust agrees that they had better get out of there but regrets not possessing the beautiful Duchess of Parma. Mephisto promises him an Empress in place of the Duchess as they mount Kasperle's dragon and ride away to Constantinople.

Busoni uses the visions of Solomon with the Queen of Sheba and Samson with Delilah, but then adds a scene in which Salome (resembling the Duchess) appears with John the Baptist (Faust) and an Executioner (the Duke). Faust tells the Duchess that Salome has only to give the signal and John will die. "Er darf nicht sterben!" ["He must not die!"] the Duchess cries, involuntarily revealing her love for Faust. The entertainment ends and, as in the puppet play, all retire to dinner except Faust and Mephistopheles. But Busoni now makes a radical change in the story. The Duchess returns to an empty stage and sings an aria of love and passionate desire for Faust:

Duchess.
> (*She enters as if in a dream, holding her arms out before her.*)
> He calls me, he calls me with a thousand voices,
> draws me to him with a thousand arms.
> And ev'ry moment seems to me a thousand,
> each single moment speaks to me of him alone.
> All that I was once, all that I used to think
> is now forgotten, forgotten. . .
> I see only the path that leads, see only the path,
> the path that leads to my lover, see only the path to my lover.
> Yes, yes, yes I come, I walk at your side
> through endless realms of wonder.
> The earth will be my kingdom, I, its anointed queen.
> And all that future ages shall discover, one day is
> it all mine, soon will all be mine, soon will all be mine!
> I take his hand and walk with him beyond the farthest horizon.
> With you, with you, with you, oh measureless delight,
> Faust, oh my love, I come. . .
> Faust, oh my love, Faust! Faust, I follow you!
> (*She goes out slowly.*)[67]

There is a lapse of time during which Faust and the Duchess make their escape together with the help of Mephistopheles. The devil does not realize that the lovers can defeat him in his struggle for Faust's soul.

In the puppet play, the scene shifts back to a street in Mainz. Faust prays before a carved figure of the Virgin that is attached to a house. He would repent, but cannot. Twelve years have passed and he has found neither joy nor gladness. The gold he has obtained has turned to dross. The foaming bowl of pleasure has left bitter dregs in his mouth. He would pray to God, but cannot. He asks Mephisto if he can still come to God and—since he can—the devil provides a final temptation to secure his triumph. He has promised Faust true love and now he offers his victim Helen of Troy. Faust denies God for the last time and takes Helena to his house but, once again, is cheated. As he tries to embrace her, she turns into a hellish serpent and Faust falls to the floor sickened and choked by the loathsome emanations from her mouth. He asks the devil if this is his idea of faithful service.

Mephistopheles laughs and replies that cheating is his trade. Not only will Faust *not* partake of the sexual pleasures provided by Helen of Troy, his time is up. At midnight, the contract expires.

Kasperle appears in the street as night watchman and announces the hours as they advance toward midnight. Faust tries again to pray before the figure of the Virgin on the wall of the house, but it turns into an image of Helen of Troy:

Faust.

Pray! Can I yet pray? Let me try.

(*Kneels before Madonna on house.*)

Virgo, Virginium praeclara. Oh horror! The face becomes Helena's and heavenly devotion is quenched by earthly love. Satan! That is thine accursed craft. My heart defrauded of all earthly joys, cannot rise to those of Heaven. Is there, then, no mercy?

Hollow Voice from Above.

He, who on earth would God deny,

Is lost to all Eternity.

(*Faust falls fainting to the ground.*)[68]

In the final scene of his opera, Busoni makes good use of the idea of a carved figure of the Virgin being transformed into an image of Helen of Troy. In fact, Helena, the incarnation of ideal mortal beauty for the Greeks had become, for Busoni, a symbol for the ideal of artistic perfection, an ideal he strove for all his life and never attained. Antony Beaumont has observed that Busoni "saw himself as a spiritual leader who was to guide music into higher, purer realms than it had ever, as yet, inhabited."[69] He thought of his lifelong work as a composer as a journey toward an ideal condition, "where the 'marvelous future' becomes the present, mankind would obtain perfection, and Paradise would be regained. The vision of Helena in *Doktor Faust* represented the attainment of his perfection."[70]

Busoni died before he was able to compose the scene in the Wittenberg tavern in which Helena, intended as a role for a dancer, beguiles Faust with her classic beauty. Mephistopheles tells Faust he will conjure her up from the ashes of the dead child, and that Faust shall possess her. Faust senses the nearness of perfection and sings, with an off-stage chorus, of his rapturous anticipation:

Faust (*with Chorus*).

Dream of young men, goal of wise men!
Perfect image of purest beauty.
Yes, to know thee, to exalt thee,
To instruct thee was my mission.
Thou unknowable, unattainable, thou still unfulfilled,
show thyself now!
(*Through smoke and flames, the outline of Helena becomes steadily
clearer.*)
All I longed for, all I dreamed of,
my ideal takes shape before me.
(*Helena appears, naked, wearing a transparent veil and stands motionless.
The background of the scene has changed to a southern sky at night.*)[71]

At this point in the action, Helena dances for Faust but, until recently,
there was no music for the scene. The conductor and Busoni specialist,
Antony Beaumont, has explained how he discovered two sheets of sketches
for *Doktor Faust* that enabled him to complete the opera as the composer
had imagined it.[72] Busoni intended to base Helena's dance on his "Trills
Study" of 1924 and, using this music as a source, Beaumont added 75
measures to the tavern scene. With Helena now able to dance, to approach
Faust, then turn away from him, Faust's lines and movements become more
coherent:

Faust.

I look on you! And now I will embrace you.
(*Faust approaches the figure. She draws back and begins a measured
dance. Faust follows her as she moves about the stage.*)
Only Faust has ever touched the perfect form.
You shrink away. Have you such various aspects?
I embrace you—and again not. O torment!
Finally—finally—to me!
(*As he at last thinks to hold her, the vision vanishes.*)
Ah! Cheated once again.
Now lost and gone for ever.[73]

The ideal of perfection has eluded Faust once more as it eluded Busoni
all his life. In fact, Beaumont believes that Busoni was unable to compose
the two key Helena scenes because he couldn't settle on a musical expression for ultimate perfection. This proved to be a serious stumbling block for

Philipp Jarnach as he worked to compose Faust's final monologue. He had the complete text, but the music of the climactic moment of the opera, when the image of the Virgin on the wall of the house turns into that of Helen of Troy, seemed impossible to bring to realization because the music would have to refer back to the music of the dance sequence in the tavern scene, and this music had not been composed. Jarnach solved the problem by cutting a number of key lines and hurrying on to an ending that he considered the best he could achieve under the circumstances. Antony Beaumont has been able, however, to set the missing lines in the 175 measures he added to the final scene after he completed the realization of the dance music of the previous scene. The missing lines, translated into English by Antony Beaumont,[74] throw light on the ultimate meaning of the opera, since they express the attainment of Faust to a condition, in Nietzsche's phrase, "beyond good and evil":

Faust.
[So let the work be finished,]
in defiance of you, of you all, who hold yourselves for good, whom we
call evil, who, for the sake of old quarrels take Mankind as a pretext and
pile upon him the consequence of your discord. Upon this highest insight
of my wisdom is your malice now broken to pieces and in my self-won
freedom expire both God and Devil at once.[75]

Faust performs the transmutation rite and, as his son dances off into the distance, dies in the street alone, and triumphant.

Edward J. Dent, among others, has bestowed high praise on Busoni's remarkable, almost legendary artistic achievement:

One cannot apply to *Doktor Faust* the ordinary standards of operatic
criticism. It moves on a plane of spiritual experience far beyond that of even
the greatest of musical works for the stage. On its first production a German
critic said of it that it could be compared only with *Parsifal*; it may be doubted
whether the comparison would altogether have pleased Busoni. The poem
by itself is a literary work of extraordinary power and imagination. It shows
clearly how much Busoni owed to the lifelong study of Goethe; it is not
Goethe's portrait of Faust, but it is written in Goethe's language. It combines
the simplicity of the puppet-plays with something of the concentrated agony
of Marlowe.[76]

Concentrated agony is, in fact, a convincing image for the immense intellectual and creative struggle Busoni experienced not only in bringing *Doktor Faust* to fruition, but throughout the course of his entire creative life. He labored to discover, by means of deductive reasoning, new musical devices and techniques that would enable him to express what he felt in his soul. W. H. Mellers has described the aim of his music as "spiritual autobiography" and adds that "there is no music of which it would be more correct to say that it was—in Lawrence's phrase—'art for *my* sake'."[77]

The effort consciously to express his changing spiritual states is possibly Busoni's most impressive intellectual achievement going, as it does, beyond art criticism and beyond aesthetical speculation. The continuous demands of his intellect on his creative resources enabled Busoni "to draw poetry from the same creative roots as music"[78] and, hence, achieve what is perhaps the loftiest degree of the Wagnerian ideal of the *Gesamtkunstwerk*: an artist, gifted with both histrionic and musical genius, composes his own libretto and sets it to his own music producing, thereby, a work of dramatic poetry that is truly the product of "two artistic forces against which he cannot struggle and to which he must voluntarily sacrifice himself."

Notes

1. Ernest Krenek, "Busoni—Then and Now," *Modern Music* 19 (1942), 88.

2. Ronald Stevenson, "Busoni—the Legend of a Prodigal," *The Score* (March, 1956), 18.

3. Anthony Beaumont, *Busoni the Composer* (London: Faber & Faber, 1985), 13.

4. Antony Beaumont, *Ferruccio Busoni: Selected Letters* (New York: Columbia University Press, 1987), XII.

5. H. H. Stuckenschmidt, *Ferruccio Busoni, Chronicle of a European,* trans. Sandra Morris (London: Calder & Boyars, 1920), 133.

6. Stuckenschmidt, 134.

7. Antony Beaumont, "Busoni and the Theatre," *Opera,* 37 (1986), 385.

8. Beaumont, 385.

9. Beaumont, 386.

10. Edward J. Dent, *Ferruccio Busoni, A Biography*, 2nd ed. (London: Oxford University Press, 1984), 106–7. Reprinted by permission of Oxford University Press.

11. Ferruccio Busoni, *Entwurf einer neuen Aesthetik der Tonkunst,* 2nd ed.

(Leipzig: Insel-Verlag, 1916), 4. Busoni uses these lines as one of two introductory mottos for the second edition of his book:

"Was sucht Ihr? Sagt! Und was erwartet Ihr?"
"Ich weiß es nicht; ich will das Unbekannte!
Was mir bekannt, ist unbegrenzt. Ich will
darüber noch. Mir fehlt das letzte Wort."

—Der mächtige Zauberer.

12. *Goethes Faust,* Kommentiert von Erich Trunz (Hamburg: Wegner, 1963), 44:

Geschrieben steht "Im Anfang war das Wort!"
Hier stock' ich schon! Wer hilft mir weiter fort?
Ich kann das Wort so hoch unmöglich schätzen,
Ich muß es anders übersetzen.
Wenn ich vom Geiste recht erleuchtet bin,
Geschrieben steht: "Im Anfang war der Sinn."

13. Arnold Schoenberg, *Moses und Aron,* opera in three acts, text, Arnold Schoenberg, trans. Allen Forte, piano reduction, Winfried Zillig (Mainz: Schotts, 1957), 300: "O Wort, du Wort das mir fehlt!"

14. Quoted by Stuckenschmidt (see n. 5), 140.

15. Ferruccio Busoni, *Von der Einheit der Musik, Verstreute Aufzeichnungen* (Berlin: Hesse, 1922), 299–300: "Die Idee zum *Arlecchino* gab mir die meisterhafte Darstellung eines italienischen Schauspielers . . . der die alte *Commedia dell' Arte* wieder einzuführen versuchte und in dieser die Rolle meines Helden überlegen sprach und spielte. Um die nämliche Zeit lernte ich das römische Marionetten-Theater kennen . . . Aus diesen beiden Erlebnissen heraus, von denen das erste auf die Dichtung, das zweite auf die Komposition einen merklichen Einfluß ausübten, ergab sich mein "theatralisches Capriccio" . . . *Arlecchino* ist ein dramatisiertes Bekenntnis . . . eine leichte Verspottung des Lebens und auch der Bühne, aufrichtiger Haltung . . . und mit liebevollster Besorgtheit um die künstlerische Form unternommen."

16. Ferruccio Busoni, *Arlecchino,* a theatrical caprice in one act, text, Ferrucio Busoni, trans. Edward J. Dent, piano reduction, Philipp Jarnach (Wiesbaden: Breitkopf & Härtel, 1968), 5.

17. Ferruccio Busoni, *Turandot,* a Chinese fable after Gozzi in two acts, text, Ferruccio Busoni, piano reduction, Philipp Jarnach (Leipzig: Breitkopf & Härtel, 1918), 67–80:

Turandot: Was kriecht am Boden,
    fliegt im Himmel,
was tappt im Dunkeln,
    zündet Lichter,
wühlt im Vergangenen,
    strebt in die Zukunft,
weilt im Gewohnten,
    regt sich im Neuen,
was ist besonnen
    und bäumt sich trotzig,
gesund ergeben
    und krankhaft protzig?

[What crawls on the ground,
    flies in the air,
gropes in the dark,
    strikes a light,
burrows in the past,
    strives toward the future,
lingers in the familiar
    is aroused by the new,
what is reflective
    and rears with defiance,
devoted to good health
    and morbid connivance?

Kalaf: ... *der menschliche Verstand*!

Human intellect!

Turandot: Was ist beständig
    und stets wechselnd,
heute geboten,
    morgen verpönt,
hier gepriesen,
    dort bestraft,
erst befolgt,
    später verlacht,
ein unentbehrlich
    stillschweigend Gesetz,
je weniger begründet,
    je seltner verletzt?

What is constant
    and always changing,
demanded today,
    despised tomorrow,
praised here,
    punished there,
obeyed at first,
    ridiculed later,
an indispensable
    silent principle,
the less explained
    the more invincible?

Kalaf: ... *die Sitte*!

Morals!

Turandot: Was ist, das aus
    den Wurzeln der Zeiten
dem Stamm, der Menschen—
    gemeinschaft trägt,
dem Geäste der Gewohnheiten,
    als köstlichste Blüte
zuhöchst ausschlägt,
    das jeden hinzieht,
das wenige halten;
    darüber einsam

What is it that grows
    out of the roots of time,
out of the primal tree,
    the society of man,
the branches of habit,
    as the rarest of blossoms
ripened to their fullest,
    desired by everyone,
grasped by few;
    its dominions ruled

Geweihte walten;	by the self-proclaimed,
das jegliches schönt,	beautifying all things,
an alles sich wendet,	in all people's sight,
die Menschen zu heitern,	sent from on high,
von oben entsendet?	mankind to delight?

Kalaf: *. . . die Kunst!*   *Art!*]

18. Ferruccio Busoni, *Doktor Faust*, text, Ferruccio Busoni, opera completed and ed. Philipp Jarnach, trans. Edward J. Dent, piano reduction, Egon Petri and Michael von Zadora (Wiesbaden: Breitkopf & Härtel, 1926), 212: "Nichts ist bewiesen und nichts ist beweisbar."

19. Edward J. Dent, "The Return of Busoni," *The Athenaeum* (December 17, 1920), 845.

20. Busoni (see n. 18), 317: "Ich, Faust, ein ewiger Wille!"

21. Quoted by Hugo Leichtentritt, "Ferruccio Busoni," translation by Edward J. Dent, *The Music Review* 6 (1945), 217–8.

22. Leichtentritt, 216.

23. Busoni (see n. 11), 6: ". . . die Abbildung der Natur und die Wiedergabe der menschlichen Empfindungen."

24. Busoni, 31: ". . . Gesetze aufzustellen, und nicht, Gesetzen zu folgen."

25. Busoni, 31: ". . . erstrebt im Grunde nur die Vollendung. Und indem er diese mit seiner Individualität in Einklang bringt, ensteht absichtlos ein neues Gesetz."

26. Busoni, 16: "Der größte Teil neuerer Theatermusik leidet an dem Fehler, daß sie die Vorgänge, die sich auf der Bühne abspielen, wiederholen will, anstatt ihrer eigentlichen Aufgabe nachzugeben, den Seelenzustand der handelnden Personen während jener Vorgänge zu tragen. Wenn die Bühne die Illusion eines Gewitters vortäuscht, so ist dieses Ereignis durch das Auge erschöpfend wahrgenommen. Fast alle Komponisten bemühen sich jedoch, das Gewitter in Tönen zu beschreiben, welches nicht nur eine unnötige und schwächere Wiederholung, sondern zugleich eine Versäumnis ihrer Aufgabe ist. Die Person auf der Bühne wird entweder von dem Gewitter seelich beeinflußt, oder ihr Gemüt verweilt infolge von Gedanken, die es stärker in Anspruch nehmen, unbeirrt. Das Gewitter ist sichtbar und hörbar ohne Hilfe der Musik; was aber in der Seele des Menschen währenddessen vorgeht, das Unsichtbare und Unhörbare, das soll die Musik verständlich machen."

27. Busoni, 17: ". . . die durch eine dramatisch-bewegte Szene gewonnene Stimmung in einem geschlossenen Stücke zusammenfaßte und ausklingen ließ (Arie)."

28. Busoni, 17–18: "Immer wird das gesungene Wort auf der Bühne eine

Konvention bleiben und ein Hindernis für alle wahrhaftige Wirkung: aus diesem Konflikt mit Anstand hervorzugehen, wird eine Handlung, in welcher die Personen singend agieren, von Anfang an auf das Unglaubhafte, Unwahre, Unwahrscheinliche gestellt sein müssen, auf daß eine Unmöglichkeit die andere stütze und so beide möglich und annehmbar werden.

"Schon deshalb, und weil er von vornherein dieses wichtigste Prinzip ignoriert, sehe ich den sogenannten italienischen Verismus für die musikalische Bühne als unhaltbar an."

29. Busoni, 18: "An welchen Momenten ist die Musik auf der Bühne unerläßlich?"

30. Busoni, 18: "Bei Tänzen, bei Märschen, bei Liedern und—beim Eintreten des Übernatürlichen in die Handlung."

31. Busoni, 18–19: ". . . eine Scheinwelt schaffen, die das Leben entweder in einen Zauberspiegel oder einen Lachspiegel reflektiert, die bewußt das geben will, was in dem wirklichen Leben nicht zu finden ist. Der Zauberspiegel für die ernste Oper, der Lachspiegel für die heitere."

32. Busoni, 19: "Und lasset Tanz und Maskenspiel und Spuk mit eingeflochten sein, auf daß der Zuschauer der anmutigen Lüge auf jedem Schritt gewahr bleibe und nicht sich ihr hingebe wie einem Erlebnis."

33. Busoni (see n. 15), 314–15: "Nicht nur, daß die Oper keine geringere Gattung der Musik vorzustellen braucht . . . ich erwarte von der Oper, daß sie in Zukunft die oberste, nämlich die universelle, einzige Form musikalischen Ausdrucks und Gehalts werde."

34. Busoni, 315: "Von den einfachen Lied-, Marsch- und Tanzweisen bis zu dem kunstreichsten Kontrapunkt, vom Gesang zum Orchester, vom "Weltlichen" zum "Geistlichen" reicht—und noch weiter—das Gebiet der Oper; der ungemessene Raum, über den sie verfügt, befähigt sie, jede Gattung und Art aufzunehmen, jede Stimmung zu reflektieren."

35. Busoni, 316–17: "Denn . . . eine Opernpartitur müßte indem sie der Handlung gerecht wird, auch von dieser losgelöst, ein vollständiges musikalisches Bild ergeben: einer Rüstung vergleichbar, die dazu bestimmt, den menschlichen Körper zu umhüllen, auch für sich allein—an Material, an Form, und an kunstreicher Ausführung—ein befriedigendes Bild, ein wertvolles Stück ergibt. Endlich—und es mag paradox klingen!—führt uns die Opernkomposition zur reineren und absoluteren Musik zurück; indem—durch das künftig gebotene Hinwegfallen alles Illustrativen—nur die der Musik organisch angemessenen Elemente zu ihrem Rechte gelangen: der Gehalt, die Stimmung, und die Form; gleichbedeutend mit Geist, Gemüt und Können."

36. Busoni, 318: "Es sollte vor allem die Oper nicht mit dem gesprochenen Drama identifiziert werden. Vielmehr es sollten die beiden von einander unterschieden sein, als wie Mann und Weib. Es handelt sich bei der Oper um das *musikalische* Gesamtkunstwerk; im Gegensatz zum Bayreuther "Gesamt-

kunstwerk" . . . Als oberste Bedingung erscheint mir die Wahl des Textes. Während es für das Drama fast grenzenlose Möglichkeiten des Stoffes gibt, ziegt sich bei der Oper, daß nur solche "Sujets" ihr angemessen sind, die *ohne Musik nicht bestehen,* noch zum vollen Ausdruck gelangen könnten, die nach Musik verlangen und erst durch diese vollständig werden."

37. Busoni, 321: "Denn im "zweiten Faust" ist Musik überall geboten und unerläßlich . . . und sie muß dem Schauspiel, der Darstellung zu Hilfe kommen, wie das Licht dem geschauten Bilde."

38. Busoni, 323: ". . . ein Trinklied, ein Mandolinenkonzert, ein Nachtgebet, eine Romanze (die von der Weide) . . ."

39. Busoni, 323: ". . . fast zu einer Oper."

40. Busoni, 325: "Überhaupt ist Erotik kein Vorwurf für die Kunst, sondern eine Angelegenheit des Lebens."

41. Busoni, 329: "Ist doch die Oper Schaustück, Dichtung und Musik in Einem."

42. Busoni, 330: "Eine ideelle Vereinung ist am Ende doch nur in der Lösung zu finden, daß der Komponist sein eigener Dichter sei. So wird ihm widerspruchlos die Befugnis zugestanden, im Verlaufe des Komponierens die Worte, die Szenen zu kürzen, zu ergänzen, sie umzustellen, je wie der musikalische Hergang es heischt."

43. Busoni, 331: ". . . stets aus einer Reihe kürzerer, geschlossener Stücke bestand . . ."

44. Busoni, 331: "Es ist ja nicht zufällig, daß man aus der "unendlichen Kette" des *Ringes* getrennte Nummern ziehen konnte, die im Konzertsaal zur Geltung kommen: Waldweben, Walkürenritt, Feuerzauber und weiteres."

45. Busoni, 332–3: ". . . welches Recht die Oper, die auf Unwahrscheinliches, Unglaubhaftes, Unmögliches gestellt ist, für sich in Anspruch zu nehmen die tiefsten und sittlichsten Gründe hat."

46. Hugo Leichtentritt (see n. 21), 215.

47. Vladimir Vogel, "Impressions of Ferruccio Busoni," *Perspectives of New Music* 6, no. 2 (Spring-Summer, 1968), 170.

48. Antony Beaumont (see n. 3), 317.

49. Humphrey Searle, "Busoni's *Doktor Faust*," *The Monthly Musical Record* (March-April, 1937), 54.

50. Ferruccio Busoni, *Über die Möglichkeiten der Oper und Über die Partitur des "Doktor Faust"* (Leipzig: Breitkopf & Härtel, 1926), 33: "Eine hervorragende, historische und sprichwörtliche Figur, die mit dem Zauberischen und Unenträtselten zusammenhinge, zum Mittelpunkt meines Opernspiels zu machen, war in mir Wunsch und Prinzip. Von Zoroaster bis Cagliostro bilden diese Gestalten eine Säulenreihe durch den Gang der Zeiten."

51. Busoni, 35–6: "Wie in einem Fieber, und in sechs Tagen, schrieb ich den

ersten Entwurf des *Doktor Faust* nieder; zwischen dem Ausbruche des Krieges und den Vorbereitungen zu einer Ozeanfahrt, gegen Ende 1914.

Mein eigenes Drama beginnt mit der Szene am Hofe zu Parma, und es tritt damit aus dem Mystichen in das Weltliche."

52. Busoni, 39: "Vorzüglich war es mir darum zu tun, musikalisch-selbständige Formen zu gießen, die zugleich dem Worte, dem szenischen Vorgang sich anpaßten; die jedoch, auch losgelöst vom Worte, von der Situation, ein eigenes und sinnvolles Bestehen führten."

53. Busoni, 44: "Einfall ist Begabung, Gesinnung Sache des Charakters, aber erst das Formen macht den, der jene ersten Eigenschaften besitzt, zum Künstler."

54. Philip M. Palmer & Robert P. More, *The Sources of the Faust Tradition from Simon Magus to Lessing* (New York: Oxford University Press, 1936), 241.

55. Busoni (see n. 18), 12:

Besah mir nah die schlicht geformten Bilder
die waren schöner jetzt, durch höheres Alter;
ich firnißte, hantierte als Vergülder—
(es wirkt die Zeit nicht minder als Zerspalter)
ich schärfte Eines, Andres strich ich milder,
und aus der Larve flog herauf ein Falter:
ins Altgewebte flocht ich neue Maschen,
vergess'nes Muster wird euch überraschen.

So stellt mein Spiel sich wohl lebendig dar,
doch bleibt sein Puppenursprung offenbar.

56. Palmer and More (see n. 54), 258–9.

57. Busoni (see n. 18), 15–30.

58. Palmer and More (see n. 54), 275–7.

59. Busoni (see n. 18), 32–66.

60. *Medieval Legends No. 1,* "Dr. Johannes Faustus", Puppet Play (London: David Nutt in the Strand, 1893), 19.

61. *Karl Simrocks Puppenspiel* in *Gestaltungen des Faust,* ed. H. W. Geissler, I "Die vorgoethesche Zeit" (Munich: Parcus, 1927), 246:

Faust (*für sich*).
Soll ich mit meinem Blut die Seele dir verschreiben,
Dies ist wohl ein Moment das Blut hervorzutreiben.
Da quillt es schon heraus und überströmt die Hand.
Buchstaben bildet's zwei, gleich hab' ich es erkannt,
Ein grosses *H*, ein *F*: die sollen mich wohl warnen?

Homo fuge! flieh Mensch! und laß dich nicht umgarnen.
Doch *F* kann Faustus sein, *H* Herrlichkeit versprechen.
Vielleicht ist's Zufall nur: wozu den Kopf zerbrechen?
Und schon ist es zu spät, geschrieben steht es klar—
Doch halt' ich es noch fest: mir wird so sonderbar.
Ein ängstliches Gefühl durchrieselt mir die Glieder,
Ich weiß nicht von mir selbst, ohnmächtig sink' ich nieder.

62. Busoni (see n. 18), 67–70:

Faust.
Willst du mir dienen?
Mephistopheles.
Fragt sich, fragt sich in welcher Weise?
Faust.
Beschaffe mir für meines Lebens Rest
die unbedingte Erfüllung jeden Wunsches:
Laß mich die Welt umfassen, den Osten und den Süden,
die mich rufen. O laß mich, laß mich
des Menschen Tun vollauf begreifen,
und ungeahnt erweitern, Gib mir Genie,
und gib mir auch sein Leiden.
 . . .
Mephistopheles.
Was noch mehr?
Faust.
Mache mich frei! Mache mich frei!

63. Busoni, 83–104:

Chor.
Credo in unum Deum Patrem omnipotentem,
creatorem coeli et terrae visibilium
omnium et invisibilium.
Faust.
Was verlangst du noch?
Mephistopheles.
Ein kurzes Schreiben mit deinem Blut gezeichnet,
rot auf weiss.
Faust.
So gib her.

Mephistopheles.

Brav.

Faust.

Wo ist mein Wille, wo mein Stolz geblieben!

Unseliger Faust, das Höllenwerk begann.

(*Tritt an das Fenster.*)

Wie wird mir—!

(*Es wird Tag. Osterchor. Glocken.*)

Chor.

Et resurrexit tertia die—secundum scripturam—et ascendit in coelum,
sedet ad dexteram Patris.

Faust.

Ostertag! Da ziehen die Guten zum Münster.

Tag meiner Kindheit!

Mephistopheles.

Kehr' dich nicht an das Gesäusel. Still!

Chor.

Et iterum venturus est cum gloria
judicare vivos, et mortuos.

Faust.

Du, Faust, bist nun ein Toter.

Ich werde gerichtet! Wer hilft mir?

Wer hilft mir?

(*Ein Rabe fliegt herbei, Feder im Schnabel, die Mephistopheles ihm
abnimmt.*)

Mephistopheles.

Ein Mann, Faust, du hast dein Wort zu halten:

Vollziehe! Vollziehe! Vollziehe!

Faust.

Noch hat es Zeit. Fauch' mich nicht an!

Es gibt kein Erbarmen. Es gibt keine Seligkeit,

keine Vergeltung, den Himmel nicht und nicht

die Höllenschrecken: den Jenseits trotz' ich!

Mephistopheles.

Tüchtig, tüchtig! Das nenn' ich fortgeschritten:

nun seid Ihr eben auf der rechten Fährte!

Faust (*zitternd, indem er das unterschriebene Blatt Mephistopheles
entgegenstreckt*).

Hier: nach Schwinden meiner Frist—es wird sich

ziegen—vielleicht unterliegst noch du—

bin ich—nicht dein Herr—!

(*Er fällt ohnmächtig zum Boden.*)
Chor.
Gloria in excelsis Deo et in terra pax.
(*Mephistopheles weidet sich eine Zeit lang an dem Anblick seines Opfers . . . und entreißt ihm das Blatt.*)
Mephistopheles.
Gefangen!
Chor.
Allelujah!

64. Simrock (see n. 61), 259–60:

Mephistopheles (*als Herold*).
Man spielt hier Eisenmann—wir werden doch nicht stören?
Herzogin.
Was Ihr zu melden habt, das laßt mich immer hören.
Mephistopheles (*vorstellend*).
Mein Herr, der Doktor Faust—ein großer Nekromant.
Herzogin.
Ich hab' von ihm gehört.
Faust.
      Wie? in dies welche Land,
Das freut mich überaus, ist schon mein Ruf gedrungen?
Mephistopheles.
Es wird bald allerwärts davon gesagt, gesungen.
Herzogin.
Im Teufelsbannen auch seid Ihr ein großer Meister?
Faust.
Durch Salomonis Ring gehorchen mir die Geister.
Herzogin.
So laßt uns hier sogleich doch eine Probe schauen.
Faust.
Gehorchen möcht' ich gern der schönsten aller Frauen—
Doch hier am hellen Tag—
Mephistopheles.
      O das hat nichts zu sagen.
Ihr laßt auf Euern Wink es nachten oder tagen.
Faust.
Wohlan ich bin bereit.
Herzogin.
    Nur einen Augenblick—

Gemahl, was rennt ihr noch nach jenem Galgenstrick?
Dieweil ihr Zween den Knecht gehetzt in eitler Jagd,
Hab' ich den Meister selbst in unsern Dienst gebracht.
Der große Doktor Faust, ein Herzog aller Geister—
Faust (*für sich*).
Sie stellt ihr selbst mich gleich und macht mich immer dreister.
Herzogin.
Will unser Hochzeitfest durch seine Kunst verschönen.
Mephistopheles.
Und Eur gekröntes Haupt zum andern Male krönen.
Herzog (*setzt die Krone wieder auf*).
Ich bin noch ganz im Schweiss, Herr Doktor, seid willkommen!
Herzogin.
So werde hier sogleich der Zauber vorgenommen.

65. Busoni (see n. 18), 151:

(*Faust, von oben, und von weitem, langsam herankommend, müßte ein fantastisches Gefolge—schleppentragende Mohren-Knaben, oder Affen— haben; und es sollte sein Erscheinen auffällig, wenn auch nicht marktschreierisch wirken. Der Zeremonienmeister, halb führend, halb einladend, tänzelt der Gruppe voran.*)

66. Busoni, 157–63:

Herzogin (*für sich*).
Er ist ein Fürst in Wesen und Gebärde,
noch niemals hat ein Mann mich so bestrickt.
Herzog (*für sich*).
Mich dünkt, die Hölle, die Hölle hat ihn hergeschickt!
Mephistopheles (*für sich*).
Der Wachthund bellt. Es blökt die Herde.
Chor.
Seltener Mann, seltsamer Gast! Was wird sich zeigen?
Faust (*für sich*).
Du stolzeste der Frauen, sollst mir der Preis sein!
Herzog.
Herr Doktor, seid an unserem Hof begrüßt,
und Dank, daß eure Kunst ihr uns erschließt.
Wir hoffen, daß ihr die Fürstin nicht enttäuscht.
Mögt Ihr beginnen?

Herzogin (*leise für sich*).
Was wird sich zeigen?
Faust (*halb für sich*).
Seid unbesorgt! Es sei!
(*Er erhebt die Hände. Kurze Beschwörungsgeste oder Handlung Fausts.
Ein Schwarm faunartiger Teufelchen dringt von allerwärts herein, und
verteilt sich behende in die Büsche.*)
Chor.
Ah! Ha ha ha ha ha!
Faust.
Verzeiht, wenn ich zu eigen handle:
Tag ist dem Wunder abgewandt.
Licht, sei verbannt, in Nacht dich wandle.
Sterne herauf, am Himmels Rand!
(*Es wird sternenhelle Nacht.*)

67. Busoni, 184–90:

Herzogin (*tritt auf die Bühne, wie im Traume schreitend, die Arme
           vorgestreckt*).
Er ruft mich . . . zieht mich . . .
Er ruft mich wie mit tausend Stimmen,
zieht mich wie mit tausend Armen,
ich fühl in einem, tausend Augenblicke
und jeder einzelne verkündet ihn, ihn allein,
und jeder einzle Augenblick verküdet ihn.
Wer ich gewesen und was ich vorstellte
ist mir entschwunden, entschwunden . . .
Seh nur den einen Weg, seh nur den einen Weg,
den Weg zum teuren Manne, seh nur den Weg zum teuren Manne.
Ja, ja, ja ich komme, schreite mit dir
durch unbegrenzte Räume. Die Erde wird mein Reich,
ich ihre Königin!
Was späte Zeiten einst zu Tage fördern,
bald ist dies Alles, bald wird dies Alles,
bald wird dies Alles mein, mein!
Ich schreite dann an seiner Hand, in unbegrenzte Bezirke,
Bei dir, bei dir, bei dir die Unermeßlichkeit,
Faust, du mein Faust, ich komme . . .
Faust, du mein Faust! Faust, ich folge dir!
(*Sie schreitet langsam hinaus.*)

68. Simrock (see n. 61), 274:

Faust.
Beten? Kann ich noch beten? Ich will's versuchen.
(*Kniet vor dem Marienbilde.*)
Virgo virginium praeclara!
Weh mir! Ihre Züge wandeln sich in Helenas! Die unbefriedigte Lust
vergiftet die frömmsten Gefühle. Satan! Das ist deine verruchte List.
Darum hast du mich um alle irdischen Freuden betrogen, daß ich die
himmlichen nicht inbrünstig begehren könne. Ist denn keine gnade?
Dumpfe Stimme (*von oben*).
Gott verschworen,
Ewig verloren!
(*Faust sinkt ohnmächtig nieder.*)

69. Beaumont (see n. 3), 28.
70. Beaumont, 29.
71. Busoni (see n. 18), 258–66:

Faust (*mit Chor*).
Traum der Jugend, Ziel des Weisen,
reinster Schönheit Bildvollendung,
dich zu üben, dich zu preisen,
dich zu lehren, war mir Sendung.
Unerkannte, Unerreichte, Unerfüllte, tritt hervor!
(*Durch Rauch und Flamme treten die Umrisse der Figur stetig deutlicher
hervor.*)
Was ich sehnte, was ich wähnte:
höchsten Wunsches Rätselformen.
(*Ein vollkommen schönes, junges Weib, in durchsichtigem Schleier, im
übrigen nakt, steht unbeweglich. Zugleich hat der neue Hintergrund das
Bild der Schenkstube völlig verdrängt.*)

72. Beaumont (see n. 7), 388–91.
73. Antony Beaumont, *Doktor Faust*, completion of the second and last scenes
(Wiesbaden: ©by Breitkopf & Härtel, 1984), 266, 266a–d, 267:

Faust.
Ich schaue dich! Und nun, werd' ich dich halten.

(Faust nähert sich der Gestalt. Sie entweicht und führt einen gemessenen Tanz aus. Faust folgt, nach ihren Bewegungen.)
Nur Faust berührte je das Ideal.
Du weichst, entfliehst:
Kannst du dich vielgestalten?
Ich greife dich, und wieder nicht.
O Qual!
Endlich, endlich zu mir!
(Als er sie, endlich, zu halten wähnt, zerfließt die Gestalt in Nichts.)
Ach, abermals betrogen!
Entschwunden nun für immer!

74. Beaumont (see n. 3), 325.
75. Beaumont (see n. 73), 312–16:

Faust.
[So sei das Werk vollendet!]
Euch zum Trotze, euch Allen, die ihr euch gut preist, die wir nennen böse, die ihr, um eurer alten Zwistigkeiten Willen, Menschen nehmet zum Vorwand und auf sie ladet die Folgen eures Zankes. An dieser hohen Einsicht meiner Reife bricht sich nun eure Bosheit. Und in der mir errung'nen Freiheit erlischt Gott und Teufel zugleich.

76. Dent (see n. 10), 304. Reprinted by permission of Oxford University Press.
77. W. H. Mellers, "The Problem of Busoni," *Music and Letters* 18 (1937), 243. Reprinted by permission of Oxford University Press.
78. Vogel (see n. 47), 172.

CHAPTER THREE
Allegory in the Opera House: Arnold Schoenberg

In October 1990, thirty-three years after its first stage production at the Opernhaus Zurich, Arnold Schoenberg's great allegorical opera, *Moses und Aron* arrived at the New York State Theater, home of the New York City Opera, to an enthusiastic press and sold-out houses. Perhaps the long wait for this craggy, twelve-tone masterpiece of twentieth-century dramatic poetry made it all the more exciting when it finally arrived in the Land of the Golden Calf.

Schoenberg wrote his own libretto, concentrating the Biblical story of the Exodus of the Israelites from Egypt into a few trenchant scenes organized into three acts. He completed the music for only the first two acts, however, and the work remains a fragment. But what a fragment! The City Opera's thrilling performances soundly confirmed the prevailing opinion that the ending of the second act, in which the Jewish people begin their epic journey out of Egypt toward the Promised Land, indeed ends the opera and that the surviving dialogue from the third act, in which Aron falls dead, must be regarded as an epilogue that Schoenberg, for whatever reasons, did not set to music.

This impression is confirmed more from performance in the theater than from reading the score. On the stage, it becomes abundantly clear that the chorus, representing the Jewish people, constitutes—like the chorus of Russian peasants in Musorgsky's *Boris Godunov*—the collective hero of the opera, while Moses, Aron, the Elders, virgins and other characters exist only on the periphery of the troubled history of the Jews. Since the major personages of the opera seem to be symbols of various ideas associated with the Exodus of the Jews from Egypt, the work must be regarded as an allegory for the theater, in the style and mood of Bert Brecht's *The Good Woman of Setzuan,* for example, or of *Our Town* by Thornton Wilder.

Arnold Schoenberg possessed a natural instinct for allegory, a style of dramatic poetry that enables the poet to assume the role of teacher and expound ideas to an audience in a theater. Fundamentally, Schoenberg was a born teacher. The lives of most composers are marked off by musical activities before the public, such as conducting symphony orchestras (Mendelssohn, Strauss and Mahler), virtuoso recitals (Liszt, Busoni and Rachmaninov) or playing the organ in church (Bach and Bruckner). But the course of Schoenberg's life was punctuated by his teaching positions, from his first, at the Stern Conservatory in Berlin, to his last, as Professor of Music at the University of California, Los Angeles. During this period, from 1901 to 1944, he both taught in educational institutions and gave private lessons in composition to promising students. One of his biographers, Willi Reich, has spoken of Schoenberg's "genius for teaching",[1] and there is no doubt that the composer possessed that quality of mind and character that stimulates a student to mature in his subject to the utmost limits of his potential.

Schoenberg regarded clarity of expression as a manifestation of clarity of thought. If a student didn't understand a teacher, perhaps the teacher himself didn't adequately understand his subject. All his life, Schoenberg struggled to understand the art of music and to express his understanding as clearly as humanly possible, both in his composing and in his teaching.

Arnold Schoenberg was born September 13, 1874 in the second district of Vienna. His father, the owner of a small shoe shop, came from Preßburg in Slovakia and his mother from Prague. Both parents were musical and their son began to study the violin at the age of eight. Soon he was composing solo and duet pieces for violin but formal training in music at a conservatory was denied him and as a musician, Schoenberg was largely self-taught. An early mentor was Alexander von Zemlinsky, who helped him with harmony and whose sister, Mathilde, Schoenberg married in 1901.

He soon began composing chamber music, including a sextet (later arranged for chamber orchestra), *Verklärte Nacht* [*Transfigured Night*], after poems by Richard Dehmel, which has remained to this day one of his most popular pieces. He also began work on a song cycle for soloists, chorus and orchestra, *Gurrelieder* [*Songs of Gurre*], settings of poems by the Danish author Jens Peter Jacobsen.

Vienna did not embrace the young composer and, in 1901, he and his bride moved to Berlin. It was here that Richard Strauss helped Schoenberg obtain his first teaching position, at the Stern Conservatory, where he discovered that teaching can be a useful way to support a family while simultaneously permitting a modest amount of time for composing. He put what time he had to good use, composing a symphonic poem on the subject of Maeterlinck's play *Pelléas and Mélisande*.

After two years in Berlin, Schoenberg returned to Vienna where Zemlinsky helped him obtain a post teaching harmony and counterpoint at the Schwarzwald School in the first district of Vienna. Although some of his students came from the University of Vienna, none of them measured up to Schoenberg's expectations and he soon began accepting only talented pupils for private lessons at his apartment in the Liechtensteinstraße. It was here, in 1904, that Schoenberg began teaching the young men who later became his most famous students—Egon Wellesz, Anton von Webern, Alban Berg and Erwin Stein, among others.

Like many a teacher before him—and after—Schoenberg found the available teaching materials inadequate and began working on a text of his own, *Harmonielehre* [*Theory of Harmony*], which he completed in 1911. The foreword to this brilliant work discloses Schoenberg's emerging view of himself as a teacher:

I have learned this book from my students.

While I was teaching, I never tried "to tell a student simply what I knew." Rather, I looked for what *he* didn't know. But that was not the main thing either, although it led me to develop something new for each student. My plan was to reveal to him the essence of the matter from the ground up. In this way, I didn't have to employ all those entrenched rules designed to tie a student's brain in knots. Instead, I developed guidelines that didn't constrain the student any more than they did the teacher. If the student didn't need them, he worked without them. But the teacher needs the courage to acknowledge mistakes. He must not don the mantle of infallibility—one who knows all and errs never. Instead, he must become the tireless searcher, who sometimes finds. Why pretend to be a demigod? Why not a human being?

I have never tried to persuade my students of my infallibility—only a voice teacher needs to do that—but rather have taken the risk of saying something I later had to take back or, I offered guidance that proved, in practice, to be wrong and had to be corrected. I don't think my mistakes either helped or harmed a student, but the fact that I admitted them may have got him to thinking. For myself, since my guidance was the result of untested thought, it often proved to be wrong, had to be thought out anew, and then revised.

This is how my book came about. I learned how to guide my students from the mistakes they made due to things I had taught them that were inadequate or incorrect. So, I began to recognize the soundness of my teaching method after my students stopped making mistakes, although I didn't let this lead me to think I had solved all the problems. I think this method profited both my students and myself. If I had taught them simply what I knew, they would have known that and no more. As it is, they knew even less. But they have learned what matters: *to seek*! . . .

Well, it seems clear that the first task of the teacher is to give the student a good shaking up. Then, when the air clears, it will be seen that things have fallen into place.

And something else happens!

This kind of teaching can come back with profit to the teacher himself, another example of how I learned my book from my students. And I take this occasion to thank them.[2]

In 1910, the year before he completed his *Harmonielehre*, Schoenberg found himself in serious financial difficulties. He had moved from his cramped quarters in the Liechtensteinstraße to a roomier apartment in the Vienna suburb of Hietzing since he had been appointed *Privatdozent* [Adjunct Professor] at the prestigious Imperial and Royal Academy for Music and the Performing Arts. So pressed was he that he had to beg a loan for his rent from his friend and supporter Gustav Mahler, who obliged him by return mail.[3]

But Schoenberg had great inner strength. He was soon back to teaching, writing, composing and caring for his family. In fact, his variegated personality is disclosed in another letter written in an ironic, satirical tone a year earlier (August 24, 1909) to Ferruccio Busoni in Berlin. The latter had written Schoenberg concerning his ideas about perfection as a goal in both life and art, to which Schoenberg replied:

Do you really set such infinite store by perfection? Do you really consider it obtainable? . . . I find even God's works of art, those of Nature, highly imperfect. I find perfection only in the works of joiners, gardeners, pastrycooks and hairdressers.[4]

Throughout his life, Schoenberg wrote short essays on a variety of subjects, many of which have been collected by Leonard Stein and published in the book *Style and Idea*. In one of these essays, "Problems in Teaching Art" (1911), Schoenberg added another thought to his philosophy of teaching:

> I believe art is born of "I must," not of "I can." A craftsman "can": whatever he was born with, he has developed, and so long as he wants to do something, he is able to . . . But the artist *must*. He has no say in the matter, it is nothing to do with what he wants; but since he must, he also can.[5]

During these years in Vienna, Schoenberg managed to complete his *Gurrelieder* while fulfilling his teaching assignments at the Academy. His struggles with poverty continued, however, and this, together with the violent hostility of the Viennese music critics, who not only attacked his music but tried, as well, to denigrate his reputation as a teacher, led him, in 1911, to renew his contract with the Stern Conservatory in Berlin, where he was to spend four reasonably comfortable years teaching, writing and composing. It was during this time that he composed a *Melodrama*, a song cycle on poems by Albert Giraud in a German translation by Otto Erich Hartleben, *Pierrot Lunaire*, for speaker-singer and chamber orchestra. *Melodrama*, in its original sense, refers to a scene in which dialogue is spoken over music, as in the finale of the Venetian scene in Offenbach's *Tales of Hoffmann*. Schoenberg's literary talent enabled him to devise a new way of projecting spoken lines over music. He calls on the speaker-singer to maintain exact rhythmic values but allows him freedom merely to approximate the pitch of the notes. He called his new method of vocal expression *Sprechstimme* and described it as a form of *rhythmische Deklamation* [rhythmical declamation]. In the *Vorwort* to the score of *Pierrot Lunaire*, he explains the technique as follows:

> Aside from specially marked exceptions, the melody notated as *Sprechstimme* is not intended to be sung. The task of the performer is to transform it into a *speech melody* by paying careful attention to the indicated pitches. He does this by
> I. keeping the rhythm and the note values as exact as if he were singing; that is, by taking no more liberty than he would allow himself if performing a sung melody; and
> II. by making himself aware of the exact difference between *sung tone* and *spoken tone*. The *sung tone* holds the pitch firmly, without change. The *spoken tone* announces the pitch but quickly leaves it, going either down or up. The performer must take the precaution, however, not to

fall into a "sing-song" declamation. That is absolutely not intended. It is by no means to be a realistic-naturalistic speech. On the contrary, the difference between ordinary speech and speech that interpenetrates musical form must be made clear. But also, it must not sound like a song.[6]

Sprechstimme proved to be a very useful literary means in opera for achieving variety in vocal expression. A composer may employ spoken dialogue, *Sprechstimme* and sung lines all in the same work. In *Moses und Aron*, Schoenberg uses all forms in the choral sections while setting the lines of Moses in *Sprechstimme* and those of Aron in song. Alban Berg employs this means of expression in both *Wozzeck* and *Lulu* and has commented on the technique as follows:

It has become clear that this means of handling the voice permits the preservation of all those forms of absolute music that have been lost— through recitative, for example. And that it is not only an excellent method of rendering clear enunciation of the words—especially in opera—but also, that it has enriched the art of the opera through a means of genuine artistic expression derived from the purest sources of music, ranging from a toneless, whispered word to an authentic *bel parlare* of wide ranging speech melodies.[7]

There is no question that *Sprechstimme* has become the *bel parlare* of many modern operas.

While teaching in Berlin, Schoenberg found time to compose *Die glückliche Hand* and to conduct his *Gurrelieder, Pelleas und Melisande* and *Pierrot Lunaire* in several European cities. The outbreak of war forced a curtailment of his guest-conducting activities, however, and in 1915 he returned to Vienna.

Earlier, in 1912, several of Schoenberg's students contributed "teacher evaluations" to a book entitled *Arnold Schoenberg, in höchster Verehrung von Schülern und Freunden* [*Arnold Schoenberg, in Deepest Reverence from Students and Friends*] that give a good idea of the understanding they had for his teaching methods.

Anton von Webern writes:

Some are of the opinion that Schoenberg teaches his own style and forces his student to use it. That is totally wrong.

Schoenberg teaches no special style. He advocates neither the old artistic methods nor the new ones . . . What Schoenberg says to his student about his work grows organically out of the work itself, never from preconceived artistic principles.

This is how Schoenberg teaches creativity.

He tries energetically to discover the real personality of the student, tries to deepen it, tries to help it break out. In short, he struggles to give the student "the courage and strength to develop a view of things that turns whatever he sees into a particular case because of the way he sees it."

This is education in total truthfulness with oneself.[8]

It is a rare teacher in the arts who is genuinely able to suppress his own way of seeing things in order to try to comprehend and encourage the student's vision, especially when that vision is foreign to his own.

Another of Schoenberg's students, Erwin Stein, contributed the following succinct comments to the book:

Schoenberg teaches you to think. He urges a student to look at a thing with open eyes, in his own way, as though he were the first person who had ever observed it. What has been thought before is no longer the norm. Not that our thought is better than that of others'. What really counts is not absolute truth, but the *search* for truth.[9] [Emphasis added.]

After his return to Vienna in 1915 and a period of military service in the armed forces of the Austro-Hungarian Empire, Schoenberg began developing that theory of composition for which he is most famous, his *Method of Composing with Twelve Tones Which are Related only with one Another*. Basically, this method involves arranging the twelve notes of the chromatic scale that are to be found in any key into a new sequence of the composer's own devising. The result is not called a "key" anymore but rather a "basic set". This basic set can then be played in reverse, from last note to first, resulting in a retrograde. The set can be inverted, and this inversion can be played in reverse, giving four distinct variations: the basic set, the retrograde, the inversion and the retrograde inversion. Since the set can begin on any of the twelve notes of the chromatic scale, a total of forty-eight variations is possible.

In this system, every note of both horizontal melody and vertical harmony shows its relationship to the set and its transpositions. No note recurs until the other notes of the set have appeared in some form—there is no such thing as a "free" note. Variety is achieved in rhythms and orchestral coloring, but the musical notes themselves must all be derived from the set itself, or one of its forty-eight variations.[10]

The method results in extreme economy of means. Schoenberg often states a theme horizontally and then repeats it as a chord, in which all the notes are heard at the same time—what Egon Wellesz calls "a verticalization of an idea which was first conceived horizontally."[11]

This compression of what, in Wagner, would have been extended material was continued in the work of Alban Berg, Anton von Webern, Ernst Krenek, Paul Hindemith and many others. Although popular among German and Austrian musicians, however, this system of composition is still viewed with reserve by many contemporary opera composers. It seems to be very rigid, very strict, very Teutonic. The composer is denied freedom of inspiration, invention and improvisation. The possibilities of modulation from key to key, exploited so effectively by Wagner in his *Tristan und Isolde,* for instance, are lost as is the valuable contrast of tonality between major and minor. The possibility, for example, of suggesting the relationship between Alberich's Ring and the building of Valhalla, established by shifting the Ring motif from minor to major, is denied the composer of twelve-tone opera.

Schoenberg himself was a bit diffident about his system and insisted he had not wrought some kind of a revolution in the art of music. In a letter to Nicolas Slonimsky of June 3, 1937, written in English, he comments:

As you see, it was neither a straight way nor was it caused by mannerism, as it often happens with revolutions in art. I personally hate to be called a revolutionist, which I am not. What I did was neither revolution nor anarchy. I possessed from my very first start a thoroughly developed sense of form and a strong aversion for exaggeration. There is no falling into order, because there was never disorder. There is no falling at all, but on the contrary, there is an ascending to higher and better order.[12]

In 1923, Schoenberg's wife, Mathilde, died and a year later he married Gertrud Kolisch, sister of Rudolf Kolisch, leader of the Quartet that bore his name. Busoni died in 1924 and a year later Schoenberg received an appointment to replace him as director of a master class in composition at the Prussian Academy of Arts. Once again, Schoenberg took his bride to Berlin to commence a new chapter in his life, and he was not disappointed this time. The Berlin years were active and profitable both artistically and financially. He conducted his own works in several cities, and attended some performances of *Erwartung* and *Die glückliche Hand*. He composed the first twelve-tone opera, *Von Heute auf Morgen*, wrote his play *Der biblische Weg* and developed it into the text for *Moses und Aron*. In 1932 he finished all the music he was to compose for his great opera in Barcelona, while visiting his student, Roberto Gerhardt.

In January of 1933, Adolf Hitler was named Chancellor of Germany by President Paul von Hindenburg and Schoenberg's fortunes took a turn for the worse. The Nazis promised to remove all "foreign influences" from German institutions and the Prussian Academy of Arts was not overlooked. On March 1, 1933, the President, Max von Schillings, made it clear to the faculty that the "Jewish element" must be eliminated and Schoenberg, after noting that he did not care to stay where he was not wanted, left the meeting.[13]

A short time later, in May of 1933, he left Germany and Austria forever. He paused briefly in Paris to sort out his options. One of them, an appointment as Professor of Composition at the Malkin Conservatory in Boston, looked promising and, after some hesitation, he signed a contract that required him to teach in both Boston and New York. On October 31, 1933, he arrived in the country that was to provide him a haven from European anti-Semitism for the rest of his life.

The Malkin Conservatory proved something of a disappointment for Schoenberg. For one thing, the school had no orchestra. But the faculty, though small, included the pianist Egon Petri and the composer and writer Nicolas Slonimsky. Schoenberg tried to make the best of the situation but the harsh northeastern climate, which affected his asthma, and the poverty of real teaching challenges led him to accept a position as Professor of Composition at the University of Southern California in Los Angeles. He and his family took up residence in California and the composer soon discovered that his asthma had greatly improved.

He taught at U.S.C. only one year, however, and in the fall of 1936, moved up the ladder to a professorship of composition at the University of California at Los Angeles. Here, he taught harmony, counterpoint and advanced theory to a good many students, ending his teaching career in 1944 when he was seventy, the mandatory retirement age at U.C.L.A. On the side, he gave lessons in composition to such prominent American composers living in Hollywood as George Gershwin, Oscar Levant and Max Steiner.

He was able to do some composing too, his Violin Concerto, his Fourth String Quarter, and the most performed of his later compositions, the *Melodrama* for speaker, male chorus and orchestra, *A Survivor from Warsaw* (1947), for which he wrote the text, in English, as well as the music.

His retirement pay was a modest $38 per month (later increased by U.C.L.A.) but he received regular royalty payments from A.S.C.A.P. and continued to teach privately until his death. He sums up his teaching credo in one of his last letters, written to Frank Pelleg, Head of the Music Division of the Israeli Ministry for Education and Culture, April 26, 1951, in which he accepts the post of Honorary President of the Israel Academy of Music:

> I was ever a committed teacher. I have always been driven to find what would help beginning students the most, how I could reveal to them the technical, spiritual and ethical demands of our art. And I have struggled to convince them that art is grounded in morality, that we can never give up this conviction, and will fight to the end to sustain it.[14]

Schoenberg's most significant literary accomplishments are his opera librettos and his play, *Der biblische Weg*. Although he had a well thought out concept of opera, his ideas are scattered about among his essays and letters. Some very interesting comments appear as marginal notes jotted down in his copy of the 1916 edition of Ferruccio Busoni's book *Entwurf einer neuen Aesthetik der Tonkunst*. At the passage in which Busoni argues that music ought not simply to repeat what is happening on stage but should, instead, interpret the soul states of the characters, Schoenberg writes "Splendid"[15] in the margin and then adds two interesting sentences: "The real task of the art of the theatre is different: it is to use the means of the theatre for the external representation of inner events. For the artist the theatre is exactly the same as an orchestra and the drama is a symphony, for there is only one kind of art."[16]

But later on in Busoni's text, Schoenberg begins to disagree with his Italian friend. When Busoni asks where music is indispensable on the stage, Schoenberg replies, "Nowhere."[17] When Busoni suggests dances, marches, songs and supernatural phenomena as occasions for using music, Schoenberg observes, "These are purely formal reasons."[18] And when Busoni objects to the audience devoting itself to a charming illusion as though it were an actual experience, Schoenberg protests, "Oh, no!"[19] When Busoni adds that the listener should never regard theatrical effect as reality and that artistic enjoyment should never sink to the level of human participation,

Schoenberg proclaims, "Artistic enjoyment is the highest form of human participation."[20]

All his life, Schoenberg was fascinated by the art of the opera and, at an early age, he evidently took to heart Wagner's conviction that the composer must write his own text. In June and July of 1901, he wrote his first opera libretto, *Die Schildbürger* [*The Philistines*] after a story by Gustav Schwab[21] which, however, he never set to music.

He also accepted Wagner's belief in the close relationship between opera and drama. In a short article of 1927, replying to a question about the future of opera in the *Neues Wiener Tagblatt,* he observed, "The future of the opera depends on the future of the drama . . . The coming drama will be a *verbal* drama . . . and if the drama is to be a verbal drama, then the opera will have to be an opera of *musical ideas*."[22] The belief that drama depends on ideas expressed by words and that opera depends on ideas expressed by music influenced all of Schoenberg's efforts to create dramatic poems for the operatic stage.

In 1908, he developed an idea for an opera for one character, a Woman, who searches through a forest for her lover, stumbles over his dead body and then realizes, intuitively, that he has been killed because of his relationship with another woman.

This scenario reflects Schoenberg's absorption with the interior essence of character, in contrast to the external events of traditional plot structure. He was interested in the Woman's mind, her thoughts as she searches through the forest, rather than what she finds at the end of her search. Like Debussy, he was drawn to the drama of suggestion, of dream, of idea. *Erwartung* dramatizes the inner, psychic awareness of the heroine, as *Die glückliche Hand* explores the inner life of a modern man, *Von Heute auf Morgen* satirizes modern trends and fads and his masterpiece, *Moses und Aron,* explores the kind of intuitively understood idea that defies transmission by words from one human being to another.

Erwartung is a product of the times. In developing his scenario, Schoenberg seems to have been influenced by not only Expressionism but also the newly emerging images of modern women, such as Ibsen's Nora and Hedda Gabler, Strindberg's Laura and Wedekind's Lulu. He intended to show through the story of a frightened woman who searches through a dark forest at night for her lover how, in moments of extreme tension, various half-understood episodes out of a person's life suddenly become flashingly clear.

With his scenario finished, however, Schoenberg hesitated to write out the text himself. A short time earlier, a young medical student from Preßburg, Marie Pappenheim, had come to Vienna to finish her studies and soon had made an impression in the literary magazine *Die Fackel*. In 1909, he showed her his scenario, and she agreed to compose the lines. She finished the text in a few weeks, and Schoenberg quickly set it to music. It was first performed under the musical direction of Alexander von Zemlinsky on June 6, 1924 at the Neues Deutsches Theater in Prague with the role of the Woman sung by Marie Gutheil-Schoder.

Schoenberg's text consists entirely of a series of short, ejaculatory phrases sung by the Woman as she responds to the atmosphere of the dark forest through which she wanders, a dramatic situation strongly reminiscent, in both theme and construction, of Eugene O'Neill's *The Emperor Jones,* written some years later. A brief comparison with this play, which stems from the same aesthetic as the opera, may shed some light on the nature of Schoenberg's histrionic imagination.

Both opera and play are constructed in monodrama form. The essential action of O'Neill's play begins when Brutus Jones first encounters the forest. A drum supplies a quasi-musical accompaniment that carries the intensity of the drama from one scene to the next and, as the tempo increases, helps to build suspense. The protagonists of both plays are driven by fear and both see visions in the forest.

Perhaps the most absorbing parallel is the emergence of personal memories out of the past that come crowding before their eyes in moments of extreme tension. The Woman in *Erwartung* recalls the quiet moments of her life with her lover; after she has discovered his body, she senses an indefinable barrier that had erected itself between them, a barrier that she did not perceive at the time. The implication appears to be that a moment of terrible tension can reveal an unconscious perception normally closed to the conscious mind. In *The Emperor Jones,* the hero penetrates through conscious and remembered experience to scenes and episodes that took place long before he was born but which led inevitably to his own personal existence.

Further, the two protagonists undergo a psychological strain that is outwardly dramatized, in part, by the continuous disintegration of their clothing. As the Woman becomes more and more terrified of the forest and, consequently, more perceptive and aware, the state of her clothing suggests that she is approaching the elemental in emotional sensitivity. When she enters in Scene 4, she is "exhausted, her dress torn, her hair dishevelled, her face and hands marked with bloody lacerations."[23] In *The Emperor Jones*, the disintegration of the hero's clothing serves still another purpose: as Jones returns in his visions toward the very origins of his race, his torn garments reflect the stripping away of the layers of civilization acquired by blacks after coming from Africa to America.

As they enter their respective forests, both protagonists think they see objects that exist only in their excited imaginations. Jones thinks he sees a dice player he has killed, followed by a guard and a chain gang. He then envisions a slave auction, the hold of a slave ship and, finally, a witch doctor dancing by a river. The Woman in *Erwartung*, in Scene 2, half senses what she is to discover later. She first recalls the quietude and peace behind the garden walls where "No scythes were to be heard . . . no one called or moved . . ."[24] where she had waited for her lover. Then, abruptly, the calls of the night birds of the forest interrupt her thoughts and, as she starts to go on, she cries out, "Oh, oh—what is that? A body . . . ? No, only a tree trunk."[25] Her mistaking a tree trunk for a man's body suggests that she already subconsciously perceives the outcome of her search. She has little time to dwell on this, however, as new apparitions grip her imagination: "Something black is dancing there . . . a hundred hands . . . Don't be stupid . . . only shadows . . ."[26] Large yellow mushrooms suggest the staring eyes of a beast of some kind and she rushes further into the forest.

In the final scene, the Woman senses something elemental and imperceptible that had become a barrier between her and her lover: "Ah, now I remember . . . your sigh in your half-sleep . . . like a name . . . you kissed the question away from my lips . . ."[27] And again: "Then where is she, the witch, the whore, the woman with the white arms . . . ?"[28] She accepts her discovery quietly and continues in a melancholy way to recall the events of her past relationship with her lover, whose dead body she tenderly caresses. Finally, as morning approaches and reminds her of the many mornings requiring them to part, she suddenly thinks she sees her lover approaching her in the misty half-light. "Oh, are you here? I was seeking . . ."[29] and the opera closes with a reference to "seeking", one of the most trenchant themes of Expressionism.

In an essay entitled "New Music: My Music" that Schoenberg states was written before 1930, he says that his aim in *Erwartung* was "to represent in *slow motion* everything that occurs during a single second of maximum spiritual excitement, stretching it out to half an hour, whereas in *Die*

90

glückliche Hand a major drama is compressed into about 20 minutes, as if photographed with a time-exposure."[30]

This passion for compression led Schoenberg to create one of the most striking examples in the modern theater of a genuine *Gesamtkunstwerk* in the Wagnerian sense. He not only composed the text for *Die glückliche Hand* (in June, 1910) but worked out every detail of the scenic background, the stage action, the costumes and properties, the lighting, including precise descriptions of the color to be projected by the lighting instruments and, finally, set it all to music with specific notations in the score that coordinate all elements of the visual with the musical.

Like *Erwartung, Die glückliche Hand* is a representation of the inner thoughts of one person—a Man instead of a Woman—who is experiencing a profound emotional crisis. But, unlike its predecessor, the later work is plainly autobiographical. During 1908, Schoenberg's wife, Mathilde, fell in love with a painter they both knew, and for whom she posed, named Richard Gerstl. She left Schoenberg and their two young children to live with Gerstl but, after a time, went back to her husband, whereupon the painter committed suicide. In the opera, Schoenberg represents himself as the artist-hero (a goldsmith), his wife as a nameless Woman and his rival as an also unnamed, well dressed Gentleman, who seems to stand for money and worldly prestige. There are no lines for the Woman or the Gentleman—each role is pantomimed by a dancer. There is also a Chorus in the first and last scenes consisting of six women and six men that questions the Man about his life and fears, and a group of Artisans appears in the workshop episode.

As Scene 1 begins, the stage is quite dark. The Man lies face down on the ground toward the front. On his back is perched a hyena-like, mythical beast with large bat-like wings that appears to have sunk its teeth into his neck—a symbol, perhaps, of the jealousy gnawing at his vitals. In a semicircle to the rear, green-lighted faces of the Greek-style Chorus of six men and six women appear to hang in the air. Employing constantly changing relationships between sung and spoken tones, the Chorus laments the fate of the Man, who seeks again and again for the unobtainable, who abandons himself to the siren call of his senses but who longs, at the same time, for earthly happiness. They conclude their lament with the incantation "Poor Man!"[31]

In a lecture in connection with a production of the work in Breslau in 1928, Schoenberg commented on this opening scene:

At the beginning, you see twelve light *spots* on a black background: the faces of the six women and the six men. Or rather: *their gazes*. This is part of the mime performance, thus, of a medium of the stage. The impression under which this was written was approximately the following: it was as if I perceived a chorus of stares, as one perceives stares, even without seeing them, as they say something to one. What these say here is also paraphrased in words, which are sung by the chorus, and by the colors which show on the faces. The musical way in which this idea is composed testifies to the unity of conception: in spite of the diverse shaping of some *Hauptstimmen* this whole introduction is, as it were, held fast in place by an ostinato-like chord. Just as the gazes are rigidly and unchangeably directed at the Man, so the musical ostinato makes clear that these gazes form an ostinato on their part.[32]

The Chorus-faces disappear, as does the beast. Off-stage is heard the sound of spirited music followed by a burst of shrill, mocking laughter. The Man suddenly rises and stands with bowed head for a moment. He wears a dirty, brown-yellow jacket and black trousers, one leg of which reaches only below the knee. In his lower leg is a large open wound, perhaps made by a nail. On his feet are torn and tattered shoes. His open shirt reveals a bloodied breast and his hair is shorn close to his head. At length, he raises his head and intones with deep passion, "Yes—oh yes! The blooming . . . of my desire!"[33]

Scene 2 begins as the stage brightens. The cyclorama is lighted in a heaven-like shade of blue. Harsh yellow sunlight pours in from the left.[*] Yellow-green backing cloths hang at the sides. From the left, behind the Man, appears a beautiful young Woman, clothed in a warm violet dress with yellow and red roses in her hair. She gazes at the Man with intense compassion. The Man, sensing her presence, trembles—without turning around. The Woman apparently symbolizes earthly happiness, even as the Man seems to represent the pleasures of the spirit. As he extols her beauty—without looking at her—symbolic episodes from Wagner's operas are recalled. The Woman offers the Man a goblet on which violet light falls. The goblet appears in the Man's right hand, although neither has moved. Still facing front, the Man slowly drains the contents of the cup. The Woman loses interest in the Man and runs noiselessly to a position upstage right where an elegantly dressed Gentleman appears, wearing a dark gray cloak

---

* Right and left in the German theater refer to the audience's right and left, unlike the British and American theater in which the terms refer to the actor's right and left as he faces the audience.

and carrying a walking stick. The Man continues to sing of the Woman's beauty as he crosses toward center stage. The Gentleman extends his hand toward the Woman. She goes smilingly to him, they embrace, then disappear together off right.

The Man senses what has happened, groans, crosses a few steps left and stands in an attitude of despair. After a few moments, however, the Woman comes back in—from the left—kneels before him in an attitude of humility and appears to beg his forgiveness. He accepts her, without looking at her and, as she rises, he sinks to one knee before her. Her expression again changes, to one of light sarcasm, and suddenly she exits up left. The Man appears to imagine that the Woman is still near him, however; he rises, stands on tiptoe, raises his arms over his head and sings, "Now, I possess you for ever!"[34] suggesting that his own control over himself enables him to possess the Woman in spirit, if not in body. The scene ends as lighting fades down and out.

As Scene 3 begins, lighting comes up on a wild, rocky landscape, blackish gray in color, punctuated by a few pine trees with silver gray boughs. The scene "should not be an imitation of nature but, rather, a free combination of colors and forms."[35] Back lighting throws shadows of rocks on the stage which is bathed in gray green light at first. Later, when two hidden grottos are revealed right and left, shafts of lighting from the front wash the rocks in yellow green, while dark blue violet light falls on a gorge in the middle of the stage.

Echoes of Wagner are called up again as the Man emerges from the gorge, clad as before, except for a rope-like belt around his waist from which hang two severed Turk's heads. In his hand he carries a naked, bloody sword. The sense of the hero, Siegfried, is further enhanced as he enters a grotto left of the gorge that is then illuminated by shafts of brown, red, blue, green and lemon yellow light. Within the grotto is a workshop with an anvil and a large hammer in which mechanics and goldsmiths, wearing realistic work clothing, perform various tasks, recalling the *Niebelungen* in *Das Rheingold*. The Man observes the workers a few moments and then appears to be gripped by an inspiration. He goes to the anvil, puts down his sword, picks up a piece of gold with his left hand and puts it on the anvil. With his right—or favored—hand (of the title), he picks up the heavy hammer and prepares to strike the gold on the anvil. The workers quickly surround him in a threatening manner suggesting, perhaps, the Viennese critics who so hated Schoenberg's music.

The Man strikes the anvil with the hammer and, in an action that recalls the end of Act I of Wagner's *Siegfried,* the anvil splits and the gold falls into the fissure. The Man bends over the anvil and, with his left hand, lifts out a richly jewelled diadem that he holds up for all to see. The workers again make threatening gestures at this creator of art objects. The Man laughs and throws them the diadem, then picks up his sword as the grotto is engulfed in darkness.

There follows the most richly symbolic scene of the opera. As the Man stands alone on the darkened stage, a dramatic crescendo of wind, lighting and music takes place. It seems to emanate from the Man himself and suggests that he is intuitively aware of the sexual activity in which the Woman and the Gentleman are engaged.

The lighting begins in shades of weak red, goes to brown, then a mottled green. Following the dynamics of the music and the wind, the lighting turns to a dark blue gray, followed by shades of violet. A bright shaft of dark red splits the general lighting, becoming blood red, then orange and finally reaching an intensive yellow tonality. Yellow is the color of excitement, according to Schoenberg's close friend, Wassily Kandinsky. In its extreme form, it can become "unbearable to the eye and spirit . . . a representation of insanity in color."[36]

The intense yellow light reveals another grotto, right of the gorge, into which the Woman skips from off left with light quick steps to the accompaniment of a Viennese waltz suggesting, perhaps, that she had been cheapened by her affair with the Gentleman.[37] The lighting then fades from intense yellow to a weak blue tonality and the wind stops. The Woman is dressed as she was in the first scene except that part of her dress is missing, disclosing the naked upper left part of her body down to her hip. She pauses in the middle of the grotto, then stretches her arms toward the Gentleman, who has entered from the right. He carries the missing portion of her dress in his hand and motions her to come to him.

Meanwhile, the Man's despair grows. He bends backwards, then falls on his knees and crawls on all fours toward the grotto. As he sings, "You, you, you are mine, you were mine, she was mine,"[38] the Gentleman tosses the piece of clothing toward the Man and exits right with an expression on his face of utter indifference. The Man struggles toward the grotto but the rocks are slippery and he is unable to reach it.

The stage becomes dark, then lightens somewhat in a green-gray tonality. The grotto is dark as the Woman springs out of it, picks up the piece of clothing lying near the Man and wraps it around herself. As she does so, the Man, gripped by his tragic infatuation for the Woman, sings "Beautiful one! Stay with me!"[39] He reaches out for her, but she evades him and runs up to a ledge over the gorge. The lighting changes to an uncanny green tonality. A rock takes on the appearance of the beast of Scene 1. With a light push of her foot, the Woman kicks the rock down on the Man. The stage darkens as strident, contemptuous laughter is heard off-stage. When the lighting comes up, the Man is again on the floor, face down, the mythical beast again on his back, its teeth sunk in his neck.

The Chorus of six men and six women, whose faces are now bathed in a gray-blue tonality ask, in a combination of sung and spoken tones, "Did you have to live through again what you so often lived through before? . . . Do you feel only what you touch, feel your wounds only in your flesh, feel your pain only in your body? For this you search? And torment yourself? And forgo peace? . . ."[40] The gray-blue lighting on the twelve faces of the Chorus becomes accented with red light as they sing, very quietly, the last line of the opera, "Poor Man!"[41]

John Crawford has observed that the episodes of *Die glückliche Hand* form a mirror construction in which the action proceeds to a certain point, then goes back in reverse order to the starting point, as in Strindberg's *To Damascus, Part I*. The opening scene with the Chorus is followed by the mocking laughter off-stage. The scene in which the Gentleman draws the Woman away from the Man is followed by the workshop sequence. The lighting crescendo then leads to another scene between Man, Woman and Gentleman, off-stage mocking laughter is heard again and, finally, as in the beginning, the Man once more lies on the floor while the Chorus intones its words of sympathy.

The meaning of the opera is related to this plot structure embodying, as it does, Nietzsche's idea of the "eternal return,"[42] so archetypically expressed by Sophocles in his *Oedipus the King*. A subtheme is the contrast between the Man's success in art, as revealed in the workshop scene, and his failure in life, as dramatized by his loss of the Woman he loves.

The first performance of *Die glückliche Hand* took place October 14, 1924 at the Volksoper in Vienna under the musical direction of Fritz Stiedry and achieved a considerable success with the audience. But the requirements of an orchestra of over 90 musicians and a large scenic investiture for a 23-minute allegorical work have inhibited subsequent productions of one of the seminal operas of modern times. Perhaps its most arresting attribute is its demonstration of the possibility of *Gesamtkunstwerk* in its original meaning, in which the composer himself assumes responsibility for all the elements of theatrical production—text, stage action, scenery, costumes, lighting, sound effects and—the ultimate unifying means of expression—music.

Unlike Gustav Mahler and Richard Strauss, Schoenberg was never professionally associated with an opera house. As Karl Wörner has observed, "He was an outsider. And only in the mind of an outsider could there have arisen ideas that would so shatter the framework traditionally the stage's, that are often anti-stagy, and that have at the same time opened up new perspectives for the stage."[43]

It was four years after the Vienna production of *Die glückliche Hand* that Schoenberg decided to write another opera, a satirical piece with a libretto by his wife, Gertrud, and himself, to be composed in his serial technique, thus making *Von Heute auf Morgen* the first of many twelve-tone operas of our time. An allegory, like his other stage works, the new opera is a study of manners, fashion and the cult of modernism. There are five abstract characters—the Husband, his Wife, the Tenor, the Wife's Girl Friend and the Child. The setting consists of a modern bed-sitting room with built-in cupboards and in-a-door beds. A door up center leads to a verandah and, beyond, a garden.

The Husband and Wife return from a party, wearing evening dress— the Wife's clothing is adaptable to quick change. The Wife looks in on the Child, offstage, to make sure it is asleep, while the Man extols the virtues of an attractive woman he met at the party, a Girl Friend of his Wife's, whom they haven't seen in several years. The Wife tries to get her Husband to get ready for bed but he insists on contrasting the dreary routine of his married existence with the excitement that might be his in the company of the Wife's Friend. The Wife remarks, "Always, after a pleasant evening, you are in a bad mood."[44]

She goes on to observe that her Friend has changed over the years. She used to be a plain, mousy girl but now she is gay and seductive. Of course, she is not inhibited by husband, child, cooking and housework. The Wife wonders if her Friend thinks *she* has changed, over the years. The Husband replies—No—her Friend had said she was the same girl she had known at school. The Wife remembers the tricks her Friend used to think up (for which she—the Wife—was punished). The Husband mentions a Tenor who interrupted his lively conversation with the Wife's Friend. The Wife was very drawn to the Tenor—such a beautiful voice! The Husband can't see why any woman would be attracted to a tenor simply because of his voice. The wife replies that the Tenor looked deep into her eyes, expressed dissatisfaction with the loneliness of the heights on which he dwelt, and was prepared, for her, to become a bass. "What a crazy nut!"[45] she adds, with a laugh. The Husband wants to know why she is laughing. She explains that the Tenor made advances to her. Her Husband finds this surprising. She retorts by asking him if he prefers her Friend to her? He evades the question, and she points out how dazzled he tends to be by the superficial, the surface appearance, the modish dress.

He continues to praise the Friend and his Wife decides on a plan to open his eyes. While he is gazing into space, she changes into an elegant negligee, adds color to her hair and freshens her makeup, then turns up the light in the apartment. Her Husband is astonished at the change in his Wife's appearance and, in a scene reminiscent of Ferenc Molnár's play *The Guardsman* (1910)[*], finds himself falling in love with her all over again. "What is this?" he asks. "How can you look like this? How can a person be so changed? Is this elegant being my wife? Can I believe my eyes?"[46]

His Wife responds ironically with similar questions—can this ardent admirer of hers be her husband? The Husband becomes lyrical, insisting that only he is right for her, "that no other can love you with such heat, admire you so, worship you so, deify you so: my dearest wife!"[47] She hints that someone might take her away from him. He asks—who? The Tenor, she replies. The Husband waxes scornful: "What? This brainless comedian? Who thinks only in terms of operatic plots? Who can talk only about singing?"[48] He pleads with her to promise herself to him alone, but she responds that she expects to have many lovers in the coming days whose names she will jot down in an engagement book—old but rich, young but poor, muscular, elegant, philosophers, tramps, one after the other, as she pleases. And her Husband may take his place in line, after she's had so many lovers she can't remember him.

He protests against all this, but she abruptly persuades him to dance with her, perhaps for the last time. She sings a few measures of a popular tune as they dance around the room. Their Child, awakened by the noise, enters in his nightdress to find out what is going on. The Wife displays annoyance with her Child, refuses to kiss him, and the Husband takes him

---

[*] In *The Guardsman*, it is the husband who transforms himself into an elegantly uniformed Russian officer in order to dazzle his wife.

back to bed. The Wife's plan is now clear. As a "modern" woman, she will be unfaithful, willful, expensive, indifferent to her child, interested only in the pleasures of the moment.

As the Husband returns, the doorbell rings. It is the man from the gas company, demanding payment. The Husband gave the Wife money to pay the bill but she spent it on new clothes. And, if the gas is cut off, they can move to a hotel. As she begins packing a suitcase, the telephone rings. It is the Tenor, whose voice we can hear from offstage. The Husband goes out again to promise payment to the gas man, while the Wife flirts with the Tenor over the phone. The Husband returns, puts some things of his own in the suitcase and listens to the Wife's conversation with the Tenor, the upshot of which is that they all four, Husband, Wife, Tenor and Friend, will meet in ten minutes at a bar nearby.

The Wife again changes, this time into a sexy evening dress. The Husband objects to the Tenor seeing her in this dress and admits his jealousy. She thinks this is laughable—her Husband's sentimentality is outmoded. She suggests they do something "modern"—she with the Tenor, he with her Friend. Her Husband is deeply wounded by the idea and confesses his unhappiness with all this modernism. His Wife quickly changes back to a simple housedress and alters her makeup and hairstyle to what they were at the beginning of the scene. Her Husband is delighted and sings, "I took you for a woman of yesterday, whereupon you played the role of a woman of today. I thought she was better than you but now, I know you are the one for me all my life."[49]

She puts the beds back up in the wall, observes that it is morning, and they haven't slept. She goes out to make coffee. The Husband still wonders if she wasn't, after all, attracted to the Tenor? She returns with the coffee and the receipt for the gas bill. She also explains that the sexy clothes belong to her Husband's sister, Lisl—a professional dancer.

But just as Husband and Wife seem to have reached a better under-standing, the Tenor and the Friend come in up center. They have grown tired of drinking and dancing while waiting at the bar. Husband and Wife apologize—they had forgotten. Some coffee?

A quartet begins, in which it develops that the Tenor and the Friend live in a world of cognac and gin, while Husband and Wife face life's realities in terms of coffee that is getting cold. The Tenor and the Friend accuse the Husband and Wife of refusing the new freedom everyone enjoys these days, while the latter admit that they are, perhaps, obsolete. Unlimited freedom, Schoenberg seems to be saying, leads to anarchy, while real freedom is obtained through order, sacrifice and acceptance of obligation.

Tenor and Friend depart, after which Wife, Husband and Child sit down to breakfast and deliver the last lines of the opera in *Sprechstimme*:

Wife.

Perhaps we are a bit faded, but they seem merely colorful stage figures out of the latest hit. And another difference: their lives are directed by fashion but ours—are they gone? I can dare to say it—by love.

Husband.

They don't seem very modern to me.

Wife.

That can change over night.

Child (spoken).

Mama, what are modern people?[50]

Schoenberg seems to respond to this question, in some notes regarding his opera, by saying that "the so-called modern, the merely modish exists but 'from today till tomorrow,' from a shaky hand to a greedy mouth—not only in marriage, but no less in art, in politics and in attitudes toward life."[51]

The first production of *Von Heute auf Morgen* took place at the Frankfort Opera on February 1, 1930. Schoenberg wrote to the conductor, Wilhelm Steinberg: "Throughout, the tone of the whole thing should be quite light."[52] The stage direction was by the future principal stage director of the Metropolitan Opera, Herbert Graf.

By the time Arnold Schoenberg made his third move to Berlin, early in 1926, he had begun to reexamine his religious convictions. As a child, he had been instructed in the Jewish faith by his devout mother and his more liberal father but, like many Jews in Vienna at the turn of the century, he did not take religion very seriously. In a letter of 1891, he calls himself an "unbeliever",[53] but a few years later, under the influence of a close friend, the opera singer Walter Pieau, he was baptized in the Evangelische Dorotheer Kirche on the 25th of March, 1898, after having formally left the Jewish faith a few days earlier.[54] It was in this same Lutheran church, in the heart of the old quarter of Catholic Vienna, that Schoenberg married Mathilde von Zemlinsky on October 18, 1901.[55]

Why Schoenberg chose to become a Lutheran instead of a Roman Catholic, the faith of the vast majority of the Austrian people, is not clear. He was conducting a Workers' Chorus at the time, members of which addressed him as "Comrade", and the Jewish leader of the Austrian Social Democratic Party, Victor Adler, had converted to Protestantism.[56] But it is also possible that for Schoenberg, an instinctive revolutionary in everything else, it was simply natural to adopt a religion whose fundamental reason for being is the sacred principle of protest.

Schoenberg's conversion did not lessen anti-Semitic animosity toward him in Vienna, however. In 1910, when he received a temporary appointment at the Academy of Music and the Performing Arts, his hopes of obtaining a tenured professorship were frustrated by the anti-Semitism of both faculty and officials of the government, led by the rabidly anti-Semitic mayor of Vienna, Karl Lueger. It was, in part, this attitude toward Schoenberg in his native city that drove him, in 1911, to accept a new teaching position in Berlin.

After his return to Vienna and the completion of his two terms of military service, he again took up teaching, writing and other diverse activities such as helping to organize the *Verein für musikalische Privataufführungen* [Society for Private Concerts], to which he devoted much time and energy. For time to compose, he counted on his summers and, in 1921, had found a quiet retreat at Mattsee, near Salzburg, where he could swim and work. His idyll was interrupted, however, by a number of signs and placards affixed to buildings in the town demanding that Jews get out. Schoenberg and his family were forced to leave Mattsee and seek a vacation-work spot elsewhere.

During the twenties, Schoenberg became ever more conscious of the growth of anti-Semitism in Germany and Austria. In 1923, he turned down an invitation from Wassily Kandinsky to join the teaching staff of the newly formed *Bauhaus* in Weimar because of the rumored anti-Semitism of some of its members. In a letter to Kandinsky of April 20, 1923, Schoenberg expresses himself as follows:

> If I had gotten your letter a year ago, I'd have abandoned my principles, given up my plan to compose full time and plunged head first into the adventure. Even today I hesitated, because the great pleasure I take in teaching is still easily fired up. But it cannot be.
>
> Because I was forced to learn a lesson this past year that I will never forget: that I am not a German, not a European, perhaps not even a human being— certainly Europeans prefer the worst of their brethren to me—but a Jew.[57]

In another letter to Kandinsky, May 4, 1923, Schoenberg continues his thoughts on anti-Semitism with a reference to the Mattsee affair:

I had to interrupt my first working summer in five years, leave a place where I thought I would be able to work in peace, and then was unable to find such peace anywhere else—all because the Germans will not tolerate Jews![58]

He goes on to inquire why Jews are equated with the criminal elements of their own race while Gentiles are judged by Goethe and Schopenhauer? And why does Kandinsky think he—Schoenberg—is somehow exempt from all this? If there are to be individual exceptions, what about Jews who were wounded fighting in the war? And, he adds, not all Jews are communists. "I am not one and was never one."[59] If a Jew does business effectively, thus threatening his competitors, he is attacked not only as a businessman but as a Jew as well, whereas on the other side, the Jew is not concerned with beating his Christian competitors but with beating *all* his competitors. Schoenberg then sums up:

What will anti-Semitism lead to except violence? Is that so hard to imagine? Perhaps you are pleased to see Jews deprived of their rights, see Einstein, Mahler, me and many others eliminated? But something else remains. No one can exterminate those hardy members of our race who have enabled us to survive the hostility of all mankind for twenty centuries . . . who carried out God's command—to live in exile, racially pure, heads held high—until the Hour of Salvation![60]

It took Schoenberg many years, from the time of his baptism as a Protestant in 1898 to the early 1920s, to become convinced that, as the saying goes, he couldn't wash away his Jewishness with a few drops of holy water. After Hitler's seizure of power forced him to leave Berlin and reside temporarily in Paris, he reentered the Jewish community in a ceremony at the *Union Liberale Israelite* on July 24, 1933. Among the witnesses present was the painter Marc Chagall.

According to a letter to Alban Berg of October 16, 1933, Schoenberg began thinking about his play, *Der biblische Weg*, in 1922 or 1923,[61] shortly after the Mattsee episode opened his eyes to the reality of being a Jew in Central Europe. He didn't begin work on his only play, however, until after he had settled down in Berlin, where he finished the first draft in June, 1926.[62]

The play is an allegory on the centuries-long struggle of the Jewish people to return to Jerusalem, to reestablish their identity as a people by acquiring a homeland of their own and, as Schoenberg described it in a letter, "a topical treatment (from 1926–7) of the emergence of the Jews as a people."[63]

The characters in the play represent many attitudes and shades of opinion held by Jews during the 1920s toward the great dream of establishing an independent Jewish state, either in Palestine or, perhaps, in one of the African states, newly emancipated from colonial rule, where a large tract of territory might be purchased by international Jewish capital.

In the fall of 1923, the League of Nations ratified the British mandate over Palestine and endorsed the Balfour Declaration of 1917, promising an independent Jewish state in the area west of the Jordan River, but not including all of Palestine. Jews of the time were divided over this issue. Moderates wanted to accept whatever size and shape of state the British were willing to give them, but militant Zionists such as Vladimir Jabotinsky, among others, believed that the new Jewish homeland must be established not by means of a handout but by military means, as in the heroic times of the Israelites when Joshua, following Moses as leader of the Jewish refugees from Egypt, fought his way into the Promised Land by force of arms.

Schoenberg was convinced that the security of the new Jewish state would depend on military strength rather than on international goodwill, and he may have modelled his hero, Max Aruns, on the figure of Jabotinsky. As he explains in some notes to his play, Aruns "has seized upon the idea that the liberation of the Jews must be sought in accordance with the biblical example through the appropriate use of power. (He has recognized as a fallacy the attempt to rely on the goodwill of other nations) . . . Once this idea has taken hold, all else flows forth from it."[*64]

Schoenberg's thinking proved to be right. The modern state of Israel was proclaimed by the United Nations on May 14, 1948, and on that same day, Israel was invaded by Arab armies intent on crushing the new state and driving its citizens into the sea, an intention that was thwarted by the Israeli armed forces. Israel had to fight two more short but vicious wars with its Arab neighbors in 1967 and 1973 and today, it depends for its security on its army, its air force, and its alliance with the last of the superpowers.

---

* Thirty years later, Manachem Begin wrote that the state of Israel could be summed up in one sentence: "We fight, therefore we are."

Schoenberg's play is in three acts. The first, in two scenes, takes place at a sports camp and stadium in the Alps, while the second and third are set in New Palestine, part of an imaginary African country, Ammongäa. During the first act, we become acquainted with Max Aruns (a name that suggests both Moses and Aaron), former journalist turned statesman (like Theodor Herzl), who has a plan for the establishment of a temporary Jewish state in an African country, to be followed by the establishment of the primary state in British Palestine, with Jerusalem as the capital. All the other characters are associated with Max Aruns: his wife, Christine; his secretary, Linda Rutlin; his close supporters, Pinxar, an engineer and inventor, Jonston, Kolbief, Gadman and Golban, Jr.; his spiritual adviser and nemesis, David Asseino; a messenger from Asseino, Setouras; Aruns's successor, Joseph Guido (the Joshua-figure of the story); Kaphira, representative of the Emperor of Ammongäa; Sanda, a childhood friend of Christine's and an informer, paid by Jewish groups in opposition to Max Aruns; Golban, a representative of these hostile groups and various other figures connected with the great dream of securing once more a free and independent homeland for the Jewish people.

In the first scene of the first act, details of Max Aruns's plan for New Palestine gradually become clear. His secretary and fervent admirer, Linda Rutlin, describes his recent activities:

Linda.

In the last two years, he has travelled twice around the world. Everywhere, he has organized federations, negotiated with governments, signed contracts, accepted promises and created climates of confidence. He has thoroughly explored New Palestine and visited the important centers. He has examined the reports of all the experts, has consulted with technicians, geographers, industrialists and financiers, has drawn up the plan for the emigration and settling in of our people, has worked out the execution of the plan in every detail and has suggested many improvements in it. He has devised everything, down to the smallest detail, and now we are prepared! Only months—weeks, perhaps—separate us from the departure of the first shipload of emigrants to Ammongäa.

Anyone who does not admire his achievement unconditionally and believe in its success is not one of us![65]

It develops that Max Aruns has enemies, however. Two points of view

103

regarding the return to Jerusalem become apparent. The view of Aruns is that an intermediate stage must be undertaken. It is possible, with help from international Jewish banking interests, to purchase land in Africa where the Jews could establish their own state and, later, when they have developed a credible military organization, complete the move to Palestine by force, if necessary. He thinks of this rather long, drawn-out process as being comparable to the forty years it took the ancient Israelites to achieve their Exodus from Egypt, as recorded in the Bible.

The enemies of Max Aruns, however, believe the new state should be established in Palestine, ancient domicile of the Jews, and nowhere else. Their spy in Aruns's camp, Sanda, keeps them informed of all his plans. Much of this divergence of opinion is made clear by one of Aruns's closest collaborators, Jonston, to Gadman, an interested spectator who has not committed himself to either camp as yet:

Jonston.

You are aware that we have concluded a contract with the Emperor of Ammongäa, who has agreed to make available to us an underdeveloped portion of his empire large enough to accommodate thirty million settlers, thus providing the basis for New Palestine. For our part, we have undertaken to make available to him the means of turning his country, which is rich in natural resources of all kinds, into a modern state.[66]

Jonston goes on to explain the sense of dedication that prevails among the followers of Max Aruns:

Jonston.

You have surely heard about a scandal involving Kaphira, the ambassador of the Emperor of Ammongäa. I will tell you a story about this.

We were with Aruns in Ammongäa: Pinxar, Kolbief, Eldad, some specialists and I.

We were negotiating with Kaphira who, from the very beginning, had supported our endeavours, about the border of New Palestine. Kaphira displayed real friendship for Aruns and we all believed that he loved him in the same way as everyone else who knew him.

But Aruns thought otherwise.

At one place, the border was to follow a large river. But at a certain point Kaphira suggested that it make a large bend away from the river which would greatly increase the size of our country. There was iron ore in this piece of land and, it was rumoured, radium.[67]

Jonston explains that, to their surprise, Aruns refused to accept this handsome gift and insisted that the border follow the river. After the conference ended, Aruns's followers were displeased and disappointed, but such was their discipline and devotion to their leader that no one questioned his decision. Later, the truth came out:

Jonston.
Aruns said, "I have just received a letter from Kaphira." He read it to us. It seems that Kaphira had long wanted this land for himself but didn't have enough money to buy it. Since Aruns had now indicated that he placed no value on the land, Kaphira is asking that Aruns add it to New Palestine and then sell it to him at a reduced price.[68]

Johnston concludes his story by explaining that because Aruns couldn't understand why Kaphira wanted to give them so much valuable land, he decided to refuse it in order to find out. The clarification not only put Kaphira in their debt but enhanced Aruns's own knowledge of the kinds of thinking that must accompany successful political negotiations.

When Max Aruns finally makes his entrance in Act I, the audience is well prepared for him. He discusses with his closest supporter, Pinxar, their people's need for a visible symbol of the driving force that will enable them to regain a free and independent homeland of their own. Pinxar observes:

Pinxar.
You were right when you said, "We may again need trumpets before Jericho and they will be there." And that further demonstrates the truth of your words, "From a good thought, everything else flows on its own."
Aruns.
Unfortunately, we can't show them such a miracle. The masses of people need something *visible* to believe in.
Pinxar.
Our propaganda employs the same means common to other, similar

105

strivings. We make clear our sufferings, our hopes and one thing more: our faith.

Aruns.

But our faith in an invisible and unimaginable God does not provide for any visible fulfillment.[69]

The idea of "trumpets before Jericho" is repeated several times in *Der biblische Weg* and eventually comes to stand for a new invention of Pinxar's, a ray gun that can damage an enemy position by sucking all the oxygen out of the area, leading to the suffocation of the enemy forces, a weapon not unlike a modern nuclear warhead delivered to an enemy position by means of a rocket.

The following idea, that everything flows necessarily from a good thought, is a major theme of Schoenberg's play and of his opera, *Moses und Aron*. The "good thought" of providing again a free and independent homeland for the Jewish people guarantees its ultimate realization as, in fact, happened in 1948.

Aruns's pessimistic observation that the masses of people need visible images to reinforce their faith points directly toward the central conflict of *Moses und Aron*: Moses understands the God-Idea but can't express it in words, while Aron can display to the people an image of God in the form of a Golden Calf, but his image is false. This dilemma is expressed for the first time by Aruns's lines describing God as "invisible" and "un-imaginable", a description augmented in the opening line of the opera with the adjectives "one-and-only", "eternal" and "ever-present". These mysterious attributes of God seem to Moses to rule out any kind of representation of him—by symbol, metaphor or allegory, by drawing, painting or sculpture, even by that most abstract of all representations, a musical idea.

The second scene of Act I takes place in a large sports arena in the Alps. From a platform overlooking the entire complex, Max Aruns addresses the young people who will settle New Palestine:

Aruns.

People of Israel!
What is this Festival?

A sports festival? A parade? A party convention? A people's convention?

106

Isn't this a day like all the others?

No, it is not. It is a day that will be remembered by the Jewish people for all time.

It is like that day on which the youngest man asks:

"Why do we sit here, huddled together?"

But today, he asks instead:

"Why do we all stand up? Why have we lifted ourselves up? Why don't we remain on the floor, supine, as on all the other days?"

Well, we have gotten up. We stand now on our own two feet. And we have attained a stature nobody could have dreamed of.

We have stiffened our bent backs, bent to receive the lashes that others deserved. We stand up again, like that old, tough, defiant, stiff-necked people of the Bible. But today, we are no longer in stiff-necked opposition to our God. We are *for* him, the God who chose us to be his people . . .

We are an old people:

What good to us would be a God whom we could comprehend, of whom we could make an image, on whom we could exert influence?

We need no miracles. Persecution and contempt have strengthened us, have increased our tenacity and resilience and have developed and improved organs that raise our capacity for resistance.

We are an old people.

To be sure, not every single person can grasp our God-Idea: to accept that every event depends on the highest Being, whose laws we feel and recognize although we may not question their meaning.

But when everyone has grasped the God-Idea, then the Messiah will have come.

107

The Messiah of inner confidence.

Dear young friends! Your teachers and leaders have transplanted this faith into you, have developed your spiritual capacities and have schooled your bodies . . .

Now, you are capable of facing the greatest challenges.

You possess elasticity, drive, enthusiasm, adaptability and capacity for sacrifice.

The hardest task has fallen to you.

Because everything we have striven for has been for young people like yourselves.

The future belongs to you. The time will come when no Jew will be concerned about the respect or disrespect of people of other races.

For this reason, you will take on the decisive phase of our work:

You young people! You will be the pioneers in our new country! You will prepare the soil and lay the foundation on which will be erected the proud edifice of our new state!

And that is the deeper significance of this Festival. That is why this Festival will become a Memorial Day for all time . . .

Today, here, you announce with all your strength that you are prepared to serve a knowledge higher than any known to man:

That you will make it possible for our people at last to live, at last to dream their God-Idea![70]

To the applause of the assembled young men and women of the sports clubs and the disciples of Max Aruns, the curtain falls on Act I.

Act II takes place in the Central Administration building of the Colony of New Palestine in Ammongäa, a few weeks after the end of Act I. Aruns dictates a message to his secretary, Linda, to be radioed to David Asseino. A uniformed sentry guards the door.

As he dictates, Aruns observes that they have been in New Palestine for four weeks, that he would like Asseino to join them the next day to take part in the first Feast of the Passover to be celebrated in the new, independent land of the Jews, and asks further that Asseino become the first High Priest of New Palestine. He explains, too, about the weapon invented by Pinxar with which they will be able to defend themselves against their enemies and adds that Pinxar is flying in with the last critical portion of the apparatus.

Linda interrupts to ask if such an important piece of information should be sent out by radio. What if the message were intercepted?

Aruns replies that Pinxar's code will ensure the integrity of the message. After she leaves to send the radiogram a scene between Aruns and his wife, Christine, suggests a certain amount of tension between them, derived from Christine's jealousy of Linda. Christine's possession of the only written description of the secret weapon is established.

Two officers appear, Tomlan and the younger Golban, an expert in Oriental languages. Some idea of the growing pains of the new, multilingual state is suggested by Golban, Jr.'s report of an incident connected with a construction project:

Golban, Jr.
During the building of a temporary church on the common border between the Russian and German camps, people who spoke both languages were working under a German-speaking foreman.

Yesterday, some discord developed because the foreman couldn't express some technical instructions in either Hebrew or Russian. A bit of a fight was soon settled and they all agreed to approach the Language Commission.

The Commission established that for this particular problem certain phrases borrowed from Arabic or Turkish could have been used, but doubtless they are not in universal use. I request orders that will cover future situations of this kind.
Aruns.
Were you with them?
Golban, Jr.
Yes, sir.

Aruns.

But this is your specialty. Couldn't you help them?

Golban, Jr.

I only got there when the fight was on.

Aruns.

So the language expert arrives too late! You have changed. A while back you would have missed the fight too!

Of course, we can't assign a language specialist to every little construction job. And, we can hardly expect a foreman with a fire on his hands to first call up and find out the Hebrew word for "extinguish" and how, from that, to build the imperative form![71]

Aruns concludes the discussion by saying he will not be upset if the language specialist arrives late, but hopes the military will arrive at about the right time, as it did in this case.

A message is received to the effect that Pinxar's arrival will be delayed due to damage to the plane carrying the piece of apparatus crucial for the operation of the secret weapon. The spy, Sanda, plays on Christine's jealousy of her husband to obtain the paper describing the weapon. He eventually sends it to certain Jewish interests in London that are opposed to the establishment of New Palestine.

Sanda also applies his powers of persuasion to Linda Rutlin, Aruns's secretary and devoted disciple. He explains that New Palestine is in danger of collapse, and that he will save her if she will give him the code Pinxar has devised to protect radio messages. She leads him on to try to ascertain his true position in the community, but ultimately refuses to betray Max Aruns.

Various messages come in. Pinxar will arrive in the afternoon. Golban is present and ready to sign contracts for the industrial development of Ammongäa, provided his capitalist backers may have some direct influence in the new government. And the food transport, which has been delayed, will arrive in two days.

Max Aruns rejects Golban's condition that foreign capitalists, even if they are Jewish, should have a say in the running of the new state: "The position of the big capitalists won't be any different in this state than in any other democracy."[72]

After some further discussion with his followers, Max Aruns prepares to receive Kaphira, ambassador from the Emperor of Ammongäa. He asks Linda to find his wife, who should be present on this state occasion.

Kaphira enters with his retinue and there ensues a scene of formal greetings and flattering observations:

Aruns.
It is for me a high honor and great pleasure to greet your Excellency in our country. You, the benevolent ambassador from our fatherly friend, without whose good opinion, our people could not have been freed from their sorrows, without which we could not call this country *our* country.[73]

Aruns adds that he recalls with emotion all their meetings and discussions, during which Kaphira made it clear that the fate of the Jewish people was almost as important to him as that of his own.

Kaphira responds with equal enthusiasm. He has looked forward fervently to the moment when he would meet again with the man whose God has marked him with distinction by enabling him to perform one of the unique deeds of history, the man who puts all his warmest love, ability, understanding, and feeling at the disposal of his people, "the man who has the strength and the courage to carry through his idea in spite of the opposition of the entire world, the man who ultimately succeeds in his work, the man of success, who is able not only to imagine an idea but also has the perseverance and the luck to achieve it."[74]

As Alexander Ringer has observed, Kaphira's words probably describe Arnold Schoenberg's own opinion of himself[75] as he spent his years fighting with unflagging conviction for his musical as well as his political ideals.

Kaphira announces that the Emperor of Ammongäa has empowered him to sign the agreements providing the Jews a homeland and those providing the Emperor with his compensation. After Kaphira withdraws, tension among the Jewish leaders increases. Where is Pinxar? Sanda has been seen driving away with Aruns's wife, Christine. The food transports are moving with unexplained slowness. It is reported that Christine's room is in disarray, that somebody must have been searching for something. Aruns guesses that Pinxar's design for their secret weapon may have been stolen. A letter then informs him that his wife has indeed deserted him.

Aruns.
She has run away with Sanda—the traitor!

After all these years of faithfulness and trust!

Is my destiny turning?

Now that I am so close to my goal? . . .

Am I too dependent on people?

Have I lost her because I am too absorbed in my work? . . .

Well—no vanity! It is only the man in me that is injured . . .

Perhaps this sacrifice was necessary . . . Perhaps I must stand now entirely alone. . . .

Perhaps I am only now capable of finishing my work . . .

I must triumph over this blow!

Or, is my destiny turning?[76]

Once again, Schoenberg relives the feelings that engulfed him when his wife, Mathilde, left him for the painter Richard Gerstl and, as earlier in *Die glückliche Hand*, expresses them here in the climax of Act II of *Der biblische Weg*.

Act III takes place the following day, the first day of Passover, in the same setting except that the building is pushed farther off-stage to increase the size of the acting area.

Pinxar still has not arrived. The people of the settlement are uneasy because of the shortage of food. Is there a relationship between the dilatory progress of the food transports from Ammongäa and the delay in Pinxar's arrival? People have been trying to break into the food-storage warehouses. Plans for possible food rationing are discussed. An old man reports a rumor that Kaphira is deliberately holding up the food transports.

David Asseino appears and he and Aruns engage in the most philosophical exchange in the play. Two distinct "Biblical ways" are developed: Max Aruns's way of war and Asseino's way of spirit.

Asseino.

May you be blessed, because you have raised our people up again and led them back to belief in the sublimity of our religion.

You were on the right path when you based your work on the word of God, when you said that God has chosen this people, before all others, to believe in the one-and-only, and unimaginable God. . . .

God has blessed your work up to now and will bless it further if you remain faithful to his word and trust in spiritual power alone.[77]

Pamela White has noted that it is in this speech of Asseino's that Schoenberg first employs the "important, incantationlike words *'Einziger, ewiger, unsichtbarer und unvorstellbarer Gott'* which resonate in the opening of the opera [*Moses und Aron*]."[78]

Max Aruns replies to Asseino that he senses an undertone of rebuke to his belief that the new state must stand on its own two feet and not depend for its survival on the benevolence of foreign countries.

The new state must be prepared to fight, if necessary, for its independence. Asseino replies with words that sum up the very essence of the conflict in *Moses und Aron*: "Max Aruns, you want to be Moses and Aron in one person! Moses, to whom God gave the Idea but not the power to express it; and Aron, who failed to grasp the Idea but was able to repeat it and stir the people to action."[79]

This paradoxical view of God, that he is unimaginable but also wants himself revealed to the people, is at the heart of both *Der biblische Weg* and *Moses und Aron*. God, in the Judeo-Christian scheme of things, is both transcendent (outside the universe) and immanent (within the universe). As Michael Cherlin has observed, "For Moses, God's immanence is the bridge to God's transcendence, and it is God's transcendence that makes Him the object of worship . . . For Aron . . . God's transcendence can be only an article of faith, and because Aron himself cannot understand the nature of God's transcendence, he cannot nurture that idea in the Volk."[80] On the basis of this failure of perception, Aron causes to be erected before the people a Golden Calf, an image of God that satisfies nearly everybody.

Max Aruns continues to press Asseino for a more liberal interpretation of the ancient ways of Jewish life so that the people of New Palestine may survive modern competition and not have to live by laws established 5,000 years earlier. As he puts it, "Modern people cannot cool down the blast furnaces and cut off the electricity every Friday."[81]

Asseino responds that what Max Aruns asks of him is tantamount to Aron's asking Moses to help with the erection of the Golden Calf. Max Aruns depends too much on material things, on machines and weapons rather than on the power of the divine spirit. He depends on "striking the rock", as Moses did, instead of "speaking to the rock" as God had told him to do. For this reason, just as Moses was denied entrance into the Promised Land, so Max Aruns will not live to see the fulfillment of his dream.

Asseino leaves Aruns, saying he can no longer support him or his undertaking. In an aside to the audience, Aruns wonders,

Aruns.
Was this just a scholarly dispute?

Is it possible that he is right? Was I presumptuous? Have I expected too much of myself? Have I strayed from my Idea?

Is my destiny turning?[82]

Linda arrives with disturbing news. Sanda has called to say that the food transports are not coming, and that Pinxar's design for the ray-gun weapon has been stolen. She urges Max Aruns to save himself for the sake of the cause. He asks her if she really thinks he would run away in the face of danger? "If I am defeated now, I am defeated for all time. The Idea itself was wrong, everything I did was wrong and, therefore, I must pay."[83]

A phone message conveys the news that Pinxar is dead. His transport plane was attacked for a second time the day before, and he died defending it. Only Eldad, who made the report, survived—badly wounded. Christine returns, throws herself at her husband's feet and begs his forgiveness. She confirms that Sanda has stolen Pinxar's weapon design. Kaphira enters to say that the Emperor of Ammongäa no longer supports the settlement of New Palestine because he is under severe pressure from a foreign power.

Suddenly, a multitude of emigrants, bearing arms, bursts onto the stage demanding an accounting for the lack of food from the Commander-in-Chief, the Leader, the Prophet, the King of the Jews. In the ensuing melee both Gadman and Golban, Jr. lose their lives, and Max Aruns falls to the ground, mortally wounded. In his last moments, he addresses God:

114

Aruns.

God, you have struck me down. This means that I have deserved it. This means that Asseino was right, that I was presumptuous in trying to be Moses and Aron in one person. This means that I betrayed the Idea when I relied on a machine instead of the holy spirit.

God, only now do I realize this and beg of you: take my blood in payment.

But don't let these poor, innocent people suffer for my sins.

God, save them! Give them a sign that you punish only me for my sin against the spirit, but you will not let the Idea be defeated.

God, I am vanquished, beaten, flogged.

I die, but I feel: you will let the Idea live. And I die gladly, because I know you will always give men to our people who will die gladly for the Idea of the one-and-only, eternal, invisible and unimaginable God.[84]

The bodies of Max Aruns, Gadman and Golban, Jr. are placed on biers in the center of the stage. The people stand near them, in deep mourning. Joseph Guido appears, accompanied by soldiers, and addresses the crowd. He shows Jonston a paper indicating that he is the successor to Max Aruns should the latter suffer a fatal accident. He relates that Pinxar had placed the secret weapon in another plane, to be flown by himself (Guido), that the loading of Pinxar's plane was a fake operation (*Scheinmanöver*), designed to lure their enemies into attacking it. The operation worked as planned. Pinxar died defending the decoy plane while Guido managed to fly the vital portion of the secret weapon to safety. The weapon is being deployed even now, so the security of New Palestine is assured.

Guido orders Kaphira to hand over the documents of agreement with the Emperor. The ambassador does so, and departs quietly. An air of authority and confidence settles over the young community as Guido delivers a funeral oration over the body of the dead hero, Max Aruns:

Guido.

Even though we may now have the power to make ourselves masters of this earth, we wish to declare, in the name and the spirit of this dead man, that such a thing is far from our thoughts.

The Jewish people live an Idea: belief in a one-and-only, immortal, eternal, unimaginable God. They will allow only this Idea to become their ultimate law; in its purest form, it may one day become the ultimate law of the world.

And, as we are so little concerned to direct the newly discovered death-bringing rays of a material power to any point in the world, just so little do we concern ourselves with revenge or winning power over another people. On the contrary, we are concerned with spreading everywhere the enlightening rays of our Idea, so that they may call forth a new spiritual life for all.

The time will come when all these material rays will symbolize only that which can flow from a good thought. They are nothing other than rays of thought which, however, will encounter the rays of spirit and will be, therefore, excluded from the higher reality.

But striving for universal acceptance of our ideals is an enterprise for the future. For the present, we must concern ourselves only with matters that are clearly within our immediate interests.

We have a further goal. We want to feel *safe* as a people. We want to be sure that no one can force us into something, and that no one can prevent us from doing something.

We do not wish to exert undue influence on other peoples.

We have enough to do among ourselves!

As with every ancient people, we possess the desire to *spiritualize* our existence, to separate ourselves from the material.

And one final goal: we must all learn to understand God as one-and-only, eternal and unimaginable.

We wish to lead spiritual lives, without disturbance from others.

We wish to obtain fulfillment of the spirit and to dream our dream of God—like all ancient peoples who have transcended the material world.[85]

It is clear that *Der biblische Weg* supplied Schoenberg with the basic elements around which he built his libretto for *Moses und Aron*. In Act I, scene 9, Asseino pronounces two of the five words that describe God at the beginning of the opera—"eternal" and "unimaginable". Asseino also states a major theme of the opera in Act II, scene 3—that Moses understood the God-Idea as revealed to him through the Burning Bush but couldn't express it in words, while Aron was able to influence the masses with a retelling of the Idea even though he didn't understand it. This dichotomy resolves itself into a perennial question that is fundamental to both play and opera: how to realize the God-Idea by means that will not destroy the Idea itself. The people of the modern state of Israel are still struggling with this ancient challenge to the wisdom of the human race.

Schoenberg vastly improved his play by rewriting it as an opera libretto. He cut the long, prolix, philosophical sections to the bone, reestablished the duality of Max Aruns as Moses and Aron and succeeded in dramatizing his thematic ideas in place of merely discussing them. Still, it must be said of his awkward but original play that he made a remarkably prophetic and convincing political statement in the theatrical mode. After all, we can see in the history of Israel from 1948 to the present that Max Aruns was right. The Biblical Way *is* the way of war, of the ultimate means of legitimate self-defense, as the people of modern Israel discovered when they had to fight three times for their very lives. Schoenberg's idea of a powerful weapon, capable of wreaking devastation on the enemies of New Palestine is replicated today by Israel's possession of atomic weapons that can be delivered to her enemies by means of her air force. Negotiation, accommodation and diplomacy have their place in the political spectrum, but it is a melancholy commentary on the nature of the human race that most of the significant conflicts of history have been settled by means of war, that continuation of politics by violent means.

Der biblische Weg was not produced on the stage in Schoenberg's lifetime. He showed it to Max Reinhardt, who seems to have become interested in the idea of the play if not the play itself. After he read it, according to Alma Mahler Werfel, he "ordered a Biblical cavalcade from Werfel, 'a kind of St. Matthew's Passion' as he put it, encompassing the whole Old Testament. The play, which Werfel called *The Eternal Road,*[*] was to be produced in New York, with music by Kurt Weill."[86]

Although *The Eternal Road,* with its climactic scene of a dance around the Golden Calf, had a good success in New York in 1937, Schoenberg's epic drama continues to languish in obscurity. If it were adapted into English by an experienced playwright and produced with the kind of conviction that infused the recent New York City Opera production of *Moses und Aron*, it might achieve a surprising success in the spoken theater.

Schoenberg himself intuitively identified more with Moses the prophet than with Aron the priest, and his opera is, to a considerable extent, a projection of himself as the more sympathetic of the two Biblical figures. Thus, it is Moses who speaks the first line of the opera, in which the dream of God expounded in *Der biblische Weg* is invoked in five incantatory descriptions: "one-and-only, eternal, ever-present, invisible and unimaginable God!"[87]

Voices from the Burning Bush call on Moses to enlighten the Israelites and lead them out of Egyptian slavery. To Moses' objection that his tongue is not fluent *(ungelenk),* the Voices reply that Aron, his brother, will speak for him. They also tell him that his people are chosen to be the worshippers of the one-and-only God, that they will suffer for their convictions but, in the end, will enjoy salvation.

In scene 2, Moses meets Aron in the desert and they prepare to convey the word of God to their people. They will make it clear to the Israelites that they are a chosen people—chosen to proclaim the one-and-onliness of God; chosen to lead the races of the world away from the polytheism of the past to the monotheism of the future; and chosen to reveal by the example of their worship that God is both invisible and unimaginable:

Moses.
Our people, chosen to know the invisible, to reflect on the unimaginable.
Aron.
Our people are chosen to love the one-and-only God for ever, with a thousand times more love than that bestowed by other peoples on their many gods. Invisible! Unimaginable![88]

Aron adds a question, however, that is to dominate the rest of the opera: "But can our people, even if chosen by the one-and-only, worship what they

---

* *Der Weg der Verheißung* [*The Promised Way*].

118

cannot imagine?"[89] He remains doubtful about this and his thoughts eventually lead him to recognize the need of the people to bow down before a divine image of God, something they can see, a need he satisfies with his Golden Calf.

In scene 3, the Israelites await the return of Moses and Aron from the desert. Two points of view are expressed. One group counsels caution—no new god is likely to be more powerful than Pharaoh's gods:

> **Chorus** (first group).
> Don't believe the liars!
> The gods love us not!
> Who is it that could be
> Stronger than Pharaoh's gods?[90]

The other group sings the praises of the new god:

> **Chorus** (second group).
> He will make us free!
> We want to love him!
> We want to sacrifice to him![91]

They become aware of the approach of Moses and Aron in the distance and eagerly await tidings of the new God.

In scene 4, the people greet Moses and Aron warmly and offer to make sacrifices to the new God, including the sacrifice of life. Moses replies that God requires no sacrifices, that he is invisible and unimaginable. The people protest against the fact that they may neither see God nor try to imagine what he looks like. They need a figure to revere, a face to look upon, a being before whom they may kneel down in worship.

Moses is overwhelmed by the people's refusal to accept the new God: "All powerful One, I have reached the end of my strength. My thought is powerless in Aron's word!"[92] He stands in the background as Aron steps forward. In order to persuade the people to believe in the new God, Aron performs three miracles that the people can see with their own eyes. For the first miracle, he seizes Moses' staff, turns it into a snake from which the people recoil, then turns the snake back into the staff. He interprets this miracle as revealing the firmness of the Law when in his brother's hand, and the suppleness of persuasion when in his own. But in the end, it remains

119

the staff of Moses: "Behold the power that this staff bestows on our Leader!"[93]

The people respond favorably to the first miracle, so Aron performs a second. When the Priest observes that although the rod establishes the Law for the Jews, it does not free them from Pharaoh, Aron points to Moses' hand. The hand is healthy but the heart is sick, like the hearts of the people who fear the power of Pharaoh. As Moses places his hand over his heart, it becomes leprous, and the people express repugnance. But Moses' heart is suddenly filled with God's will, and his hand is healed. Aron observes, "Behold your own spirit: your courage will overcome Pharaoh!"[94]

The people rejoice in the significance of this second miracle, that reveals the power of God to put courage into the hearts of his people. But the Priest again protests: "Madmen! How will you find sustenance in the desert?"[95]

Moses replies that pureness of thought (*die Reinheit des Denkens*) will sustain the people in their journey across the desert. But Aron adds, characteristically, something more attuned to bodily needs. After performing a third miracle, in which he turns water from the Nile to blood, signifying that through the power of God, the Israelites' own blood will render the desert land fruitful, he promises "that God will lead them to that land where milk and honey flow."[96] The Israelites respond with the conviction that they are, indeed, the Chosen People, and Act I ends with a hymn of praise for their new God, their decision to plunge forward into the desert and to leave their Egyptian slavery behind forever.

Between Act I and Act II, the Israelites have escaped the Egyptian forces that were drowned in the Red Sea and have paused in their journey in the shadow of Mount Sinai. As Act II begins, the Elders express fear at the forty-day absence of Moses. Where is he? When will he return? Aron doesn't know what is keeping his brother.

In scene 2, the people enter, greatly agitated. They, too, demand to know where Moses is. Aron replies that Moses is near God on Mount Sinai. But perhaps he got too close. "He is a powerful God. Perhaps he killed my brother."[97] The people demand a resolution of their situation. Either show the power of the new God, or they will return to the older ones. Aron, sensing that he must act in the absence of any sign at all from the new God, decides to give the people what they want until Moses returns to enlighten him.

At the beginning of scene 3, Aron reveals an altar and a Golden Calf before which the people may worship and make sacrifice: "This image reveals that God lives in all things. A law, unchangeable. He lives in the gold you have given . . . worship yourselves in this image!"[98]

There follows one of the most gripping scenes in modern opera, a triumphant display of dramatic action expressed through music, words, dance, scenery, costumes, and lighting, a *Gesamtkunstwerk* in its purest form. Processions of laden camels, asses, horses and wagons enter the stage from many directions. They bring offerings of gold, grain, wine and animal skins. These are unloaded and piled up. Herds of animals are driven in to be slaughtered. They are decorated with flowers and the butchers, waving their knives in the air, dance wildly around them.

It grows dark. Torches are lighted as the animals are slaughtered. Male and female beggars offer the last of their clothing and food to the Golden Calf, after which old men and women offer the last moments of their lives by killing themselves. More tribal leaders come riding in on horseback and dismount. An emaciated youth protests against this idol worship and is quickly dispatched. Wine flows. Gifts are exchanged. Wild dancing, revelry, drunkenness and fighting take place in every corner of the stage. The Elders observe the scene with satisfaction: "The people are blessed. Great is the miracle of their joy and rapture."[99]

Four naked virgins are sacrificed to the Golden Calf, after which destruction and suicide become rampant. Objects are flung about and destroyed. People throw themselves on swords, leap into the fire and run flaming across the stage; a naked youth tears the clothing off a girl, lifts her high and conveys her to the altar. Others follow his example shouting "Holy is creative strength", "Holy is fertility" and "Holy is desire".[100]

The naked men and women disappear into the background, the stage grows dark and the remaining revellers sink down in exhaustion.

In scene 4, Moses comes down from Mount Sinai bearing the Tables of the Law. With a wave of his hand, he dismisses the Golden Calf: "Begone, figure of impotence, who would enclose the infinite in a finite image!"[101] The idol vanishes, the people withdraw, and scene 5 begins with a dialogue between Moses and his brother.

Moses berates Aron for providing the people with an image of God. The Idea of God is primary—any image of God must be false. Aron replies in his defense that the Tables of the Law that Moses has brought down from the Mountain of Revelation are also images, only a small part of the reality of God. Moses agrees with his brother and smashes the Tables of the Law.

In the distance, a new sign of the presence of God appears—a pillar of fire. The people come forward, convinced that they are indeed chosen and follow the pillar toward the Promised Land. Aron follows too, but Moses remains behind, lamenting his impotence: "So, everything that I thought was madness, and cannot and must not be spoken! Oh word, word that I lack!"[102]

Structurally, Schoenberg's dramatic poem terminates with the end of Act II, although a prose sketch for a third act exists. In this uncomposed scene, Moses has taken Aron prisoner. He accuses him once more of influencing the people by means of image rather than spirit. Aron defends himself again by arguing that common people must be given something to worship that they can see. Moses orders the soldiers to release Aron but, upon gaining his freedom, Aron falls down dead.

This scene, which embodies Schoenberg's final statement on the relationship between Moses and Aron, is curiously lacking in interest. Perhaps this is because the Jewish people are not present. They have already resumed their epic, forty-year migration from Egypt to Palestine, and it is this great chapter in the history of the Jewish race that is central to Schoenberg's opera.

Oscar Wilde once said that every work of art is the conversion of an idea into an image, and *Moses und Aron* is no exception. Schoenberg, perhaps unconsciously, created an unforgettable image of his people in the great choral scenes of his opera, and it is this image of a people at the climax of their worship of the gods of materialism and hedonism, coupled with the mysterious feeling that they are about to grasp the Idea of a single, transcendental God of spirit who will lead them out of bondage to freedom, that renders *Moses und Aron* a significant work of modern dramatic poetry.

Just how significant, of course, is hard to say at close range. Mozart's operas were not very popular in his own lifetime, nor were the plays of Heinrich von Kleist in his. Time alone will tell the truth about *Moses und Aron*, but a tentative judgment is possible even at this early stage in what many signs indicate will be a long and distinguished performance history.

In addition to *Boris Godunov,* the primacy of the chorus in Schoenberg's opera calls to mind the great prototype of the operatic genre— Greek tragedy. Especially, one is reminded of the third play in the *Oresteia* trilogy of Aeschylus, *The Eumenides,* in which the Attic poet dramatizes one of the great forward steps taken by the human race on its way from barbarism to civilization: Athena's transformation of the Furies into the Eumenides, of the powers of hate and revenge into those of law and order.

So moving is this great scene that at a production of the trilogy at London's National Theatre, directed by Peter Hall, the entire audience rose to its feet and applauded as the transformed chorus made its exit up the center aisle of the Olivier Theatre.

In a similar way, Schoenberg dramatizes another great turning point in human history, the rejection by the Jewish people of their multi-god religion in favor of the "one-and-only, eternal, ever-present, invisible and unimaginable" God of Moses. Seldom in dramatic poetry has idea been rendered into image with such power and conviction.

Notes

1. Willi Reich, *Schoenberg, A Critical Biography,* trans. Leo Black (London: Longman, 1971), 13.

2. Arnold Schoenberg, *Harmonielehre,* 3rd ed. (Vienna: Universal, 1922), V–VII (used by permission of Belmont Music Publishers, Pacific Palisades, CA 90272):

"Dieses Buch habe ich von meinen Schülern gelernt.

Wenn ich unterrichtete, suchte ich nie dem Schüler bloß, 'das zu sagen, was ich weiß.' Eher noch das, was er nicht wußte. Aber auch das war nicht die Hauptsache, obwohl ich dadurch schon genötigt war, für jeden Schüler etwas Neues zu erfinden. Sondern ich bemühte mich, ihm das Wesen der Sache von Grund auf zu zeigen. Darum gab es für mich niemals diese starren Regeln, die so sorgsam ihre Schlingen um ein Schülerhirn legen. Alles löste sich in Anweisungen auf, die für den Schüler so wenig bindend sind wie für den Lehrer. Kann es der Schüler ohne die Anweisungen besser, dann mache er es ohne sie. Aber der Lehrer muß den Mut haben, sich zu blamieren. Er muß sich nicht als der Unfehlbare zeigen, der alles weiß und nie irrt, sondern als der Unermüdliche, der immer sucht und vielleicht manchmal findet. Warum Halbgott sein wollen? Warum nicht lieber Vollmensch?

Ich habe meinen Schülern niemals eingeredet, ich sei unfehlbar—das hat nur ein 'Gesangsprofessor' nötig—sondern habe oft zu sagen riskiert, was ich später widerrufen, Anweisungen zu geben, die sich, angewendet, als falsch herausstellen, die ich später verbessern müßte: mein Irren hat dem Schüler vielleicht nicht genützt, aber kaum viel geschadet; doch daß ich es offen zugab, mag ihm zu denken gegeben haben. Mich aber, der ich Unerprobtes, Selbsterdachtes gab, zwang der bald sich zeigende Irrtum zu neuerlicher Prüfung und besserer Formulierung.

So ist dieses Buch entstanden. Aus den Fehlern, die meine Schüler infolge ungenügender oder falscher Anweisungen machten, habe ich gelernt die richtige Anweisung zu geben. Gelungene Lösungen bestätigten die Richtigkeit meines Versuchs, ohne mich zu dem Irrglauben zu verleiten, daß ich damit das Problem wirklich gelöst habe. Und ich denke, wir sind beide nicht schlecht dabei gefahren. Hätte ich ihnen auch bloß das gesagt, was ich weiß, dann wüßten sie nur das und nicht mehr. So wissen sie vielleicht sogar weniger. Aber sie wissen, worauf es ankommt: *aufs suchen*! . . .

Dann wäre es klar, daß es die erste Aufgabe des Lehrers ist, den Schüler recht durcheinanderzuschütteln. Wenn der Aufruhr, der dadurch entsteht, sich legt, dann hat sich wahrscheinlich alles an den richtigen Platz begeben.

Oder es kommt nie dahin!

Die Bewegung, die auf solche Art vom Lehrer ausgeht, kommt wieder zu ihm zurück. Auch in diesem Sinn habe ich diese Buch von meinen Schülern gelernt. Und ich muß die Gelegenheit benützen, ihnen zu danken."

3. Alma Mahler, *Gustav Mahler: Memories and Letters,* ed. Donald Mitchell, trans. Basil Creighton (London: John Murray, 1968), 340–1.

4. Quoted by Antony Beaumont, *Busoni the Composer* (Bloomington: Indiana University Press, 1985), 28.

5. Arnold Schoenberg, "Problems in Teaching Art" in *Style and Idea,* ed. Leonard Stein, trans. Leo Black (London: Faber & Faber, 1975), 365.

6. Arnold Schoenberg, *Pierrot Lunaire,* trans. Otto Erich Hartleben, piano reduction, Erwin Stein (Vienna: Universal, 1923), *Vorwort*. (Used by permission of Belmont Music Publishers, Pacific Palisades, CA 90272):

"Die in der Sprechstimme durch Noten angegebene Melodie ist (bis auf einzelne besonders bezeichnete Ausnahmen) nicht zum singen bestimmt. Der Ausführende hat die Aufgabe, sie unter guter Berücksichtigung der vorgezeichneten Tonhöhen in eine *Sprechmelodie* umzuwandelm. Das geschieht, in dem er.

I. den Rhythmus haarscharf so einhält, als ob er sänge, d. h. mit nicht mehr Freiheit, als er sich bei einer Gesangsmelodie gestatten dürfte;

II. sich des Unterschiedes zwischen *Gesangston* und *Sprechton* genau bewußt wird: der *Gesangston* hält die Tonhöhe unabänderlich fest, der *Sprechton* gibt sie zwar an, verläßt sie aber durch Fallen oder Steigen sofort wieder. Der Ausführende muß sich aber sehr davor hüten, in eine 'singende' Sprechweise zu verfallen. Das ist absolut nicht gemeint. Es wird zwar keineswegs ein realistisch-natürliches Sprechen angestrebt. Im Gegenteil, der Unterschied zwischen gewöhnlichem und einem Sprechen, das in einer musikalischen Form mitwirkt, soll deutlich werden. Aber es darf auch nie an Gesang erinnern."

7. Quoted by Willi Reich in his *Alban Berg* (Vienna: Reichner, 1937), 165: "Dabei hat sich herausgestellt, daß diese Art der Stimmbehandlung— wohlgemerkt: bei voller Wahrung aller absolut-musikalischen Gestaltungsmöglichkeiten, die ja beim Rezitativ z. B. wegfallen—, daß diese melodramatische Art der Stimmbehandlung nicht nur eines der besten Verständigunsmittel

darstellt—das muß die Sprache ja hin und wieder auch in der Oper sein—, sondern daß sie auch—vom tonlos geflüsterten Wort bis zum wahrhaftigen *bel parlare* ihrer weitgeschwungenen Sprechmelodien—die Opernmusik um ein vollwertiges und aus den reinsten Quellen der Musik geschöpftes Kunstmittel bereichert hat."

8. *Arnold Schoenberg, in höchster Verehrung von Schülern und Freunden,* (Munich: Piper, 1912), 85-6: "Man ist der Meinung, Schoenberg lehre seinen Stil und zwinge den Schüler, sich diesen anzueignen. Das ist ganz und gar falsch.

Schoenberg lehrt überhaupt keinen Stil; er predigt weder die Verwendung alter noch die neuer Kunstmittel . . . Was dann Schoenberg dem Schüler an der Hand von dessen Arbeit erklärt, ergibt sich alles organisch aus dieser; von außen trägt er keinen Lehrsatz dazu.

So erzieht Schoenberg tatsächlich im Schaffen.

Er folgt mit höchster Energie den Spuren der Persönlichkeit des Schülers, sucht sie zu vertiefen, ihr zum Durchbruch zu verhelfen, kurzum dem Schüler 'den Mut und die Kraft' zu geben, 'sich so zu den Dingen zu stellen, daß alles, was er ansieht, durch die Art, wie er es ansieht, zum außergewöhnlichen Fall wird.'

Das ist eine Erziehung zur äußersten Wahrhaftigkeit gegen sich selbst."

9. *Arnold Schoenberg,* 82: "Schoenberg lehrt Denken. Er hält den Schüler an, mit eigenen, offenen Augen zu sehen, als wäre er der Erste, der die Erscheinungen betrachtet. Was sonst gedacht wurde, soll nicht Norm sein. Ist auch unser Denken nicht besser als das anderer—nicht auf die absolute Wahrheit kommt es an, sondern auf das Suchen nach Wahrheit."

10. Arnold Schoenberg, "Composition with Twelve Tones" (see n. 5), 218–26.

11. Egon Wellesz, *Arnold Schoenberg,* trans. W. H. Kerridge (London: J. M. Dent, Ltd., 1925), 90.

12. Nicolas Slonimsky, *Music since 1900,* 4th ed. (New York: Scribner's, 1971), 1316.

13. Reich (see n. 1), 187.

14. *Arnold Schoenbergs Briefe,* sel. and ed. Erwin Stein (Mainz: Schotts, 1958), 297: "Ich war immer ein passionierter Lehrer. Es hat mich immer gedrängt, herauszufinden, was Anfängern am besten hilft, wie man sie mit den technischen, geistigen und ethischen Erfordernissen unserer Kunst vertraut machen könne; wie ihnen beizubringen, daß es eine Kunst-Moral gibt, und warum man nie aufhören darf, sie zu pflegen, jeden aber, der sie verletzt, aufs schärfste zu bekämpfen."

15. H. H. Stuckenschmidt, *Schoenberg, his Life and Work,* trans. Humphrey Searle (London: John Calder, 1977), 225.

16.–20. Stuckenschmidt, 226.

21. Stuckenschmidt, 44.

22. Schoenberg, "The Future of Opera" (see n. 5), 336-7.

23. Arnold Schoenberg, *Erwartung* (Monodram), text, Marie Pappenheim, piano reduction, Eduard Steuermann (Vienna: Universal, 1922). Used by permission of Belmont Music Publishers, Pacific Palisades, CA 90272. P. 16: ". . .

erschöpft. Gewand ist zerissen, die Haare verwirrt, blutige Risse an Gesicht und Händen."

24. Schoenberg, 9: "Keine Sensen mehr . . . kein Rufen und Gehn . . ."

25. Schoenberg, 11–12: "Oh, oh, was ist das? . . . Ein Körper . . . Nein, nur ein Stamm."

26. Schoenberg, 12–13: "Dort tanzt etwas Schwarzes . . . hundert Hände . . . Sei nicht dumm . . . es ist der Schatten . . ."

27. Schoenberg, 33: "Ah, jetzt erinnere ich mich . . . der Seufzer im Halbschlaf . . . wie ein Name . . . Du hast mir die Frage von den Lippen geküßt."

28. Schoenberg, 36: "Wo ist sie denn, die Hexe, die Dirne, die Frau mit den weißen Armen . . . ?"

29. Schoenberg, 47: "Oh, bist du da? Ich suchte . . ."

30. Schoenberg, "New Music: My Music" (see n. 5), 105.

31. Arnold Schoenberg, *Die glückliche Hand*, drama with music, text, Arnold Schoenberg, piano reduction (four hands), Eduard Steurermann (Vienna: Universal, 1923). Used by permission of Belmont Music Publishers, Pacific Palisades, CA 90272. P. 8: "Du Armer!"

32. Quoted by John C. Crawford, "*Die glückliche Hand*: Schoenberg's *Gesamtkunstwerk*," *The Musical Quarterly* 60 (1974), 593. Copyright 1974, The Musical Quarterly. Oxford University Press. Used with permission.

33. Schoenberg (see n. 31), 8–9: "Ja, o ja! Das Blühen; o Sehnsucht!"

34. Schoenberg, 15: "Nun besitze ich dich für immer!"

35. Schoenberg, 16: ". . . soll nicht die Nachahmung eines Naturbildes, sondern eine freie Kombination von Farben und Formen sein."

36. Quoted by Crawford (see n. 32), 588.

37. Crawford, 595.

38. Schoenberg (see n. 31), 27: "Du, du, du bist mein . . . du warst mein . . . sie war mein . . ."

39. Schoenberg, 29: "Du Schöne, bleib bei mir!"

40. Schoenberg, 31–9: "Mußtest du's wieder erleben, was du so oft erlebt? . . . Fühlst du nur, was du berührst, deine Wunden erst an deinem Fleisch, deine Schmerzen erst an deinem Körper? Und suchst dennoch! Und quälst dich, und bist ruhelos . . . ?"

41. Schoenberg, 40: "Du Armer!"

42. Crawford (see n. 32), 585.

43. Karl H. Wörner, "Arnold Schoenberg and the Theater," *The Musical Quarterly* 48 (1962), 444. Copyright 1962, The Musical Quarterly. Oxford University Press. Used with permission.

44. Arnold Schoenberg, *Von Heute auf Morgen*, opera in one act, text, Max Blonda (Mainz: Schotts, 1961). Used by permission of Belmont Music Publishers, Pacific Palisades, CA 90272. P. 7: "Immer nach einem vergnügten Abend bist du schlecht gelaunt."

45. Schoenberg, 24: "So ein verrückter Kerl!"

46. Schoenberg, 45–6: "Was ist das? Wie siehst du aus? Wie kann man sich so verändern? Ist dieses elegante Wesen meine Frau? Soll ich meinen Augen trauen?"

47. Schoenberg, 54: "... daß keiner sonst dich so heiß liebt, dich so bewundert, dich so anbetet, dich so vergöttert: mein liebes Weib!"

48. Schoenberg, 57–8: "Was? Dieser hirnlose Komödiant, der nur in Opernzitaten denkt, und immer irgendwie vom Singen redet?"

49. Schoenberg, 118: "Ich hielt dich für die Frau von gestern; da gabst du die Frau von heute: die stellt' ich höher als dich. Nun weiß ich: du bist die Frau fürs Leben."

50. Schoenberg, 160–1:

Frau.
Wir vielleicht schon verblaßte, sie heute noch in beliebten Farben strahlende Theaterfiguren. Aber noch ein Unterschied: Regie führt bei ihnen die Mode, bei uns jedoch . . . sind sie schon weg? Dann wag ich's zu sagen: Die Liebe . . .
Mann.
Und dabei finde ich sie heute schon nicht einmal mehr ganz modern.
Frau.
Das ändert sich eben von heute auf morgen.
Kind (spricht).
Mama, was sind das, moderne Menschen?

51. Quoted by Alexander L. Ringer, *Arnold Schoenberg: The Composer as Jew* (Oxford: Clarendon Press, 1990), 85. Reprinted by permission of Oxford University Press.

52. Quoted by Wörner (see n. 43), 452.

53. Stuckenschmidt (see n. 15), 34.

54. Stuckenschmidt, 74.

55. Pamela C. White, *Schoenberg and the God-Idea: The Opera, "Moses und Aron"* (Ann Arbor, MI: UMI Research Press, 1985), 54.

56. Ringer (see n. 51), 120.

57. Schoenberg (see n. 14), 90: "Wenn ich Ihren Brief vor einem Jahr bekommen hätte, würde ich alle meine Grundsätze fallen haben lassen, hätte auf die Aussicht, endlich komponieren zu dürfen, verzichtet, und hätte mich, den Kopf voran, in das Abenteuer gestürzt. Ja ich gestehe: noch heute habe ich einen Augenblick geschwankt: so groß ist meine Lust zu unterrichten, so leicht entzündlich bin ich noch heute. Aber es kann nicht sein.

Denn was ich im letzten Jahre zu lernen gezwungen wurde, habe ich nun endlich kapiert und werde es nicht wieder vergessen. Daß ich nämlich kein Deutscher, kein Europäer, ja vielleicht kaum ein Mensch bin (wenigstens ziehen die Europäer die schlechtesten ihrer Rasse mir vor), sondern, daß ich Jude bin."

58. Schoenberg, 91: "Ich meinen ersten Arbeitssommer nach 5 Jahren unterbrechen mußte, den Ort verlassen, an dem ich Ruhe zur Arbeit gesucht hatte, und die Ruhe dazu nicht mehr zu finden imstande sein konnte? Weil die Deutschen keinen Juden dulden!"

59. Schoenberg, 93: "Ich bin keiner und war keiner!"

60. Schoenberg, 95: "Wozu aber soll der Antisemitismus führen, wenn nicht zu Gewalttaten? Ist das so schwer, sich das vorzustellen? Ihnen genügt es vielleicht, die Juden zu entrechten. Dann werden Einstein, Mahler, ich und viele andere allerdings abgeschafft sein. Aber eines ist sicher: Jene viel zäheren Elemente, dank deren Widerstandsfähigkeit sich das Judentum 20 Jahrhunderte lang ohne Schutz gegen die ganze Menschheit erhalten hat, diese werden sie doch nicht ausrotten können . . . die ihnen ihr Gott angewiesen hat: Im Exil sich zu erhalten, unvermischt und ungebrochen, bis die Stunde der Erlösung kommt!"

61. *The Berg-Schoenberg Correspondence,* eds. Juliane Brand, Christopher Haily, Donald Harris (New York: W. W. Norton, 1987), 446.

62. Ringer (see n. 51), 56.

63. Schoenberg (see n. 14), 197: ". . . behandelt in aktuelle Weise (geschrieben 1926–27) die Volkwerdung der Juden."

64. Quoted by Alexander Ringer, "Arnold Schoenberg and the Politics of Jewish Survival," *Journal of the Arnold Schoenberg Institute,* 3 (1979), 21.

65. Arnold Schoenberg, *Der biblische Weg*, a play in three acts (Los Angeles: The Arnold Schoenberg Institute, unpubl. MS.), 10a:

Linda.

Er hat in diesen zwei Jahren die Erde bereist, hat überall Bünde organisiert, mit Regierungen verhandelt, Verträge geschlossen, Zusagen erhalten, Gewißheiten geschaffen. Er hat Neupalästina in verschiedenen Richtungen durchquert und die wichtigsten Punkte selbst besichtigt, hat die Berichte der Sachverständigen geprüft, mit Technikern, Geographen, Industriellen und Finanzleuten verhandelt, den Plan der Besiedlung und Einwanderung selbst entworfen, die Ausführung in allen Details erwogen, Verbesserungen vorgeschlagen—er hat alles bis ins Kleinste ausgedacht und nun sind wir vorbereitet: Nur Monate, Wochen vielleicht, trennen uns noch von dem Augenblick, wo das erste Auswandererschiff abgeht.

Wer da nicht widerspruchlos bewundert und an den Erfolg glaubt, ist unfähig dazu!

66. Schoenberg, 21:

Jonston.

Sie wissen, wir haben einen Vertrag mit dem Kaiser von Ammongäa geschlossen, dem zufolge dieser uns einen bisher wenig kultivierten Teil seines Reiches, groß genug um dreissig Millionen Menschen dort anzusiedeln, zur Gründung Neupalästinas uberläßt. Wir haben dagegen die Verpflichtung übernommen, Ammongäa, welches reich an natürlichen Schätzen aller Art ist, die Mittel zur Verfügung zu stellen, welche es ihm ermöglichen ein moderner Staat zu werden.

67. Schoenberg, 21:

Jonston.

Sie haben gewiß von einem Skandal gehört in den Kaphira, der bevollmächtigte Vertreter des Kaisers von Ammongäa, verwickelt war. Davon will ich Ihnen eine Geschichte erzählen.

Wir waren mit Aruns in Ammongäa: Pinxar, Kolbief, Eldad, einige Sachberater und ich.

Man verhandelte mit Kaphira, der sich von allem Anfang an für unsere Bestrebungen eingesetzt hatte, über den Verlauf der Grenze Neupalästinas. Kaphira bezeugte Aruns große Freundschaft und jeder glaubte Kaphira liebe Aruns, wie jeder ihn liebt, der ihn kennt.

Aruns dachte scheinbar anders darüber.

Die Grenze sollte an einer Stelle einen großen Fluß entlang gehn. An einem bestimmten Punkte jedoch, sollte sie, nach einem Vorschlag Kaphiras in einem großen Bogen vom Fluß abweichen, wodurch unser Gebiet um ein beträchtliches Stück vergrößert wurde. In diesem Landstrich befinden sich große Erzlager und wie man vermutet, auch Radium.

68. Schoenberg, 22–3:

Jonston.

Aruns sagte . . . "Ich habe eben einen Brief von Kaphira bekommen." Er las ihn vor: Kaphira hätte dieses Landstück schon lange gerne selbst erworbern, besitze aber nicht genug Geld. Da nun Aruns keinen Wert darauf lege, es zu besitzen, so hoffe Kaphira, es von ihm zu einem billigen Preis zu erhalten und bitte deshalb Aruns, es für Neupalästina zu übernehmen.

69. Schoenberg, 24:

Pinxar.
Daß Sie recht hatten, als Sie sagten: "Wir werden vielleicht wieder Posaunen vor Jericho brauchen und darum werden sie da sein." Und daß sich somit auch die Wahrheit Ihres Wortes bewiesen hat: "Aus einem guten Gedanken fließt alles von selbst."
Aruns.
Leider können wir ihnen dieses Wunder noch nicht zeigen. Eine Volksmasse aber begeht *sichtbare* Erfüllungen.
Pinxar.
Unsere Propaganda bedient sich derselben Mittel, wie alle ähnlichen Bestrebungen. Wir haben unsere Leiden, unsere Hoffnungen und eins mehr: unseren Glauben.
Aruns.
Dieser Glaube aber: an einen unsichtbaren und unvorstellbaren Gott, bietet keine sichtbaren Erfüllungen.

70. Schoenberg, 43–6:

Aruns.
Volk Israels!

Was ist dieses Fest?

Ist es ein Sportfest? Eine Parade? Eine Parteiversammlung? Eine Volksversammlung?

Ist dieser Tag denn nicht ein Tag, wie alle andern?

Nein das ist er nicht, sondern er ist einer, der sicherlich ein Gedenktag bleiben wird für alle Zeiten des Judentums.

So wie es jener Tag ist, an welchem der jüngste Mann fragt:

"Warum sitzen wir heute angelehnt?"

Aber hier wird er anders fragen müssen:

"Warum stehn wir heute alle? Warum haben wir uns erhoben? Warum
bleiben wir nicht sitzen, am Boden, niedrig, wie alle andern Tage vorher?"

Wir sind aufgestanden, wir haben uns erhoben und aufgerichtet zu einer
Größe, die niemand geahnt hätte.

Wir haben wieder aufgerichtet die runden Rücken, die gekrümmt waren,
weil sie gewärtig sein mußten, jeden Streich zu empfangen, der andern
gebührte. Wir stehen wieder da, wie das alte, zähe, trotzige, halsstarrige
Volk der Bibel: aber nicht mehr, wie dort, sind wir heute halsstarrig gegen
unsern Gott, sondern *für* ihn, der uns zu seinem Volk bestimmt hat . . .

Wir sind ein altes Volk:

Was könnte uns ein Gott sein, den wir verstehn, von dem wir uns ein Bild
machen, den wir beeinflussen können?

Wir brauchen kein Wunder: Verfolgung und Verachtung haben uns
gestärkt, haben unsere Zähigkeit und Ausdauer vervielfältigt, Organe
erzeugt und gekräftigt, die unsere Widerstandsfähigkeit erhöhten.

Wir sind ein altes Volk.

Noch kann zwar nicht jeder Einzelne unsern Gottesgedanken ganz erfas-
sen: sich damit abfinden, daß alles Geschehn von einem höchsten Wesen
abhängt, dessen Gesetze wir fühlen und erkennen, aber nach ihrem Sinn
nicht fragen dürfen.

Sobald aber jeder bis zum Letzten das kann:

Dann ist der Messias gekommen.

Der Messias des inneren Gleichgewichts!

Liebe junge Freunde! Eure Lehrer und Führer haben diesen Glauben in euch verpflanzt, haben euren Geist entwickelt und euren Körper geschult . . .

Nun also seid ihr fähig, die große Aufgabe zu lösen!

Ihr besitzt Elastizität, Schwung, Begeisterung, Anpassung und Opferfähigkeit.

Euch ist die schwerste Aufgabe zugefallen.

Denn für die Jugend geschieht alles, was wir erstreben.

Ihr gehört die Zukunft; sie wird es genießen, wenn kein Jude mehr nach Achtung oder Nichtachtung Andersrassiger wird fragen müssen.

Darum soll sie den entscheidenden Anteil an der Arbeit haben:

Ihr jungen Menschen, ihr sollt Pioniere sein im neuen Land; ihr sollt den Boden bereiten, das Fundament legen, auf dem sich der stolze Bau dieses Staates erheben wird.

Und das ist der tiefere Sinn diese Feste und darum wird es ein Gedenktag für alle Zeiten werden . . .

Und heute, hier, bekundet ihr mit eurer Kraft, daß ihr einen höhern Wissen dienen wollt, als es Menschenweisheit ist:
Daß ihr eurem Volk es ermöglichen wollt, seinen Gottesgedanken zuende zu leben, zuende zu träumen!

71. Schoenberg, 52–3:

Golban, Jr.
Bei der Aufstellung eines provisorischen Gotteshauses an der gemeinsamen Grenze des russischen und deutschen Lagers arbeiteten Angehörige beider Sprachen unter Leitung eines deutschsprechenden Vorarbeiters.

Gestern war nun ein Zwist entstanden, weil der Vorarbeiter einige technische Kommandos weder auf hebräisch, noch auf russisch sagen konnte.

132

Eine kleine Prügelei war bald beigelegt und man einigte sich, an die Sprachenkommission heranzutreten.

Dort wurde nun konstatiert, daß für die betreffenden Begriffe bereits lehnwortartige Bildungen aus Arabischen, respektive Türkischen vorgesehen, aber zwiefelos noch nicht in allgemeinem Gebrauch sind. Ich soll Befehle für künftiges Verhalten erbitten.

Aruns.

Waren Sie dabei?

Golban, Jr.

Jawohl!

Aruns.

Das ist doch Ihr Fach. Haben Sie da nicht helfen können?

Golban, Jr.

Ich kam gerade noch zur Prügelei zurecht.

Aruns.

Die Sprachwissenschaft ist also zu spät gekommen!

Wie haben Sie sich verändert! Früher wären Sie zur Prügelei zu spät gekommen!

Man kann natürlich nicht zu jedem kleinen Bau einen Sprachgelehrten delegieren. Auch ist es unmöglich, daß der Vorarbeiter, wenn es brennt, erst telephonisch anfrägt, wie löschen auf Hebraisch heiße und wie der Imperativ gebildet werde.

72. Schoenberg, 69: "Die Stellung des Kapitals wird in diesem Staate keine andere sein, als in jedem, demokratisch regierten, anderen."

73. Schoenberg, 73:

Aruns.

Es ist mir eine hohe Ehre und große Freude, Eure Excellenz in unserem Lande zu begrüßen; Sie den wohlwollenden Stellvertreter unseres väterlichen Freundes, ohne dessen hohe Gesinnung unser Volk nicht von seinen Leiden hätte erlöst werden können, ohne den wir dieses nicht *unser* Land nennen dürften.

74. Schoenberg, 73: ". . . den Mann, der die Kraft und den Muth besitzt, seine Idee gegen den Widerstand der ganzen Welt durchzusetzen; und den Mann schließlich, dem sein Werk geglückt ist, den Mann des Erfolges, der einen

Gedanken nicht nur fassen kann, sondern auch die Ausdauer und das Glück hat, ihn zu verwirklichen."

75. Ringer (see n. 51), 63.

76. Schoenberg (see n. 65), 77–9:

Aruns.

Sie ist weg mit Sanda, dem Verräter!

Nach so vielen Jahren der Treue und des Vertrauens!

Wendet sich mein Geschick?

Jetzt, wo ich dem Ziele so nahe bin? . . .

Hänge ich noch zu sehr an Menschen?

Und doch habe ich sie vielleicht nur verloren, weil ich zu sehr an meiner Sache hing? . . .

Nur jetzt keine Eitelkeit! Es ist nur der Mann in mir verletzt . . .

Aber vielleicht war dieses Opfer nötig . . . Vielleicht muß ich ganz allein stehn . . .

Vielleicht bin ich jetzt erst fähig, mein Werk zu vollenden? . . .

Ich muß diesen Schlag verwinden!

Oder: Wendet sich mein Geschick?

77. Schoenberg, 86–7:

Asseino.

Seien Sie gesegnet, denn Sie haben unser Volk wieder aufgerichtet und zum Glauben an die Erhabenheit unserer Religion zurückgeführt.

Sie waren auf dem richtigen Weg, als Sie Ihr Werk auf Gottes Wort stützen, als Sie sagten, Gott habe dies Volk auserwählt, vor allen anderen, an den einzigen und unvorstellbaren Gott zu glauben . . .

Gott that Ihr Werk bisher gesegnet und wird es weiter segnen, wenn Sie seinem Wort treu bleiben und der geistigen Macht allein vertrauen.

78. White (see n. 55), 30.

79. Schoenberg (see n. 65), 87: "Max Aruns, Moses und Aron wollen Sie in einer Person sein! Moses, dem Gott den Gedanken gegeben, aber die Macht der Rede versagt hat; und Aron der den Gedanken nicht fassen, aber wiedergeben und die Massen bewegen könnte."

80. Michael Cherlin, "The Formal and Dramatic Organization of Schoenberg's *Moses und Aron*" (Ph.D. dissertation, Yale University), 296–7.

81. Schoenberg (see n. 65), 88: "Aber ein Volk von heute kann nicht jeden Freitag die Hochöfen ausblasen und die Elektrizitätswerke sperren."

82. Schoenberg, 91:

Aruns.

War das nur ein Gelehrtenstreit?

Ist es möglich, daß er recht hat? War ich anmaßend, habe ich mir zuviel zugemutet? Bin ich von meinem Gedanken abgewichen?

Wendet sich mein Geschick?

83. Schoenberg, 93: "Wenn ich jetzt geschlagen werde, bin ich für immer geschlagen. Dann war der Gedanke falsch, war alles Irrtum und dafür muß ich büßen."

84. Schoenberg, 96:

Aruns.

Herr, du hast mich geschlagen; so habe ich es also verdient. So hat also Asseino Recht, daß ich mich überhoben habe, also ich Moses und Aron in einer Person sein wollte. So habe ich also den Gedanken verraten, da ich mich auf eine Maschine, statt auf dem Geist stützte.

Herr, jetzt erst weiß ich es und bitte dich: nimm mein Blut als Sühne.

Aber lasse nicht dies arme, unschuldige Volk für meine Sünde büßen.

Herrgott rette sie! Gib ihnen ein Zeichen, daß du nur mich für meine Sünde

135

gegen den Geist gestraft hast, aber den Gedanken nicht wirst unterliegen lassen.

Herrgott, ich bin besiegt, geschlagen, gezüchtigt.

Ich sterbe, aber ich fühle: du wirst den Gedanken leben lassen. Und ich sterbe gerne, denn ich weiß, du wirst unserm Volk immer Männer schenken, die gerne für den Gedanken des einzigen, ewigen, unsichtbaren und unvorstellbaren Gottes sterben.

85. Schoenberg, 101–2:

Guido.

Nun, wo wir die Macht hätten, uns zu Herren dieser Erde zu machen, wollen wir im Namen dieses Toten und in seinem Geist verkünden, daß uns derlei fernliegt.

Das jüdische Volk lebt einem Gedanken: Dem Glauben an einen einzigen, unsterblichen, ewigen, unvorstellbaren Gott. Diesem Gedanken allein will es zur Herrschaft verhelfen; er wird vielleicht einst in seiner reinsten Form die Welt beherrschen.

Uns so wenig wir daran denken, die neuentdeckten, todbringend Strahlen einer materiellen Macht an irgend einen Punkt dieser Welt zu lenken, so wenig wir daran denken, an irgendeinem Volk Rache oder Gewalt zu verüben; so sehr denken wir dagegen daran, die lauchtenden Strahlen unseres Glaubensgedankens überall hin zu verbreiten, damit sie neues, geistiges Leben hervorrufen.

Und so mögen diese materiellen Strahlen in einiger Zeit nur ein Symbol dessen darstellen, was auch aus dem Gedanken von selbst fließt. Sie sind auch nicht anderes, als eine Ausstrahlung des Gedankens, eine aber, die den Strahlen des Geistes entgegengesetzt, durch diese aus der höheren Wirklichkeit ausgeschlossen wird.

Aber solche Expansionsbestrebungen sind uns höchstens ein Zweck fernster Zukunft, beschäftigen uns derzeit nicht mehr, als Werbung in unserem Interesse liegt.

Wir haben ein nächtes Ziel: wir wollen uns als Volk *sicher* fühlen. Wir wollen sicher wissen, daß uns niemand zu etwas zwingen, daß uns niemand an etwas hindern kann.

Aber wir wünschen keinen wie immer gearteten Einfluß auf andere Völker.

Wir haben mit uns genug zu tun:

Wie jeden alten Volkes, so ist es auch unsere Bestimmung: uns zu *vergeistigen*. Uns von allem Materiellen loszulösen.

Wir haben ein Ziel mehr: Wir müssen alle den Gedanken vom einzigen, ewigen, unvorstellbaren Gott denken lernen.

Wir wollen unser geistiges Leben führen und niemand soll uns dabei stören können.

Wir wollen uns geistig vervollkommen, wollen unsern Gottestraum träumen dürfen—wie alle Völker, die die Materie hinter sich haben.

86. Alma Mahler Werfel, *And the Bridge is Love* (New York: Harcourt Brace, 1958), 228.

87. Arnold Schoenberg, *Moses und Aron*, opera in three acts, text, Arnold Schoenberg, trans. Allen Forte, piano reduction, Winfried Zillig (Mainz: Schotts, 1957). Used by permission of Belmont Music Publishers, Pacific Palisades, CA 90272. P. 2: "Einziger, ewiger, allgegenwärtiger, unsichtbarer und unvorstellbarer Gott!"

88. Schoenberg, 32–4:

Moses.
Volk, auserwählt, den unsichtbaren zu wissen, den Unvorstellbaren zu denken.
Aron.
Auserwähltes Volk, einen einzigen Gott ewig zu lieben mit tausendmal mehr der Liebe, mit der alle andern Völker ihre vielen Götter lieben. Unsichtbar! Unvorstellbar!

89. Schoenberg, 34–5: "Volk, auserwählt dem Einzigen, kannst du lieben, was du dir nicht vorstellen darfst?"

90. Schoenberg, 59–60:

Chorus (1. Hälfte).
  Glaubt nicht den Betrügern!
  Die Götter lieben uns nicht!
  Wer ist es, der stärker sein will,
  als Pharaos Götter?

91. Schoenberg, 59–60:

Chorus (2. Hälfte).
  Er wird uns befrein!
  Wir wollen ihn lieben!
  Wir wollen ihm opfern!

92. Schoenberg, 96: "Allmächtiger, meine Kraft ist zu Ende: Mein Gedanke ist machtlos in Arons Wort!"

93. Schoenberg, 103: "Erkennet die Macht, die dieser Stab dem Führer verleiht!"

94. Schoenberg, 126–9: "Erkennet euch auch darin: Euer Mut wird Pharao besiegen!"

95. Schoenberg, 140: "Wahnsinnige! Wovon soll euch die Wüste nähern?"

96. Schoenberg, 147–8: "Er wird euch führen in das Land wo Milch und Honig fließt . . ."

97. Schoenberg, 182: "Er ist ein strenger Gott: Vielleicht hat er ihn getötet."

98. Schoenberg, 206: "Dieses Bild bezeugt, daß in allem, was ist, ein Gott lebt. Unwandelbar, wie ein Prinzip, ist der Stoff, das Gold, das ihr geschenkt habt . . . Verehrt euch selbst in diesem Sinnbild!"

99. Schoenberg, 236–42: "Selig ist das Volk, und groß zeigt ein Wunder, was Begeisterung, was Entzückung imstande."

100. Schoenberg, 263: "Heilig ist die Zeugenskraft! Heilig ist die Fruchtbarkeit! Heilig ist die Lust!"

101. Schoenberg, 270: "Vergeh, du Abbild des Unvermögens, das Grenzenlose in ein Bild zu fassen!"

102. Schoenberg, 299–300: "So war alles Wahnsinn, was ich gedacht habe, und kann und darf nicht gesagt werden! O Wort, du Wort, das mir fehlt!"

CHAPTER FOUR

Spoken Drama into Music Drama: Alban Berg

Arnold Schoenberg's distinguished pupil, one of the masters of the art of the opera, came from a middle-class Viennese family, the members of which were interested in both commerce and art. Berg's father, Conrad Berg, was the successful proprietor of an export-import business and his mother, Johanna, brought to the family a lively enthusiasm for art and music. The third of their four children, Albano Maria Johannes Berg, was born February 9, 1885, and grew up in the family's spacious apartment in Vienna's First District on Tuchlaubengasse, a short street that runs into the Graben, not far from St. Stephen's Cathedral.

Alban Berg and his brothers and sister received scant artistic education in the Viennese public schools of the time, but their parents tried to compensate for this in various ways. One example of Conrad Berg's concern for the artistic development of his family was his purchase, at auction, of the organ from the old Burgtheater that he had installed in his apartment. Among those who played the instrument for the delight and edification of the Berg family was Anton Bruckner, one of the first notable musicians with whom Berg became acquainted.[1]

As a child, Berg displayed as much interest in literature, plays and drawings as he did in music. Theodor Adorno has observed that Berg "measured and multiplied his strengths against the problem of binding himself to a particular medium. At first, he seems to have thought of himself as a poet and only secondarily as a composer, like many highly gifted adolescents, including Wagner."[2] This inclination explains, perhaps, why he never did approach the study of music through the formal, conservatory route. He obtained his entire musical education from tutors, a process that reached a fruitful climax in 1904 when he was accepted for private study by a tutor of genius, Arnold Schoenberg.

Schoenberg began by providing his talented student with a solid foundation in harmony, counterpoint and orchestration from the classical

139

and Romantic periods of music. The last thing he imparted to Berg was his new method of composing with twelve tones, a system that Berg employed only in his second opera, *Lulu*.

The young musician married Helene Nahowski in 1911 and settled down to a quiet life of composing, both in Vienna and at his family's country home in Carinthia. At first, his compositions did not provide sufficient financial sustenance for a young married couple, so he made ends meet by collecting the rent every month from tenants living in his mother's apartment buildings in Vienna and by making piano reductions of various orchestral scores[*] for Universal Edition, Vienna's leading music publisher. After the substantial success of *Wozzeck* in Berlin in 1925, however, his fortunes changed for the better, and he lived on the income from his musical compositions from then until his death in 1935.

On July 28, 1914, the Austro-Hungarian Empire declared war on Serbia, and Europe was thrown into the holocaust of the First World War. Millions died in the trenches and both Berg and Schoenberg were lucky to survive. Berg failed his army physical in 1914 and was able to continue composing for a time. The war was constantly on his mind, however, and on December 15, 1914, he wrote Schoenberg about a new weapon he had invented,[**] "a new ballistics invention that would give us—should guns and cannon of this kind be manufactured soon (which would, however, require extensive technical and mathematical experiments) that would, as I say, give us such an enormous advantage over our enemies that we could defeat any superior power."[3]

Berg was inducted into the Austrian army in 1915 but, due to his asthma, was assigned to a desk job in Vienna. Here, he found time to adapt Georg Büchner's 1837 play *Woyzeck*[†] into a prose libretto of three acts of five scenes each for his first opera. The end of the war, in 1918, enabled him to devote all his energies to composing and orchestrating *Wozzeck* and, in 1922, he completed the opera that has come to be recognized as one of the singular achievements of twentieth-century dramatic poetry. That *Wozzeck* was Berg's very first effort to express himself through the art of the

---

[*] Among the works for which Berg prepared piano reductions was Franz Schreker's opera *Der ferne Klang*, a piece that made a strong impression on him.

[**] Did Schoenberg recall this letter when he planned the secret weapon that would defend the people of New Palestine from their enemies in his play, *Der biblische Weg*?

[†] Büchner's spelling is "Woyzeck"; Berg spells it "Wozzeck".

opera discloses the range of his histrionic, as well as his musical imagination.

Even his teacher, Arnold Schoenberg, seems to have been surprised by this unexpected eruption into a new and complex world but, after seeing the score prior to orchestration, he wrote a letter to Emil Hertzka, head of Universal Edition, on October 24, 1921 urging him to put *Wozzeck* under contract: "It left me with a very strong impression. It works so well that one would think Berg had never done anything but write for the theater."[4]

Hertzka declined Schoenberg's advice, however, and Berg resolved to pay out of his own pocket for the printing and binding of a limited edition of the piano score, which had been prepared by his student Fritz Heinrich Klein. He sold some family heirlooms and borrowed some money from Alma Maria Mahler (to whom he dedicated *Wozzeck*) and sent copies to opera house directors, conductors and important critics in Germany and Austria.

And his gamble paid off. One of the recipients of his piano score was Erich Kleiber, *Generalmusikdirektor* of the Berlin Staatsoper Unter den Linden who, after some soul-searching, scheduled the world premiere of the opera for the 1925–26 season. *Wozzeck* achieved a substantial success in Berlin and Berg soon began to enjoy an international reputation as the successful composer of a great modern opera.

In looking about for a congenial play to adapt as his next opera libretto, Berg first settled on Gerhart Hauptmann's *Und Pippa tanzt!* [*And Pippa Dances!*], a piece that would provide some opportunities for dance music in the mood of *Salome*, but Hauptmann and his publisher demanded so much in royalties that Berg and Universal Edition (who, by now, had taken on *Wozzeck*) decided they couldn't afford it. Berg's negotiations with Tilly Newes Wedekind over the opera rights to Wedekind's plays *Erdgeist* and *Die Büchse der Pandora* were more fruitful. The widow asked only a reasonable royalty on her late husband's most famous works for the theater, and Berg soon set about adapting the two plays into an opera libretto in a prologue and three acts to be entitled, *Lulu*.

With his libretto completed, Berg composed the entire opera in short score and had orchestrated the prologue and the first two acts before he was stung by a wasp during the summer of 1935, while working on *Lulu* at the Waldhaus, his summer residence on the Wörthersee. He had been laid up before, in 1932, by an attack of wasps, to whose venom he was severely allergic and, although he recovered from the earlier attack, the later one proved fatal and, on December 23, 1935, in the Rudolfspital in Vienna, he died of blood poisoning. His death mask was taken by Anna Mahler, the daughter of Alma and Gustav Mahler.

After her husband's death, Helene Berg asked Arnold Schoenberg to orchestrate the third act of *Lulu,* but he sent the materials back to her with a negative response, possibly because of the unpleasant character of the Jewish banker, Puntschu, who sells worthless stock in Act III, scene 1. Anton von Webern and others also turned down this project and the opera had to be performed in a prologue and two acts until Friedrich Cerha's orchestration of the third act made possible the first performance of the work in its entirety at the Paris Opéra, conducted by Pierre Boulez with stage direction by Patrice Chereau, on February 24, 1979.

As Douglas Jarman has observed, Alban Berg greatly expanded the range of traditional operatic subject matter by setting Büchner's *Wozzeck* to music.[5] His choice of this brooding play from the early nineteenth century as a viable text for a twentieth-century opera discloses a histrionic sensibility strongly susceptible to the outer limits of the dramatic poetry of his day. Instead of choosing to set still another play by Goethe, Schiller, Kleist, Hebbel or Grillparzer, he found, in Büchner's tale of a desperate soldier in the peacetime Prussian army of the post-Napoleonic era, a subject with whom his fellow Europeans of the 1920s, after their experiences of the unprecedented horrors of World War I, could readily empathize. Not only did Büchner's play depict the lives of the common people in and around a nineteenth-century Prussian army post, it explored in detail the signals of approaching schizophrenia in the hero, a subject that is rare in the spoken and lyric drama. The worldwide success of *Wozzeck* made it clear that many another story about the lives of poor people, repressed, exploited, even driven to madness by those who are better off than they could be formed into librettos, set to music and performed in modern opera houses. It is hard to imagine the creation of, for instance, Britten's *Peter Grimes,* Menotti's *Saint of Bleecker Street* or Weill's *Street Scene* prior to the appearance of *Wozzeck* in the lyric theater.

Alban Berg first saw Georg Büchner's play, *Woyzeck,* at the Residenzbühne on Rotenturmstraße in Vienna on May 5, 1914, as attested to by a friend who saw him there. Berg was strongly moved by the play, which had been performed in total darkness, without intermission, for three hours* and said to his friend that someone ought to set this play to music.[6]

---

* Some recent productions of Berg's opera also have been performed without intermissions.

His later experiences in the Austro-Hungarian army contributed to his sympathy for his hero, who hears voices, behaves strangely and murders his common-law wife out of jealousy and despair, and he worked on his libretto throughout the years of the First World War.

Berg's choice of Büchner's play as the text for his opera is, in itself, a manifestation of his histrionic imagination. The catholicity of his taste for the theater is clear from his regular attendance at performances not only of the classics of world drama at the Burgtheater and the Theater in der Josefstadt but, also, at those small, often private avant-garde houses that dotted the Viennese theatrical landscape of the time. His approach to rendering Büchner's play into music was both conservative and avant-garde:

> Aside from my wish to compose good music, to fulfill the spiritual content of Büchner's immortal drama by means of music, and to render his poetic speech into musical speech, I desired—in the moment when I decided to write an opera—nothing more, even in regard to the techniques of musical composition, than to render to the theater what belongs to the theater, to shape the music so that it *constantly* fulfills its duty to serve the needs of the drama. And further, the music must do everything necessary to achieve the transposition of the written play to the reality of the boards; hence the *composer*, through his music, must fulfill the function of an ideal stage director.[7]

Berg's reference to an "ideal stage director" discloses his particular concern that his opera be put on the stage as he saw it in his imagination. All modern dramatic poets, influenced as they are by Ibsen and Wagner, try to assure reasonably authentic stage productions by including in their texts specific instructions to the stage director and to the scene, costume and lighting designers. In fact, the more gifted the poet is in visualizing his work on the stage—in front of a certain setting, the performers wearing costumes representative of the period of the action, the whole lighted by a particular group of color tonalities and intensities—the more likely he is to fill his text with production notes and directions. And, in view of the trouble Berg took to relate these stage directions to the music of *Wozzeck*, it is painful to sit through productions of his opera in which the stage director and the designers shamefully ignore his wishes.

Several aspects of Büchner's play must have appealed to Berg: the power of the narrative and the gripping verisimilitude of the situations in which the major characters find themselves, the demented psyche of Woz-

143

zeck, the imaginary voices he hears, the sounds of men marching along underground (hinting at incipient schizophrenia), the military music associated with the Drum Major, the folk songs sung by Andres, Marie, Wozzeck and the apprentices and, finally, the overall atmosphere of the play itself, redolent with images of persecution and sadism, sexual passion, jealousy and despair. In preparing his libretto, Berg appears to have made use of the edition of Büchner's play that was published by Paul Landau in 1909,[8] which was, in turn, derived from the version published by Karl Emil Franzos in 1879. In fact, the verbal texts are identical, but Landau rearranges the order of the scenes.

In Landau's version, the first scene of the play depicts Wozzeck shaving his Captain to earn extra money he needs for his common-law wife, Marie, and their little son. Berg tends to set Büchner's lines to music as he finds them (with few exceptions) but, as noted above, his histrionic instincts led him to add many stage directions to the original text. At the beginning of the scene, for example, Büchner describes the setting simply as *"Room. The Captain and Wozzeck. Captain on a chair. Wozzeck shaves him."*[9]

Berg, however, adds some further instructions: *"The Captain's room. (Early in the morning). The Captain sits on a chair before a mirror. Wozzeck shaves the Captain."*[10] It is characteristic of Berg's sensitivity to the visual aspect of his opera that he prescribes the lighting for each scene—here, early morning.

The Captain's first speech runs along as in the play except that after he complains to Wozzeck, "You make me dizzy . . ."[11] Berg adds the stage direction *"covers his forehead and eyes with his hand. Wozzeck stops his work. The Captain pulls himself together."*[12] These directions enable the singer performing the Captain to effect a complete change of mood as he wonders what he will do with the extra time he will have on his hands because Wozzeck will finish shaving him ten minutes early. Since all this is plainly reflected in the music, it is the duty of the stage director to make sure the performers execute the business as Berg has prescribed it.

At the end of the scene, Berg makes a small change in Büchner's text. Instead of the Captain's "You may go now and don't run. Slow. Nice and slow. Right down the middle of the street!",[13] Berg substitutes, "You may go now and don't run! Walk slowly down the street, exactly in the middle. Slow, nice and slow."[14] As George Perle has observed: "By transposing the Captain's key word *langsam* ["slowly"] so that it becomes the last as well as the first word of the scene, Berg emphasizes the recapitulative function

144

of the Reprise and establishes the Captain's '*langsam*' as one of the verbal *Leitmotive* of the work."[15]

For scene 2 of his opera, Berg follows Landau's ordering of Büchner's scenes but, again, adds stage directions. In Büchner, Scene 2 is described merely as an "*open field with the town in the distance.*"[16] Berg alters this to "*Open field. The town in the distance. (Late afternoon). Wozzeck and Andres cut firewood in the bushes.*"[17]

Again, Berg discloses his concern for the stage lighting by specifying the time of day and, with the skill of a born playwright, he develops this visual element of his opera by calling for a considerable change in the lighting toward the end of the scene: "*The sun is on the point of setting. The last rays fill the sky with an uncanny light. Then, quite suddenly (like descending darkness), twilight follows, to which the eye gradually becomes accustomed.*"[18] Wozzeck, betraying his incipient delusional schizophrenia, shouts, "A fire! A fire! It goes up from the earth to heaven and, down below, a great noise, like trumpets. How it thunders!"[19]

At the beginning of the third scene of Act I, in Marie's room, Berg indicates that the action involving Marie, Margret, the Drum Major and—later—Wozzeck takes place in the early evening. At the end of the scene, as Marie ponders Wozzeck's eccentric behavior, he adds stage directions that are not in Büchner's text: *Marie goes away from the window. She is alone with her child and regards him anxiously.*[20] After Marie sings about Wozzeck's distracted condition, that he has no eyes for his child, and that his mind will crack under his delusions, her next lines in Büchner, which Berg sets, "It's getting so dark. You'd think you're blind. No light from the street lamp,"[21] have been clearly anticipated. The lighting will have been dimming all through the scene and will have reached a very low level as she sings, "Ah! Us poor folks. Can't stand it any longer. Scared . . ."[22]

Following Landau's arrangement, Berg places the scene between Wozzeck and the Doctor fourth in Act I. Again, the lighting is clearly specified: "*The Doctor's study. A sunny afternoon. Wozzeck enters. The Doctor hurries toward him.*"[23] It is in this scene that Berg changes a word he considered vulgar to a word less likely to offend the conservative tastes of German opera house managements. In Büchner, the Doctor scolds Wozzeck for breaking their agreement: "I saw it, Wozzeck! You pissed in the street. Pissed against a wall, like a dog!"[24] Berg replaces the word "piss" with "cough": "I saw it Wozzeck, I saw you coughing again, out in the street, barking like a dog!"[25]

145

In spite of his keen histrionic sensibility, Berg evidently didn't comprehend the dramatic significance of Wozzeck's urine. Perhaps he wasn't very well acquainted with the military milieu of early nineteenth-century Europe and was not aware that, from 1812, when Napoleon lost 100,000 men to hunger and cold in his retreat from Moscow, the old military gospel that an invading army could live off the food produced by the land it occupied had become discredited. All over Europe, army medical staffs were experimenting with rations that the foot soldier could carry on his back, the objective being the most calories for the least weight. In Büchner's play, the Doctor pays Wozzeck (who has volunteered for this duty) a modest sum to eat only certain foodstuffs for prescribed amounts of time, and Wozzeck's urine is the principal means of determining what effect the diet is having on his system. A popular view, today, that the Doctor in *Wozzeck* is some kind of a sadist, performing cruel and heartless experiments on helpless human beings, a precursor of the infamous medical men of Auschwitz, is not convincing.

Berg ends Act I of his opera with the scene in Landau's edition in which the Drum Major seduces Marie. In doing so, he cut three short but expressive scenes from Büchner's play—the scene of Marie and Wozzeck at the fair, the following scene in which they watch a trained monkey and the scene in which the Doctor throws a cat out of a window to test his theories of gravity. Although useful in developing character, the three scenes are probably well sacrificed to the cause of dramatic unity that governed Berg's work on his libretto.

To begin Act II, Berg employed Landau's Scene 9, in which Marie is admiring the earrings the Drum Major has given her. Again, he indicates the lighting by specifying *"morning sunshine"*.[26] His other stage directions, however, follow those of Büchner.

In scene 2 of Act II, Berg uses Landau's Scene 10 in which the Captain and the Doctor reveal to Wozzeck the barracks-room gossip that his common-law wife, Marie, has been unfaithful to him with the Drum Major. Berg condenses Büchner's text, however, by cutting some of the Captain's opening lines, such as the one in which he expresses how sorry he feels for horses when he thinks about how they have to go everywhere on foot. Berg also adds a new stage direction. As the Captain and the Doctor torment Wozzeck with their hints about Marie and a man with a long beard, the Doctor is required to *"mark time with his walking stick as though it were a drum major's baton,*"[27] so that poor Wozzeck won't be left in any doubt about the identity of Marie's seducer.

For the central scene of Act II, and of his entire opera, Berg chooses Landau's Scene 11, in which Wozzeck confronts Marie with her infidelity. Again, he adds stage directions. In place of Büchner's *"Marie's room"*,[28] he substitutes *"a narrow street before the door to Marie's house. (A dull day). Marie stands before her door. Wozzeck comes quickly along the sidewalk towards her."*[29] The exterior setting allows the lighting to be changed as the scene progresses in a way not compatible with an interior setting. Berg thus deepens the pathos of Wozzeck's emerging schizophrenia as he exclaims, "Man is an abyss. It makes you dizzy to look down there—(*exiting*)—makes you dizzy . . ."[30]

Berg goes next to the first tavern scene (Scene 13 in Landau), which becomes his Act II, scene 4. This scene dramatizes a further loss to Wozzeck of his self-esteem as he watches Marie dancing with the Drum Major. Berg specifies that the lighting is to depict *"late evening."*[31] Another manifestation of Berg's histrionic sensibility is his employment of three distinct forms of word expression to convey to the audience the essence of this complicated crowd scene—song, *Sprechstimme* and spoken dialogue.

The scene begins with a song sung by two Apprentices, followed by general dancing of the crowd, Marie and the Drum Major among them. Wozzeck enters and watches the dancing. He speaks his first words in rhythm to the orchestral accompaniment: "He—she—the devil!"[32] Marie and the Drum Major dance by him singing, "On and on! On and on!"[33] Wozzeck's next utterance, which repeats the words of Marie and the Drum Major, is neither spoken nor sung, but is delivered in the *Sprechstimme* style of half-singing, half-speaking that Arnold Schoenberg had invented many years earlier. Berg also employs this vividly expressive device later in the scene, when one of the Apprentices delivers a mock-sermon to the assembled patrons of the tavern, thus insuring that the audience will readily understand the words as they are pronounced by an opera singer in a large opera house.

Berg eliminates the next scene in Landau in which Wozzeck and Andres are trying to sleep in the barracks, sleep that is denied Wozzeck as he sees visions of Marie dancing with the Drum Major and hears voices from a wall telling him he must stab someone with a knife. Although this scene develops Wozzeck's dementia and plants the idea of the knife, and—ultimately—the murder of Marie, Berg must have decided that it was simply too short to include in his plot structure. He then goes on to the last scene of his Act II and, characteristically, finds an unconventional sound to convey the atmosphere of an army barracks room at night—the unnerving racket of many sleeping soldiers snoring in atonal harmony. The sound begins before the rise of the scene curtain and continues for a time after it is up. The effect may have been suggested to Berg by his own experiences of barracks life during the war.

The beating of Wozzeck by the sadistic Drum Major that closes the second act establishes in the mind of the hero the most significant of all the psychological preconditions for paranoid schizophrenia, "a catastrophic loss of self-esteem coupled with severe feelings of inadequacy and inferiority."[34] From here on, Wozzeck finds he is incapable of resisting the voices he hears, commanding him to stab Marie to death.

Berg begins Act III with Scene 17 in Landau, in which Marie, in her gloomy room, reads from the Bible by candlelight. To fill out the short sequence, Berg adds some lines from Landau's Scene 19 in which an old woman relates a story about a poor child with no mother and no father, that cries all day and all night. He then cuts Landau's Scene 18, a pawnshop where Wozzeck buys a knife from a Jew, as well as Scene 20, in which Wozzeck gives some of his clothing to Andres, and proceeds to Scene 21—*"forest path by a lake. It is dark."*[35]

During the scene, Berg indicates in his stage directions the rising of the moon. Both Marie and Wozzeck comment on it, especially its redness— "like a bloody knife,"[36] Wozzeck says, whereupon he kills Marie by stabbing her in the throat with his knife. He leaves, whispering the word "dead".[37] Berg cuts Büchner's line, "Murder! Murder!"[38]

Following Landau, Berg uses the second tavern scene for his Act III, scene 3. In place of Büchner's stage directions, *"Tavern. Apprentices dance with servant girls"*,[39] Berg substitutes *"A seedy tavern. (Night, dim light). Apprentices and servant girls (Margret among them) dance a wild, fast polka"*.[40] He also tightens Büchner's original scene by assigning Käthe's lines to Margret (whom we have already met in Act I, scene 2), giving her as well the lines spoken by the *Wirthin* and a peasant pointing out the blood on Wozzeck's arm.

For Act III, scene 4, Berg employs Landau's next scene, No. 23, which takes place again by the lake. Wozzeck has returned to the place of his crime to dispose of the murder weapon. When he finds the knife, he throws it into a shallow part of the lake, then goes to get it and throws it to a deeper part. As he does so, Berg inserts a lighting direction that is not in Büchner, "*the moon rises blood red behind the clouds*",[41] recalling the similar lighting that ended the open-field scene in Act I and the murder scene in Act III. It is in the glow of this sinister light that Wozzeck drowns, a stage direction that was inserted into Büchner's original manuscript by his first editor, Karl Emil Franzos and was retained by Berg. It is possible that Büchner intended to continue his play about the barber, Woyzeck, up through his trial and execution in Leipzig, since there is a surviving scene in which a surgeon, a doctor and a judge[42] comment on the murder. But Berg wisely brings his opera to an end with the death by drowning of his hero, his instinctive sense of dramatic form—of Aristotle's beginning, middle and end—having been vindicated by countless performances of *Wozzeck* in the world's opera houses.

In rounding out the suicide scene, Berg assigns the lines of Büchner's first and second passers-by to the Doctor and the Captain, again strengthening his dramatic poem by reducing the list of characters. He also arranges the sequence of lines so that the Captain speaks last, "Come. Come quickly."[43] George Perle has observed that as it was the Captain, in both the play and libretto, who was given the first word, ("slowly"), Berg has managed, in an economical way to provide "1) a verbal association that has important structural significance; 2) an ironic comment on a characteristic feature of the Captain's personality and speech, for in his previous appearances in the work he had repeatedly urged first Wozzeck and then the Doctor to 'take your time'; 3) a counterpart to Act II, scene 2, the only other scene in which the Captain and the Doctor . . . are shown together."[44]

Finally, to end *Wozzeck*, Berg makes use of Landau's Scene 25, in which some children tell the little son of Wozzeck and Marie that his mother is dead. The boy doesn't understand, and continues to play on his hobby horse. This scene becomes a kind of epilogue, that comments both on the meaninglessness of the lives of Wozzeck and Marie and, at the same time, on the enduring (although inexplicable) will of the human race to survive.

With his formal, carefully prepared text on his desk, Alban Berg set about the task of composing his opera by employing various forms of absolute music, some of which were new to the opera house, although familiar in the concert hall and the church. To his first biographer, Willi Reich, he offered the following table of relationships between dramatic action and musical form in *Wozzeck*:

SCENE		MUSIC
	ACT I	
Wozzeck in relation to his environment		*Five character sketches*
Wozzeck and the Captain	*Scene 1*	Suite
Wozzeck and Andres	*Scene 2*	Rhapsody
Marie and Wozzeck	*Scene 3*	Military march and cradle song
Wozzeck and the Doctor	*Scene 4*	Passacaglia
Marie and the Drum Major	*Scene 5*	*Andante affetuoso (quasi rondo)*
	ACT II	
Dramatic development		*Symphony in five movements*
Marie and child, later Wozzeck	*Scene 1*	Sonata movement
Captain and Doctor, later Wozzeck	*Scene 2*	Fantasy and fugue
Marie and Wozzeck	*Scene 3*	Largo
Tavern garden	*Scene 4*	Scherzo
Barracks room	*Scene 5*	Rondo with introduction
	ACT III	
Catastrophe and Epilogue		*Six Inventions*
Marie and the child	*Scene 1*	Invention on a theme
Marie and Wozzeck	*Scene 2*	Invention on a tone
Seedy tavern	*Scene 3*	Invention on a rhythm
Wozzeck's death	*Scene 4*	Invention on a six-tone chord
	Orchestral Interlude	
Children playing	*Scene 5*	Invention on an equal movement in eighth notes[45]

Berg did not intend, however, that these complex musico-dramatic relationships should intrude on the spectator's enjoyment of the opera. In the latter part of his article "Das Opernproblem", mentioned above, he makes it clear that he does not want the audience to have any idea of the presence of these forms from the world of absolute music:

No matter how much a person may understand of the musical forms that can be found in the opera, how precisely and logically it is all "worked out", how artfully it is planned in every detail . . . from the moment the curtains open until they close for the last time, people in the audience should have no idea of all these diverse fugues and inventions, suite and sonata movements, variations and passacaglias. Nobody should be absorbed in anything but the overall, thematic *idea* of the opera, an idea that goes far beyond the particular fate of Wozzeck. And in this, I believe, I have been successful![46]

Berg's belief that it would be best if all the telltale signs of the abstract musical forms in his opera passed unnoticed by the members of the audience was reflected in the considerable success of the first performance of *Wozzeck* at the Staatsoper Unter den Linden in Berlin, December 14, 1925. The work was conducted by Erich Kleiber, Franz Ludwig Hörth directed and the scenery and costumes were designed by Panos Aravantinos. After mentioning some unfavorable notices, Douglas Jarman has observed that "the reviews in those papers not politically or artistically biased make it clear, however, that both the public and the majority of critics recognized that *Wozzeck* was a milestone in the history of opera."[47]

And what was Alban Berg's reaction to his big success in Berlin? Theodor Adorno has described it as follows:

After the world premiere of *Wozzeck* in Berlin, he was honored at a dinner party at Restaurant Töpfer, where he said scarcely anything and appeared quite the shy youngster. Afterward, I was with him until late that night literally endeavouring to comfort him over his success. That a work conceived like one of Wozzeck's visions in the open field, a work measuring up to Berg's own highest standards, could please a first-night theater crowd was incomprehensible and argued against the worth of the opera.[48]

Whether for the right or the wrong reasons, *Wozzeck* continued to make the rounds of the world's opera houses and, in 1930, Berg wrote down some production notes for conductors, stage directors and scene designers that he intended his publisher, Universal Edition, to distribute with the opera's performance materials. His advice to conductors is concerned mainly with questions of tempo, dynamics, balance between orchestra and voices, voice timbre and *Sprechstimme*, among other musical matters. But his histrionic instincts prompted him to offer equally detailed advice on matters of staging, scenery and lighting.

He begins this section of his notes by assuming that the production staff has a close acquaintance with both the play and the music he has composed to express it in the theater, at least with regard to its dramatic implications. He feels that he is leaving the designer sufficient leeway to develop his own visual interpretation of the scenes, but this concept should "establish a reality of design that informs the audience immediately and without question exactly where all the dramatic action takes place."[49]

Berg goes on to observe that the diversity of musical forms should lead the designer toward a similar diversity of scenic representation among, for instance, the three interior rooms (those of the Captain, the Doctor and Marie), the two street scenes (before Marie's house and in the town), the first and second tavern scenes, the scenes of the open field and those by the lake. In the open-field scene of Act I, Berg calls for a convincing sunset effect, that might seem uncannily foreboding to Wozzeck, and asks also for a realistic depiction of the positioning of the moon in the lake scenes, "where the moon, near the horizon the first time (Act III, scene 2), is seen to be the second time (Act III, scene 4), somewhat higher in the sky as it breaks through the clouds."[50] Berg adds that the image of the water in the lake (thrown on the cyclorama by a wide-angle lens projector capable of projecting moving images) might convey "a sense of gentle movement at measure 275, such movement to reach a climax at measure 285–6, and then slowly die down at measure 302, after which all is again still."[51]

Berg does not adhere to realistic representations throughout the work, however. He suggests that the second tavern scene (Act III, scene 3), placed as it is between the two lake scenes, "might have an otherworldly, even ghostly quality about it, for which the setting need be merely suggested."[52]

In pointing out that such treatment of the second tavern scene would enable the backstage crews to shift the scenery and props quickly from the lake to the tavern and then back to the lake again, he adds that all changes of scene must be achieved in the time permitted by the short musical interludes between scenes. These interludes must not be stopped because the scenery isn't in place, so the shifts have to be practiced until they fit exactly within the prescribed number of minutes and seconds of music.

Berg next makes clear that he expects the house curtain to fall only at the end of an act, while the scenes within each act are marked off by the use

152

of scene curtains or blackouts. And each rise or fall of any curtain must correspond precisely to the notation in the score. He even suggests that control over the rise and fall of all the curtains be located in the orchestra pit rather than backstage "because the noise backstage during a scene change tends to prevent the orchestra from being heard, making the vital linkage between curtain and music nearly impossible to achieve."[53]

Berg goes on to emphasize the importance of establishing the time of day or night of the fifteen scenes. He notes that the twilight of the last scene of Act I, the seduction of Marie by the Drum Major, must be clearly set off from the lighting of the other scenes using the same setting—Wozzeck's confrontation of Marie in Act II and the children's scene of Act III. There must also be distinct lighting differences inside Marie's room between the evening light of the scene in Act I when the Drum Major goes by, the morning light of the opening of Act II when Marie admires her new earrings, and the nighttime of the beginning of Act III, when Marie reads from the Bible by candlelight.

Continuing his thoughts on the lighting of *Wozzeck*, Berg observes that, in the barracks-room scene at the end of Act II, the lighting becomes brighter at measure 761 "because, as the Drum Major enters, he carries a light with him which he puts down somewhere. When he goes out with the light at measure 800, the initial darkness and atmosphere of the scene is restored."[54] By requiring the Drum Major to carry a lantern of some kind when he enters the barracks room, Berg motivates the need for brighter light on the ensuing sequence in which Wozzeck fights with the Drum Major. And, after Wozzeck has been beaten up and his tormentor has gone with his lantern, there is no longer any need for extra light as the soldiers go back to sleep and Wozzeck mutters his inchoate protest, "One after the other."[55]

Berg continues with some admonitions to the stage director, remarking that he, too, must possess an intimate knowledge of the relationship between music and dramatic action. He notes that, in the murder scene, Marie is stabbed by Wozzeck only once (at measure 103), and the musical development that follows refers only to Marie and her death. Hence, other extraneous stage activity should be avoided. Also, in the second lake scene, most of the music depicts Wozzeck's search for the knife and his drowning, except for measures 239–49, which refer to Marie. Here, Berg suggests a brightening of the light on Marie during the playing of these measures, which then goes down again to leave her body in darkness to the end of the scene.

In spite of these specific instructions, Berg feels that he has left the stage director ample opportunity to exercise his own histrionic imagination while working out the staging of *Wozzeck*. For instance, the scene in the Doctor's study might benefit from various bits of business involving medical examinations of Wozzeck, and the two tavern scenes offer possibilities for the director's inventiveness, as long as he preserves the light, gay atmosphere of the first scene in contrast to the surrealistic, almost daemonic mood of the second.

But even in such scenes, Berg warns, musical representation of character must be carefully considered. When the Idiot enters (Act II, measure 643), the tavern noise dies down so that his scene with Wozzeck can be developed without needless distraction. And, when the Doctor and the Captain appear at the end of the second lake scene, "both of them who, up to now, have been standing more or less to one side, should speak their lines in an almost muted manner because, at this point, the main concern is the music, the stage setting and the lighting."[56]

Finally, Berg concludes his admonitions to the stage director and his staff by warning that the scenes in which the child of Marie and Wozzeck appears require special consideration. He thinks the child should be played by a little girl since girls are more talented at that age than boys, and that all the children should be carefully rehearsed with the orchestra before the final dress rehearsal because, for children, the rehearsal piano is no substitute for the sound of the orchestra.

The world success of *Wozzeck* since 1926 has established its preeminence among the significant achievements of twentieth-century dramatic poetry. Berg himself summed up the universal thematic idea that permeates the work while speaking of a particular harmonic effect during a lecture he prepared for the first production of *Wozzeck* at Oldenburg, in 1929: "These fifths (piano score, Act I, page 48, measures 425–6) are . . . associated with the character of Marie. (I would say that this quiet moment suggests her aimless waiting for death, that alone can provide a resolution for her existence.)"[57]

Not only Marie, but all the personages of Berg's opera seem to be aimlessly passing the time until they die, like the characters in Samuel Beckett's most famous play, all of whom are waiting for "Godot" (*der Tod*). Berg's opera even hints at the ultimate tragedy: not only the individual human being but the entire human race is aimlessly waiting for extinction.

A feeling of the allegorical suffuses Berg's second opera, *Lulu*. Whereas *Wozzeck* projects a series of sharply drawn characters who symbolize nothing beyond their own essential selves, the central figure of *Lulu* is an image of the very essence of woman, as Wedekind understood it: passionate, calculating, naive, vulnerable, born with a prodigious talent for sex, a talent for which she makes no apology. A female Don Giovanni, she experiences—during the course of the two plays—heterosexual relations with a doctor, a painter, an African explorer, a publisher, the publisher's son, her butler, an acrobat, a schoolboy, a procurer, a professor, a Negro and Jack the Ripper. An Electra complex is suggested in her scenes with her foster father, Schigolch; she engages in homosexual relations with Countess Martha Geschwitz; and, while her husband is answering the doorbell, we watch as she indulges herself in a few satisfying moments of autoerotism.

Alban Berg probably read the first play of Wedekind's duology, *Erdgeist*, in either 1903 or 1904.[58] And on May 29, 1905, sitting in the sixth row of the private Trianon Theater in Vienna, he saw *Die Büchse der Pandora* as staged by the literary critic and editor of *Die Fackel*, Karl Kraus. The production featured Wedekind himself playing Jack, with his future wife, Tilly Newes, as Lulu.[59] The director-critic gave a short lecture on the play to which Berg listened closely. Kraus commented on Lulu's character as follows:

> I see in the image of this woman whom men think "to have," while it is really they who are being had by her, a woman who is different to every man, who shows every man a different face. . . . I see in her the ultimate vindication of immorality. She is a totally fulfilled woman with a genius for forgetting, a woman without inhibitions, who lives beyond the doubts of conscience and consigns every experience to oblivion. She longs for sex but not for children . . . a sleepwalker of love who only "wakes" when she is summoned, ever the giver, ever the loser. As an articulate panhandler in the play says of her, "She can't live by love because her life is love." But, in our hidebound world, the fountain of joy inevitably becomes Pandora's box and, it seems to me, the entire play has grown out of this infinitely deplorable fact of life.[60]

By the time Berg had begun working on his new opera, in 1928, there had been several productions in Germany that combined the two plays into a single evening's entertainment. One version, staged by Otto Falckenberg in Munich in 1928, made use of film sequences to bridge gaps between scenes, a device Berg employs in his opera in order to segue from scene 1 of Act II to scene 2.[61]

Although Berg retains most of Wedekind's characters, he changes some of them into quasi-allegorical figures by designating them not by their names, as in the plays, but by their professions or titles, such as "Medical Specialist", "Painter", "Acrobat", "Marquis", "School Boy", "Banker" and so forth. Only the five main personages—Lulu, Schigolch, Dr. Schön, Alwa and Countess Geschwitz—retain their names. Berg also changes Alwa from a writer to a composer and hints that it was Alwa who has composed *Wozzeck*.

Another of Berg's innovations is to assign pairs of roles to the same singer. The Medical Specialist, Lulu's first husband, also enacts the silent role of the Professor, her first client as a prostitute in the London scene at the end of Act III. Her second husband, the Painter, sings the role of the Negro—her second client—who kills Alwa. And the performer singing Dr. Schön, her third husband, also sings the role of Jack the Ripper, who kills both Lulu and the Countess. This doubling of roles, usually done in a theater to save money, in Berg's opera takes on an especially sinister significance since the audience knows, as these personages appear for the first time, what will happen when they appear for the last.

Berg seems to have encountered a number of special obstacles in preparing his libretto for *Lulu*. In a letter to Schoenberg of August 9, 1920, he writes:

> Aside from the composition, the twelve-tone style of which still doesn't permit me to work quickly, the libretto slows me down a lot, too. Because finalizing the text goes hand in hand with composing. Since I have to cut four-fifths of the Wedekind original, selection of the remaining fifth is torture enough. How much worse when I try to make the text fit the musical forms (large and small) without destroying Wedekind's idiosyncratic language.[62]

This letter makes it clear that Berg was writing the libretto while composing the music. He adds, "That's why I could send you only the 'text' of what I have composed so far; but I would rather wait until the whole thing is finished."[63] Douglas Jarman has commented on the context of this letter as follows:

> "Making the text fit the musical form" was, to Berg, a vital step in producing a work that met his conception of music drama as a genre in which the musical

and dramatic design were inextricably linked; a genre in which the musical structure fulfilled all the requirements of self-contained instrumental music while, at the same time, reflecting both the overall shape and the most detailed nuances of the drama. Such an intimate relationship between the demands of "absolute" musical structure and those of dramatic action could only be achieved by the composer acting as his own librettist.[64]

Of the ninety-seven lines Wedekind composed for his Prologue to *Erdgeist*, Berg sets only forty, the most important of which accompany the action in which Lulu is brought on stage in her Pierrot costume of the next scene. The Animal Tamer describes her to the audience, however, as a snake:

Animal Tamer.
She as the root of all evil was created;
To snare us, to mislead us she was fated,
And to murder, with no clue left on the spot.[65]
—Translated by Arthur Jacobs

The Prologue concludes as the Animal Tamer invites the audience into his tent to see how his snake interacts with all the other wild animals of his menagerie.

Berg cut the first and second scenes of Wedekind's *Erdgeist,* Act I, in which the playwright carefully establishes the portrait of Lulu, costumed as Pierrot, that was commissioned by her first husband, Dr. Goll. The portrait appears in every scene of the two plays and is used by Wedekind as a kind of objective correlative that dramatizes the profound effect Lulu has on her lovers. With his cuts, Berg also lost Wedekind's sketch of Dr. Goll, a pompous, elderly medical man who is intensely jealous of his young wife, information that helps us in the audience to understand what happens to him when he breaks into the Painter's studio. Still, Berg was probably right in believing that all this would become clear anyway as the action progressed. For example, the concept of the portrait as objective correlative is made clear in the London scene when Alwa, standing before the portrait, exclaims:

Alwa (*suddenly rejuvenated*).
But why—? Looking at this picture, I feel my self-esteem returning. I understand my destiny. (*With rapture*). Whoever can stand before these ripe, swelling lips, these huge, innocent child-eyes, this throbbing rose and

157

white body, whoever can remain indifferent, in the grip of his middle class morality, let him cast the first stone at us.[66]

Berg begins his own Act I, scene 1 with the entrance of Alwa, and continues with Alwa's departure with his father, the scene of the Painter's lust for Lulu, the violent entrance of Dr. Goll and his sudden death from a stroke. The way is prepared for Dr. Schön to arrange Lulu's second marriage—to the Painter.

For the second scene of his first act, Berg employs Wedekind's *Erdgeist,* Act II which takes place in the elegant drawing room the Painter and his bride now share. Lulu's portrait hangs on the rear wall. She wears a negligee and converses with her husband in spoken dialogue about the morning's mail. One letter concerns the sale of a recent painting of Lulu as a dancer for 50,000 marks, the third substantial sale since their marriage. Another announces the forthcoming marriage of Dr. Schön to his longtime fiancée, Charlotte von Zarnikow.

As in *Wozzeck*, Berg places many careful stage directions in his new work for the theater. After commenting on the letters, the Painter starts to exit to his studio off left but, sexually aroused, returns to Lulu, who is reclining on the chaise longue. She, too, is in the mood for sex, but the doorbell rings. The Painter hesitates. "Damn! Someone's at the door!"[67] She tries to keep him from leaving her. "Stay here! No one home! We just won't answer!"[68] The Painter counters, "But suppose it's the picture dealer?"[69] Lulu: "And suppose it's the Emperor of China?"[70] But the Painter is overcome by an urge to answer the door. "Just a minute,"[71] he says, and hurries out up center.

Left alone, in a state of aroused sexual desire, Lulu lies back on the chaise longue and masturbates. In Wedekind, she exclaims, as though seeing a vision, "You? You?"* then closes her eyes,[72] after which Schwarz returns to report that it is a beggar at the door. Berg carefully elaborates these stage directions to make clear what Lulu is doing between measures 441 and 460. As the Painter exits, Lulu is *"alone, in an ecstatic, dreamy state."*[73] She sings softly *"as though seeing someone in a vision,* 'You—you—' then *closes her eyes."*[74] The music describes her reaching a sexual climax at measure 453, after which it falls away as she *"comes to herself, clearly displaying a release of tension."*[75]

---

* Probably Alwa.

As in *Wozzeck*, where he changes "pissing" to "coughing", Berg goes to some trouble to avoid irritating the official censors, not to mention the conservative managers of the tax-supported opera houses of his time. A masturbation scene on the stage is, even today, offensive to many theatergoers, and this particular activity in Berg's opera is often omitted in production.

Berg also adds unusually detailed stage directions to the end of scene 3 of Act I of *Lulu*, during which Lulu dictates Dr. Schön's letter of renunciation to his fiancée. As she dictates *"emphatically*—'My dear lady . . .'"[76] Dr. Schön responds by writing, in close accord with the accompanying music, "My dear lady . . ."[77] This repetition of Lulu's lines and Dr. Schön's measured acceptance of their import continues to the end of Act I, a testimonial to his emotional, erotic and psychological bondage to his mistress during the years since he first met her, in her childhood.

Berg sets Wedekind's *Erdgeist*, Act IV, which he makes Act II, scene 1 of his opera much as written except for various cuts. In order to strengthen the development of Lulu's character, he retains her soliloquy, "Wenn sich die Menschen" in which we hear from her own lips her instinctive understanding of her essential self:

Lulu (*in a decisive, self-confident tone*).
Men may have killed themselves for my sake, but that doesn't depreciate my worth. You knew just as well why you made me your wife as I knew why I accepted you. You had betrayed your best friends with me—you couldn't very well betray yourself with me, too. If you have sacrificed your later years for me, you have received in return the enjoyment of my youth. I have never in the world tried to be what I'm not, and no one in the world has ever thought me to be other than what I am.[78]

Since Berg planned the two scenes in Dr. Schön's home to be scene 1 and scene 2 of his second act, and since Wedekind ended his first play with the first scene and used the second to begin his second play, Berg had to devise a transition of some kind to get from one scene to the next. His solution to his problem was to call for a film that would depict all the action between the arrest of Lulu and her escape from prison one year later. Since the music for the film moves forward to a certain point and is then played backwards to the starting point, the action of the film must follow the same pattern. Berg explains this as follows:

During the transitional music a silent film is to indicate the course of Lulu's fortunes in the next year. The film sequence—in accordance with the symmetrical course of the music—should also be quasi-symmetrical (i.e., it should run forwards and then backwards.) To this end the events that correspond, together with their accompanying phenomena, should be fitted together as closely as possible. This yields the following series of scenes (following the direction of the arrows):

Arrest	**En route to her final liberation** ↑
The three people concerned in the arrest	The three people concerned in the liberation
Lulu in chains	Lulu at liberty (disguised as the Countess Geschwitz)
Detention pending trial	**Isolation ward**
Nervous expectancy	Nervous expectancy
Her hopes disappearing	Growing hopes
Trial	**Medical council**
Her guilt	The illness
Judge and jury	Doctor and students
The three witnesses	The three helpers in the liberation
The judgement	
Her transfer in the police van to the . . .	Her transfer in the ambulance from the prison
Prison	**Prison**
The prison door shuts	The prison door opens
Initial resignation	Awakening will to live
Lulu's portrait—as a shadow on the prison wall	Lulu's portrait—as a reflection in a shovel

➤ **One year's imprisonment**[79]

160

After the film leads the audience to the second scene of his second act, Berg sets Wedekind's *Büchse der Pandora,* Act I, much as written except for numerous small cuts. He finds musical means to elaborate on Lulu's character, especially at the moment when she first enters her old home after her year in prison and her contraction of cholera, of which she is not yet cured.

There has been much discussion of the character of Lulu since the appearance of Berg's operatic version of the two plays. After citing some observations of Wedekind's to the effect that the central figure of his second play is not Lulu but Countess Geschwitz, Donald Mitchell writes:

> Wedekind, I think, has made his position clear; and, in *Earth-Spirit* and *Pandora's Box,* Lulu is a decisively non-developing role, "passive" throughout; events occur to, round and about Lulu, not because she "wills" but because she is—irrevocably—what she is.[80]

Mitchell goes on to argue that Berg adds an emotional dimension to Lulu's character that was not originally part of Wedekind's conception, by means of his music. As one example, he writes:

> First, compare Lulu's great cry upon her return home from prison—"Oh freedom! God in heaven!", perhaps the most moving bars in the whole opera (Act two/2)—with the corresponding passage in *Pandora's Box* (Act one). She speaks the same words, admittedly but, from her entrance into the room until the end of the act, Wedekind directs that she is to address her companions "in the most cheerful tone." Berg's music tells us most beautifully that she has suffered, and that she knows she has suffered; Wedekind's play tells us she is the same old Lulu, the same old flame, as unaffected by prison as by the deaths of her lovers.[81]

Thus, in fulfilling the fundamental obligation of music to express human feelings, Berg has "precipitated a large-scale dramatic confusion"[82] that has damaged his opera as a work of art. George Perle replies to this assertion, in an article written some ten years later, by examining more in detail the problem of the relationship of allegory and individuation in Lulu's character. He agrees that there is some element of symbolism in her dramatic portrait. For example, she responds to several names used by men in her life, such as "Mignon" (Dr. Schön), "Nelly" (Dr. Goll) and "Eve" (the Painter). The man who seems to have known her the longest, Schigolch, calls her "Lulu". Perle points out further that no one knows who her father

161

was. Schigolch says she never had a father, and Lulu agrees. "That's right," she says. "I'm a freak of nature."[83]

Perle agrees with Mitchell that Berg's music has a humanizing effect in the theater but feels that it also strengthens the allegorical elements:

> But it is precisely this art [of music] that can most effectively suggest the mythic aspect of Lulu and that can create non-verbal symbols to represent this aspect—symbols that made it possible for Berg to transform Wedekind's Lulu-dramas into a work that is simultaneously more complex and more coherent . . . Berg's humanization of Lulu makes far more dramatic sense than Wedekind's ambiguous and inconsistent characterization.[84]

Although Berg does, in fact, render Lulu more interesting, more three-dimensional than she is in Wedekind, he does not always rely on music to obtain his effects. At the end of Act II, scene 2, as Lulu is about to make love with Alwa for the first time, instead of singing her last line, Berg calls on her to speak the words over accompanying music:

Lulu (casually).
Isn't this the sofa on which your father bled to death?[85]

The effect of this "casual" question is extraordinarily intensified when hearing it spoken by a good singing actress over music, in *Melodrama* style, attesting once more to Berg's sure instinct for the art of dramatic expression in the theater.

A certain amount of ambiguity surrounds the setting for Act III, scene 1. Berg simply describes it as "a spacious drawing room in white gesso."[86] We learn from the dialogue that we are in Paris.

But who owns this spacious drawing room, with Lulu's portrait hanging on the wall, its gaming room to the rear, its large dining room to the right, its entrance doors to the left and, down left, a private door covered with wallpaper that leads to the servants' quarters? The plot summary for Act III, scene 1 in the English/German libretto, published by Universal Edition, begins, "In their new and luxurious (Parisian) home, Lulu and Alwa are entertaining guests."[87]

Somehow, all this fails to sound like either Lulu or Alwa. Setting up a gambling establishment in a Paris apartment calls for certain practical talents that neither possesses. The gaming tables have to be purchased. House players, security guards and money changers have to be hired. The

Paris police have to be bribed. Besides, the elegant blackmailer, Marquis Casti-Pianni, tells Lulu he knows Alwa has lost most of his substantial inheritance by gambling, and one doesn't lose money gambling at one's own tables.

No, the apartment must belong to Casti-Pianni but, again, Berg seems anxious to avoid offending his potential opera house patrons. It would be better if the audience didn't quite realize that Lulu has moved in with a titled Italian pimp who sells attractive young women to the better bordellos worldwide, and has even brought along her portrait to lend some excitement to his drawing room.

Nevertheless, it is in the Paris scene that the most attractive aspects of Lulu's character are dramatized. Casti-Pianni has grown tired of her and suggests a plan that he thinks will be advantageous for them both. She had given him some intimate pictures of herself that he has sent to the proprietor of a high-class whorehouse in Cairo. The Egyptian likes the pictures and is willing to pay Casti-Pianni a substantial fee in English gold for her services. She can live comfortably in Cairo, have all the sex she wants, put a little something by for her retirement and—best of all—remain well out of reach of the German police. But Lulu will have none of it:

> **Lulu** (*at first with suppressed passion*).
> I would go with you to America, to China. But I cannot sell the one thing that is mine and mine alone.[88]

She also clearly demonstrates that she is no "passive, non-developing" person who lets events take their course without protest. She bravely and resourcefully grapples with two blackmailers and manages to get clear of them both. The Acrobat tells her he'll turn her over to the police if she doesn't give him 20,000 marks that he needs so he can get married to his new girl. But she arranges for Countess Geschwitz to lure the Acrobat to Schigolch's room, which has a window overlooking the Seine, convenient for the disposal of dead bodies. And, at the end of the scene, she changes clothes with a groom and leads Alwa out through the private door just as Casti-Pianni enters through the main door with a policeman, who arrests the groom instead of Lulu.

In the London scene (Act III, scene 2), Berg reduces Lulu's four clients in Wedekind to three, by eliminating Dr. Hilti, who teaches philosophy and has never had sexual intercourse with a woman before. Also, in Wedekind's

163

play, a significant exchange takes place between Schigolch and Alwa while Lulu and Countess Geschwitz are walking the streets together:

Schigolch.
God damn it!
Alwa (*throws himself whimpering on his chaise longue*).
I don't think I can expect much more good from this world.
Schigolch.
We should have held that wench back by the throat. She'll drive away any living, breathing creature with that aristocratic Death's-head of hers.
Alwa.
She has thrown me onto a sick bed and has larded me with thorns, inside and out.
Schigolch.
Of course, she also has enough courage for ten men.
Alwa.
No wounded man will receive the coup-de-grâce with more gratitude than I.
Schigolch.
If she hadn't lured that jumping jack to my place that time, we'd still have him wrapped around our necks.[89]

As often in Wedekind, two characters are talking at cross-purposes: Alwa is thinking about Lulu, while Schigolch speaks of Countess Geschwitz. Berg condenses this dialogue as follows:

Schigolch (*pulling Alwa back*).
What right do you have to forbid your wife to work when you can't earn anything yourself?
Alwa (*groaning, as he throws himself down on the chaise-longue*).
Who else but she has thrown me onto this sickbed?
Schigolch.
She? Then she is sick?
Alwa.
She has passed on to me what she got from her Marquis. But she doesn't show any symptoms herself.[90]

Not only does Berg cut the one line that explains what happened to the Acrobat, he also changes Alwa's disease from the cholera Lulu still had when she escaped from prison to syphilis, which she contracted from Casti-Pianni, thus reducing her personal guilt in Alwa's condition. These changes are typical of the way Berg drives the action along toward the final, gruesome moments of the opera when Lulu and Countess Geschwitz meet their deaths at the hands of Jack the Ripper.

It is hard to overpraise Alban Berg's brilliant rendition of Wedekind's two plays into a single, three-act opera libretto of consummate power. As William Youngren has observed, "Berg has so perfectly imagined music that projects every expressive nuance of the text and the action—and has so expertly pruned the dead wood from *Earth Spirit* and *Pandora's Box*— that Wedekind's strangely moving celebration of sensuality, in all its destructiveness and insidious corruption takes on a grandeur and a stunning clarity not found in the original plays."[91] Not the least part of Berg's achievement is his transformation of Lulu, a near-allegorical figure in Wedekind, into a warm, fallible, fascinating human being through the expressive power of his text and music, an achievement ranking with Mozart's equally masterful humanization of the mythic Spanish womanizer, Don Juan.

Notes

1. Karen Monson, *Alban Berg* (Boston: Houghton Mifflin, 1979), 5.

2. Theodor W. Adorno, *Berg: Der Meister des kleinsten Übergangs* (Vienna: Elisabeth Lafite, 1968), 30: "Er maß und vervielfachte seine Kräfte an der Schwierigkeit, ans Material sich zu binden. Zunächst dürfte er als Dichter sich gefühlt und dazu subsidiär komponiert haben wie hochbegabte Halbwüchsige zuweilen, auch Wagner."

3. *The Berg-Schoenberg Correspondence,* eds. Juliane Brand, Christopher Hailey and Donald Harris (New York: Norton, 1987), 224.

4. Quoted by Monson (see n. 1), 161.

5. Douglas Jarman, *Alban Berg: "Wozzeck"* (Cambridge: Cambridge University Press, 1989), 2.

6. Quoted by Jarman, 1.

7. Alban Berg, "Das 'Opernproblem' ", *Neue Musik-Zeitung* 49 (1928), 285–6: "Abgesehen von dem Wunsch, gute Musik zu machen, den geistigen Inhalt von Büchners unsterblichem Drama auch musikalisch zu erfüllen, seine dichterische Sprache in eine musikalische umzusetzen, schwebte mir, in dem Moment, wo ich mich entschloß, eine Oper zu schreiben, nichts anderes, auch kompositionstechnisch nichts anderes vor, als dem Theater zu geben was des Theaters ist, das heißt

also, die Musik so zu gestalten, daß sie sich ihrer Verpflichtung, dem Drama zu dienen, *in jedem Augenblick* bewußt ist,—ja weitergehend: daß sie alles, was dieses Drama zur Umsetzung in die Wirklichkeit der Bretter bedarf, aus sich allein herausholt, damit schon vom *Komponisten* alle wesentlichen Aufgaben eines idealen Regisseurs fordernd."

8. George Perle, *The Operas of Alban Berg, Vol. I: "Wozzeck"* (Berkeley: University of California Press, 1980), 27 ff.

9. Georg Büchner, *Gesammelte Schriften*, ed. Paul Landau (Berlin: Paul Cassirer, 1909), II, 55: "*Zimmer. Der Hauptmann. Wozzeck. Hauptmann (auf einem Stuhl). Wozzeck (rasiert ihn).*"

10. Alban Berg, *Wozzeck*, opera in three acts (fifteen scenes), text, Alban Berg, piano reduction, Fritz Heinrich Klein (Vienna: Universal Edition, 1931), 9: "*Zimmer des Hauptmanns (Frühmorgens). Hauptmann auf einem Stuhl vor einem Spiegel. Wozzeck rasiert den Hauptmann.*"

11. Berg, 9: "Er macht mir ganz schwindlich . . ."

12. Berg, 9–10: "*. . . bedeckt Stirn und Augen mit der Hand. Wozzeck unterbricht seine Arbeit. Hauptmann wieder beruhigt.*"

13. Büchner (see n. 9), 57: "Geh' Er jetzt, und renn' Er nicht so, geh' Er langsam, hübsch langsam die Straße hinunter, genau in der Mitte!"

14. Berg (see n. 10), 26: "Geh' Er jetzt, und renn' Er nicht so! Geh' Er langsam die Straße hinunter, genau in der Mitte und nochmals, geh' Er langsam, hübsch langsam!"

15. Perle (see n. 8), 46.

16. Büchner (see n. 9), 57: "*Freies Feld. Die Stadt in der Ferne.*"

17. Berg (see n. 10), 30: "*Freies Feld, die Stadt in der Ferne. (Spätnachmittag). Andres und Wozzeck schneiden Stöcke im Gebüsch.*"

18. Berg, 38–9: "*Die Sonne ist im Begriff unterzugehen. Der letzte scharfe Strahl taucht den Horizont in das grellste Sonnenlicht, dem ziemlich unvermittelt die (wie tiefste Dunkelheit wirkende) Dämmerung folgt, an die sich das Auge allmählich gewöhnt.*"

19. Berg, 38: "Ein Feuer! Ein Feuer! Das fährt von der Erde in den Himmel und ein Getös herunter wie Posaunen. Wie's heranklirrt!"

20. Berg, 51–2: "*Marie geht vom Fenster weg. Allein mit dem Kind, betrachtet es schmerzlich.*"

21. Büchner (see n. 9), 60: "Es wird so dunkel, man meint, man wird blind. Sonst scheint doch die Laterne herein!"

22. Büchner, 60: "Ach! Wir armen Leut. Ich halt's nit aus, es schauert mich . . . "

23. Berg (see n. 10), 55–6: "*Studierstube des Doktors. (Sonniger Nachmittag.) Wozzeck tritt ein. Der Doktor eilt hastig dem eintretenden Wozzeck entgegen.*"

24. Büchner (see n. 9), 60: "Ich habs gesehen, Wozzeck! Er hat auf die Straße gepißt, an die Wand gepißt, wie ein Hund!"

25. Berg (see n. 10), 56: "Ich habs gesehen, Wozzeck, Er hat wieder gehustet, auf der Straße gehustet, gebellt wie ein Hund!"

26. Berg, 83: "(*Vormittag, Sonnenschein*)."

27. Berg, 112: "... *er mit seinem Spazierstock (gleich einem Tamburstab) den Takt dazu markiert.*"

28. Büchner (see n. 9), 70: "*Mariens Stube.*"

29. Berg (see n. 10), 124: "*Gasse vor Mariens Wohnungstür (trüber Tag). Marie steht vor ihrer Tür. Wozzeck kommt auf dem Gehsteig rasch auf sie zu.*"

30. Berg, 132–3: "Der Mensch ist ein Abgrund, es schwindelt Einem, wenn man hinunter schaut ... *im Abgehen* ... mich schwindelt ... "

31. Berg, 137: "*Wirtshausgarten (spät abends).*"

32. Berg, 144: "Er! Sie! Teufel!"

33. Berg, 144: "Immer zu, immer zu!"

34. Benjamin B. Wolman, "Schizophrenia: an Overview," in Benjamin B. Wolman, ed. *International Encyclopedia of Psychiatry, Psychology, Psychoanalysis and Neurology* (New York: Aesculapius, 1977) X, 47.

35. Büchner (see n. 9), 80: "*Waldeg am Teich. (Es dunkelt).*"

36. Berg, (see n. 10), 195: "Wie ein blutig Eisen!"

37. Berg, 197: "Todt."

38. Büchner (see n. 9), 81: "Mörder! Mörder!"

39. Büchner, 81: "*Wirtshaus. (Bursche, Dirnen, Tanz).*"

40. Berg (see n. 10), 198: "*Eine Schenke. (Nacht, schwaches Licht). Burschen und Dirnen (unter ihnen Margret) tanzen eine wilde 'Schnellpolka'.*"

41. Berg, 215: "*Der Mond bricht blutrot hinter den Wolken hervor.*"

42. Büchner (see n. 9), 84: "Chirurg, Arzt, Richter."

43. Berg (see n. 10), 223: "Kommen Sie! Kommen Sie schnell."

44. Perle (see n. 8), 42.

45. Willi Reich, *Alban Berg. Mit Bergs eignen Schriften und Beiträgen von Theodor Wiesengrund-Adorno und Ernst Krenek.* (Vienna: Reichner, 1937), 68:

SZENE		MUSIK
I. AKT		
Wozzeck in seinen Beziehungen zur Umwelt		*Fünf Charakterstücke*
Wozzeck und der Hauptmann	*1. Szene*	Suite
Wozzeck und Andres	*2. Szene*	Rhapsodie
Marie und Wozzeck	*3. Szene*	Militärmarsch und Wiegenlied
Wozzeck und der Doktor	*4. Szene*	Passacaglia

Marie und der Tambourmajor	*5. Szene*	Andante affetuoso (quasi rondo)

II. AKT

Dramatische Entwicklung		*Symphonie in fünf Sätzen*
Marie und Kind, später Wozzeck	*1. Szene*	Sonatensatz
Hauptmann und Doktor, später Wozzeck	*2. Szene*	Phantasie and Fuge
Marie und Wozzeck	*3. Szene*	Largo
Wirtshausgarten	*4. Szene*	Scherzo
Wachstube in der Kaserne	*5. Szene*	Rondo con Introduzione

III. AKT

Katastrophe und Epilog		*Sechs Inventionen*
Marie und dem Kind	*1. Szene*	Invention über ein Thema
Marie und Wozzeck	*2. Szene*	Invention über einen Ton
Schenke	*3. Szene*	Invention über einen Rhythmus
Wozzecks Tod	*4. Szene*	Invention über einen Sechsklang
	Orchesterzwischenspiel	
Spielende Kinder	*5. Szene*	Invention über eine gleichmäßige Achtelbewegung

46. Berg (see n. 7), 287: "Mag einem noch so viel davon bekannt sein, was sich im Rahmen dieser Oper an musikalischen Formen findet, wie das alles streng und logisch 'gearbeitet' ist, welche Kunstfertigkeit selbst in allen Einzelheiten steckt . . . von dem Augenblick an, wo sich der Vorhang öffnet, bis zu dem, wo er sich zum letztenmal schließt, darf es im Publikum keinen geben, der etwas von diesen diversen Fugen und Inventionen, Suiten- und Sonatensätzen, Variationen und Passacaglien merkt,—keinen, der von etwas anderem erfüllt ist, als von der, weit über das Einzelschicksal Wozzecks hinausgehenden *Idee* dieser Oper. Und das—glaube ich—ist mir gelungen!"

47. Jarman (see n. 5), 69–70.

48. Adorno (see n. 2), 18: "Nach der Berliner Uraufführung des *Wozzeck*, jenem Diner bei Töpfer, wo sie ihn feierten und er, jünglingshaft verlegen, kaum zu antworten vermochte, war ich bis tief in die Nacht mit ihm zusammen, um ihn

buchstäblich über den Erfolg zu trösten. Das ein Werk, selbst konzipiert wie Wozzecks Gesichte auf dem Feld; eines, das vor Bergs eigenem Maßstab bestand, einem offiziellen Publikum gefallen sollte, war ihm unverständlich und dünkte ihn ein Argument gegen die Oper."

49. Reich (see n. 45), 169: "... einer Realität des Darzustellenden festhält, die ein sofortiges und eindeutiges Erkennen und Überblicken des jeweiligen Schauplatzes sichert."

50. Reich, 169–70: "... wo der Mond das eine Mal—etwa am Horizont aufzugehen hat (III./2), das andere Mal (III./4)—schon höher oben—wieder aus den Wolken hervorbrechen muß."

51. Reich, 170: "... bei Takt 275 leise zu bewegen beginnt, welche leise Wellenbewegung bei 285/286 ihren Höhepunkt erreicht, um wieder langsam abzuflauen: bei Takt 302 wieder völliger Stillstand!"

52. Reich, 170: "... kann wirklich immateriell, ja spukhaft wirken; es genügt also die geringste Andeutung des Schauplatzes."

53. Reich, 170: "... wo infolge des Umbaues das Orchester oft nicht zu hören ist und ein Kontakt zwischen Vorhang und Musik, wie er verlangt wird, kaum zu erzielen ist."

54. Reich, 170: "... daß der heimkehrende Tambourmajor ein Licht mit hereinbringt und es irgendwohin stellt. Wenn er bei (800) wieder damit verschwindet, wird für den Rest der Szene die anfängliche Dunkelheit und Stimmung wieder hergestellt."

55. Berg (see n. 10), 180: "Einer nach dem Andern."

56. Reich (see n. 45), 171–2: "... dieser Dialog hat von beiden—die sich während der ganzen Zeit auch mehr abseits zu halten haben—quasi gedämpft geführt zu werden. Denn hier ist die Musik und das Szenenbild die Hauptsache!"

57. Hans F. Redlich, *Alban Berg: Versuch einer Würdigung* (Vienna: Universal, 1957), 318: "Diese Quinten: Klavierauszug I. Akte, Seite 48, Takt 425–426 sind ... der Figur Marie eigentümlich. (Ich möchte sagen: dieser harmonische Ruhepunkt schildert das ins Unbestimmte hinzielende Warten, welches erst in ihrem Tod den Abschluß findet.)"

58. Douglas Jarman, *Alban Berg: "Lulu"* (Cambridge: Cambridge University Press, 1991), 1.

59. Jarman, 1–2.

60. Karl Kraus, *Ausgewählte Werke, Band I, 1902–1914: "Grimassen"* (Munich: Langen Müller, 1971), 60: "Ich sehe in der Gestaltung der Frau, die die Männer zu 'haben' glauben, während sie von ihr gehabt werden, der Frau, die Jedem eine andere ist, Jedem ein anderes Gesicht zuwendet ... Ich sehe darin eine vollendete Ehrenrettung der Unmoral. In der Zeichnung des Vollweibes mit der genialen Fähigkeit, sich nicht erinnern zu können, der Frau, die ohne Hemmung, aber auch ohne die Gefahren fortwährender seelischer Konzeption lebt und jedes Erlebnis im Vergessen wegspült. Begehrende, nicht Gebärende ... eine

169

Nachtwandlerin der Liebe, die erst 'fällt', wenn sie angerufen wird, ewige Geberin, ewige Verliererin—von der ein philosophischer Strolch im Drama sagt: 'Die kann von der Liebe nicht leben, weil ihr Leben die Liebe ist.' Daß der Freudenquell in dieser engen Welt zur Pandorabüchse werden muß: diesem unendlichen Bedauern scheint mir die Dichtung zu entstammen."

61. Jarman (see n. 58), 20.

62. *The Berg-Schoenberg Correspondence: Selected Letters.* Eds., Juliane Brand, Christopher Hailey and Donald Harris (New York: Norton, 1987), 405.

63. *Correspondence*, 405.

64. Jarman (see n. 58), 56.

65. Alban Berg, *Lulu*, opera in three acts after the tragedies *Erdgeist* and *Büchse der Pandora* by Frank Wedekind, piano reduction, Erwin Stein. Orchestration of Act III completed by Friedrich Cerha. (Vienna: Universal, 1978), 12–13:

Tierbändiger.
Sie ward geschaffen, Unheil anzustiften,
zu locken, zu verführen, zu vergiften—
Und zu morden, ohne daß es einer spürt.

66. Berg, 469–71:

Alwa (*plötzlich neu belebt*).
Warum nicht gar? Diesem Bild gegenüber gewinn' ich meine Selbstachtung wieder. Es macht mir mein Verhängnis begreiflich. (*Etwas elegisch*). Wer sich vor diesen blühenden, schwellenden Lippen, vor diesen großen, unschuldsvollen Kinderaugen, vor diesem rosigweißen, strotzenden Körper in seiner bürgerlichen Stellung sicher fühlt, der werfe den ersten Stein auf uns.

67. Berg, 57: "Verwünscht! Es läutet!"

68. Berg, 57: "Bleib! Es ist ja niemand zuhaus!"

69. Berg, 58: "Vielleicht ist es aber der Kunsthändler. . . . "

70. Berg, 58: "Und wenn es der Kaiser von China wär'?"

71. Berg, 58: "Einen Moment."

72. Frank Wedekind, *Stücke* (Munich: Langen-Müller, 1970), 89: " . . . *visionär—Du?—du?—schließt die Augen.*"

73. Berg (see n. 65), 58: " . . . *allein, in einem verzückt träumenden Zustand* . . . "

74. Berg, 59: " . . . *visionär—Du . . . Du . . . schließt die Augen.*"

75. Berg, 60: " . . . *wie zu sich kommend, mit deutlichen Anzeichen der Entspannung.*"

76. Berg, 159: " . . . *mit Nachdruck* 'Sehr geehrtes Fräulein . . . ' "
77. Berg, 159: " . . . *schreibt*: 'Sehr geehrtes Fräulein . . . ' "
78. Berg, 231–7:

Lulu (*in entschiedenem, selbstbewußtem Ton*).
Wenn sich die Menschen um meinetwillen umgebracht haben, so setzt das meinen Wert nicht herab. Du hast so gut gewußt, weswegen du mich zur Frau nahmst, wie ich gewußt habe, weswegen ich dich zum Mann nahm. Du hattest deine besten Freunde mit mir betrogen, du konntest nicht gut auch noch dich selber mit mir betrügen. Wenn du mir deinen Lebensabend zum Opfer bringst, so hast du meine ganze Jugend dafür gehabt. Ich habe nie in der Welt etwas anderes scheinen wollen, als wofür man mich genommen hat; und man hat mich nie in der Welt für etwas anderes genommen, als was ich bin.

79. Alban Berg, *Lulu*, English/German Libretto. English trans. Arthur Jacobs (Vienna: Universal, 1936, 1977), 64:

Zu der nun folgenden Verwandlungsmusik werden in einem Stummen Film die Schicksale Lulus in den nächsten Jahren andeutungsweise gezeigt, wobei das filmische Geschehen, entsprechend dem symmetrischen Verlauf der Musik auch quasi symmetrisch (also vorwärtsgehend und rückläufig) zu verteilen ist, zu welchem Zweck die einander entsprechenden Geschehnisse und Begleiterscheinungen möglichst gegeneinander anzupassen sind. Dies ergibt dann folgende Bilderreihe (in Richtung der Pfeile):

Verhaftung	Am Weg zur endgültigen Befreiung
Die drei bei der Verhaftung Beteiligten	*Die drei an der Befreiung Beteiligten*
Lulu in Ketten	*Lulu auf freiem Fuß (als Gräfin Geschwitz verkleidet)*
Untersuchungshaft	**In der Isolierbaracke**
In nervöser Erwartung	In nervöser Erwartung
Schwindende Hoffnung	Steigende Hoffnung
Prozeß	**Konsilium**
Die Schuld	*Die Krankheit*
Richter und Geschworene	*Ärzte und Studenten*
Die drei Zeugen der Tat	*Die drei Helfer für die Befreiungsak-*
Verurteilung	*tion*
Überführung mit dem Gefangenenauto	*Überführung mittels Kranken-*
zum . . .	*transport aus dem . . .*
Kerker	**Kerker**
Die Kerkertür schließt sich	*Die Kerkertür geht auf*
Anfängliche Resignation	*Erwachender Lebensmut*
Lulus Bild: als Schatten an der Kerkermauer	*Lulus Bild: als Spiegelbild in einer Schaufel*

⟶ **Ein Jahr Haft** ⟶

80. Donald Mitchell, "The Character of Lulu: Wedekind's and Berg's conceptions compared," *The Music Review* 15 (1954), 272.

81. Mitchell, 272–3.

82. Mitchell, 274.

83. George Perle, "The Character of Lulu: a Sequel," *The Music Review* 25 (1964), 318.

84. Perle, 319.

85. Berg (see n. 65), 317:

Lulu (*beiläufig*).

Ist das noch der Diwan, auf dem sich dein Vater verblutet hat?

86. Berg, 320: "Ein geräumiger Salon in weißer Strukkatur."

87. Berg (see n. 79), vii: "In ihrem neuen und luxuriösen (Pariser) Domizil, empfangen Lulu und Alwa Gäste."

88. Berg (see n. 65), 347–9:

Lulu (*anfangs mit verhaltener Leidenschaft*).

Ich gehe mit dir nach Amerika, nach China. Aber ich kann nicht das Einzige verkaufen, was je mein Eigen war.

89. Wedekind (see n. 72), 221:

Schigolch.

Sakerment, Sakerment, Sakerment!

Alwa (*wirft sich wimmernd auf seine Chaiselongue*).

Ich glaube, ich habe vom Diesseits nicht mehr viel Gutes zu erwarten.

Schigolch.

Man hätte das Frauenzimmer an der Kehle zurückhalten müssen. Sie vertreibt alles, was Odem hat, mit ihrem aristokratischen Totenschädel.

Alwa.

Sie hat mich aufs Krankenlager geworfen und mich von aussen und innen mit Dornen gespikt.

Schigolch.

Dafür hat sie allerdings auch genug Courage für zehn Mannsleute im Leib.

Alwa.

Keinen Verwundeten wird der Gnadenstoß jemals dankbarer finden als mich!

Schigolch.

Wenn sie mir damals nicht den Springfritzen in meine Wohnung gelockt hätte, dann hätten wir ihn heute noch auf dem Hals.

90. Berg (see n. 65), 485–6:

Schigolch (*Alwa zurückbringend*).

Was willst du denn deinen Weib verbieten, wo du dich selbst nicht ernähern kannst?

Alwa (*wirft sich auf die Chaiselongue, stöhnend*).

Wer anders als sie hat mich auf das Krankenlager geworfen?

Schigolch.

Sie? Ist sie denn krank?

Alwa.

Sie hat es mir von ihrem Marquis übermacht, sie selbst ist längst nicht mehr dafür erreichbar.

91. William H. Youngren, "Berg's *Lulu*," *The Atlantic Monthly* 260–3 (1987), 95.

CHAPTER FIVE
Toward a Definition of Opera

Ever since the emergence of the art of the opera in early seventeenth-century Italy, the question has been debated, "Is opera a form of music or is it a form of dramatic poetry?"

There is not doubt that the earliest librettists and opera composers were strongly influenced by Greek tragedy and were, in fact, acquainted with Aristotle's definition of tragedy. They described their works for the theater by such terms as *favola in musica, favola pastorale* or *dramma per musica* ("drama by means of music"). Plato and Aristotle advanced the opinion that music is an imitation of feeling and that dramatic poetry is an imitation of human action. If opera were only an imitation of feeling, it is difficult to understand why opera composers write so much music that describes action on the stage and delineates character. In fact, the opera composers themselves, without exception, thought of their creations as works for the theater, to be performed by singers, actors and dancers before an audience gathered to witness a special kind of dramatic poem whose principal means of expression is vocal and instrumental music.

Experience in the opera house tends to confirm this view. The first thing we hear is usually an overture, a musical description of things to come. Then the curtain rises and theatrical characters appear, speaking or singing their lines. A plot begins to emerge, we become empathically involved with the characters as they struggle with one another and, at the end, when the plot is resolved, a theme, or universal idea, lodges in our consciousness, the result of a catharsis of our aroused emotion into meaning.

Thus, the fundamental element of the pleasure we take in the performance of an opera appears to be our empathic response to the comic or tragic turmoil experienced by a character on the stage. Empathy may be defined as the sympathy we feel for an unreal person in a real situation. When we empathize with Canio, for instance, as he sings "Vesti la giubba", when we respond emotionally to the anguish of a man who has certain knowledge of his wife's infidelity, yet must put on costume and makeup to perform in a

174

comedy before an audience in which his rival very likely will be present, our feeling of sympathy is as gripping as it would be in real life for a close friend in the same situation.

Pleasure begins, then, with an empathic response to a character in a particular situation or crisis and is then vastly increased by the music that expresses the situation or crisis. Both the musical beauty of Canio's great aria and the thrilling sound of the dramatic tenor voice combine to raise the level of empathic response far beyond what can be achieved by a superior performance of a great role in a spoken drama. So intense is this response that audiences everywhere applaud and cheer a tenor who can sing this aria at the artistic level established in the past by such artists as Enrico Caruso, Giovanni Martinelli, Beniamino Gigli and others.

Early operas were modelled on Greek dramatic poetry, which imitated a series of actions by three means of expression: words, music and rhythmic movement. Today, instead of one unified form, however, we are accustomed to three fairly distinct forms of dramatic poetry: spoken drama (plays, in either verse or prose), sung drama (operas, operettas and scenic cantatas) and danced drama (story ballets).

But if opera is a form of dramatic poetry is it not, therefore, a form of literature? The answer to this persistent question seems to be that it is not. As Susanne Langer has observed, the basic abstraction of literature is the word, while the basic abstraction of dramatic poetry is the act.[1] The veracity of this thesis can be illustrated by a simple hypothesis: if a person who is totally illiterate is given a copy of a play by Shakespeare, he will be unable to read it. But if he is taken to a production of the play, he will be able to enjoy it as much as anyone else in the audience if he possesses histrionic imagination.

Where, then, does dramatic poetry fit in the larger scheme of art? The classical theory of imitation, as expounded by Plato and Aristotle, argues that there are three forms of art based on the three possible objects of imitation: nature, feeling and action. The imitation of nature embodies the art of painting and sculpture, imitation of feeling that of music and the imitation of action falls into two categories, dramatic poetry (plays) and literary poetry (the epic, the narrative and the lyric). Both categories of poetry achieve the same effect as do the other forms of art: the arousal of emotion in the spectator or reader, and the catharsis of such emotion into meaning.

Aristotle's *Poetics* is an effort to analyze dramatic poetry within the

175

general framework of imitation, and very little has been added to his analysis except for various efforts to clarify his terms. For instance, he says he is defining tragedy and that he will provide us with a treatise on comedy later. But as he worked on his study of tragedy, he must have discovered that there is really very little difference between comedy and tragedy. One can test this view by attending successive performances of *Die Meistersinger* and *Tristan und Isolde*. The only differences lie in the nature of the emotions aroused through empathic responses to the situations of the principal characters. Aristotle thought that tragedy arouses emotions of pity and fear. Comedy probably arouses emotions of laughter and charm. But is accurate identification of these emotions important? Aristotle's own catharsis theory suggests not. It is the catharsis of emotion into meaning that matters, not the nature of the emotion itself. In view of this, it is plain why he never wrote a commentary on comedy—it wasn't worth the trouble. He had said all he had to say on the subject. If one simply shortens his phrase, "arousal of the emotions of pity and fear" to "arousal of emotion"[*] it can be seen that his treatise describes not only tragedy but all the other forms of dramatic poetry as well.

Aristotle's analysis of dramatic poetry is built around three fairly distinct concepts: imitation, probability and catharsis. Although he does not define imitation in his treatise, enough was written about it in Greek literature so that a definition can be reconstructed, as has been done by Richard McKeon: "Imitation is the presentation of an aspect of things in a matter other than its natural matter, rendered inevitable by reasons other than its natural reasons."[2] The key idea here is that of inevitability. A work of art is—as it *is*. It can't be changed. It can't be improved. If left unfinished at the time of the artist's death, it can't be completed by someone else. Who could compose the third and fourth movements of Schubert's "Unfinished Symphony"?

In art, inevitability is the product of the laws of art that are established by the creative imaginations of the great artists; the inevitability of a tree is determined by the laws of nature. A painting of a tree by a great artist is, thus, the presentation of an aspect of the tree by means of paint on canvas (in place of wood and leaves), which is rendered inevitable by the artist (rather than by nature.) Likewise, music is the presentation of an aspect of human feeling and poetry is the presentation of an aspect of action. And

---

* The emotion being that of empathy with the feelings of the characters on the stage.

176

inevitability is achieved in both art forms by the composer or poet, not by nature.[3]

Thus, Aristotle defines dramatic poetry as an imitation of a series of related actions, expressed by means of words, music and rhythmic movement. The "series of related actions" is described in the *Poetics* as the plot, and plot construction is thoroughly explored. The plot should have a beginning, middle and end. The episodes of the plot must be probable and the linkage between them must seem necessary. The problem of the dramatic poet, Aristotle tells us, is to make the improbable probable. A central technique in this process is that of the *hamartia,* the hero's mistake in judgment, that leads to consequences of a magnitude vastly greater than that of the mistake itself. (The translation of *hamartia* as "tragic flaw", in which the hero's downfall is brought on by a flaw in his character, is no longer defended by classical scholarship.)

Dramatic poetry is filled with examples of mistakes in judgment that have disastrous consequences. Oedipus makes a mistake in judgment when he decides to leave Corinth after hearing the prediction of the oracle that he would murder his father and marry his mother. Why didn't he confront the king and queen of Corinth with this disturbing prophecy? Surely Polybus and Merope would have told him the truth—that they were not his parents. Shakespeare builds his plots on various mistakes in judgment. Othello puts too much trust in Iago, Lear should not have divided his kingdom, Hamlet should have killed Claudius while he was praying and Macbeth should have ignored the weird sisters. In opera, Tristan should not have agreed to go back to Ireland to bring Isolde to King Mark. Rigoletto places too much trust in Sparafucile, and Azucena should have told Manrico who he really was.

If the audience is able to accept the mistake in judgment, it suspends disbelief and becomes involved emotionally with the leading personages in their struggles. The audience's empathic response to the plight of unreal personages in real situations is what Aristotle meant by arousal of emotion, and he believed that if probability is absent, emotion will not be aroused. This seems to be borne out in practice. If the action is not convincing, we lose interest in the proceedings and empathy becomes impossible. His theory of probability is perhaps Aristotle's most inspired insight into the nature of dramatic poetry.

Finally, he describes the effect that dramatic poetry has on the spectator in the audience as "achieving a catharsis of the aroused emotion." A popular interpretation of this cryptic remark holds that the word was being used in its most elementary medical meaning: that is, a cathartic is employed to rid the bowels of impurities, so the effect of dramatic poetry is to purge the spectator of unwanted emotion. But how one can be purged of emotion by means of the emotion itself has never been made clear, and students of Aristotle have turned to a more plausible interpretation of the term.

In modern psychiatry, catharsis denotes the release of emotional tension by means of verbalizing or intellectualizing the emotion during interview therapy. In Aristotle's time, intellectual concepts, philosophic speculation and deductive reasoning were thought to be closely related to feeling, emotion and intuition. It is, therefore, not out of the question that what he was saying was that the arousal of emotion in the spectator is followed by a catharsis of the emotion into meaning, understanding or knowledge. This is a special kind of knowledge, however, not the kind acquired by reading books, attending lectures or observing life. It is intuitive, *a priori* knowledge, knowledge that is prior to thought. As such, as Wittgenstein has observed, it cannot be conveyed to others by means of language. It remains locked up within us, a portion of the total storehouse of knowledge that we possess at any given moment of our lives.

This process, in which the audience senses meaning in a work of dramatic art, is the exact reverse of the way in which the dramatic poet instills meaning into a play or an opera. In his *Critique of Judgment,* Immanuel Kant ranks poetry first among the arts because poetry "raises itself aesthetically to ideas."[4] That is, "the poet renders sensuous thematic ideas about the realms of the invisible, the blessed, hell, eternity, creation, etc., as well as manifestations of experience such as death, envy and all the sins, love, fame and the like."[5] In doing so, the poet unites the worlds of thought and feeling into a single artistic statement.

How does the dramatic poet render a thematic idea sensuous? Usually, he begins with a situation involving two or three characters, a situation that provides opportunity for speculation on such ideas as, for example, jealousy (Leoncavallo's *Pagliacci*), erotic and spiritual love (Wagner's *Tristan und Isolde*) or tradition in art (Pfitzner's *Palestrina*). He then elaborates the situation into a plot structure capable of exploring the fundamental thematic idea and providing for the development of character.

Aristotle thought that character is revealed by choice, especially moral choice. For example, Macbeth's character is revealed to us by his decision to murder King Duncan while the latter is asleep in a room in Macbeth's own castle, a place where he especially owes protection to his sovereign. So the plot must allow for moral choices as well as choices of taste, jokes, clothing, food, drink and all the other kinds of activity that tell us what kind of a human being a particular person really is. If the plot makes possible the appearance on the stage of believable, well developed characters, then the audience will respond emotionally to their trials, triumphs and defeats. And if the ending of the plot makes clear the resolution of the thematic idea that underlies the dramatic poem, the audience will experience—in a mirror image of the poet's achievement of rendering the idea sensuous—an enlargement of its understanding of the idea by means of a catharsis of emotion into meaning.

The principal value of Aristotle's catharsis theory is that it enables us to separate art from entertainment. In the theater, a good performance of *My Fair Lady* is not so very different from one of *The Magic Flute*. We empathize with Eliza and Higgins just as we do with Pamina and Tamino, and the thematic idea of both plots has to do with the thirst for knowledge. But emotions aroused by the musical play die out as soon as we leave the theater, while those aroused by the opera transmute themselves into a special, incommunicable kind of knowledge about the universal human desire to know. For this reason, dramatic poetry may be regarded as an instrument of education, while entertainment in the form of dramatic poetry arouses emotion merely for its own sake.

From the foregoing, the following definition emerges:

Opera is an imitation of a series of related actions, expressed by means of music, words and rhythmic movement, acted not narrated, arousing emotion in the spectator and achieving a catharsis of such emotion into meaning.

Through statements they have made in letters, memoirs, aesthetical essays and in their creations for the lyric theater, all the opera composers who have been considered here have displayed a conviction that opera is, indeed, a form of dramatic poetry, that catharsis is achieved through audience involvement with plot and character as expressed by music, words and rhythmic movement. Although text and music need not be the product of a single creative imagination, the tendency of the times is in this direction.

Notes

1. Susanne K. Langer, *Feeling and Form, A Theory of Art* (New York: Scribner's, 1953), 306.

2. Richard McKeon, "Literary Criticism and the Concept of Imitation in Antiquity", *Modern Philology* 34 (1936), 19.

3. Sometimes, the difference between an imitation and a copy is not readily apparent. For instance, film is often described as a form of art but, since it is a copy of an imitation and not the imitation itself, it is no more art than is a print of a painting. Both film and print lack inevitability.

4. Immanuel Kant, *Kritik der Urteilskraft* in *Werke,* ed. Ernst Cassirer (Berlin: Bruno Cassirer, 1922), V, 402: "Unter allen behauptet die Dichtkunst . . . den obersten Rang . . . und sich also ästhetisch zu Ideen erhebt."

5. Kant, 390: "Der Dichter wagt es, Vernunftideen von unsichtbaren Wesen, das Reich der Seligen, das Höllenreich, die Ewigkeit, die Schöpfung u.d.gl. zu versinnlichen, oder auch das, was zwar Beispiele in der Erfahrung findet, z.B. den Tod, den Neid und alle Laster, imgleichen die Liebe, den Ruhm u.d.gl."

Bibliography

Adorno, Theodor W. *Berg: Der Meister des kleinsten Übergangs*. Vienna: Elizabeth Lafite, 1968.

Alban Berg: Letters to his Wife. Ed. and trans. Bernard Grun. London: Faber & Faber, 1971.

Aristotle. *Poetics*. Ed. and trans. Allan H. Gilbert in *Literary Criticism: Plato to Dryden*. New York: American, 1940.

Armitage, Merle. *Schoenberg*. New York: Schirmer, 1937.

Arnold Schoenberg, in höchster Verehrung von Schülern und Freunden. Munich: Piper, 1912.

Auden, W. H. *The Dyer's Hand and Other Essays*. London: Faber & Faber, 1963.

Babbitt, Milton. "Three Essays on Schoenberg." Ed. Benjamin Boretz and Edward T. Cone in *Perspectives on Schoenberg and Stravinsky*. Princeton: Princeton University Press, 1968, 47–60.

Beaumont, Antony. "Busoni and Schoenberg." *The Piano Quarterly* 28 (1979–80), 32–8.

_____. "Busoni and the Theater." *Opera* 37 (1986), 384-91.

_____. *Busoni the Composer*. London: Faber & Faber, 1985.

_____. *Doktor Faust*. Additions to the 2nd and last scenes. Wiesbaden: Breitkopf & Härtel, 1984.

Beecham, Sir Thomas. *Frederick Delius*. New York: Knopf, 1960.

Berg, Alban. "Das 'Opernproblem'." *Neue Musik-Zeitung* 49 (1928), 285-7.

_____. "Die Musikalische Formen in meiner Oper *Wozzeck*." *Die Musik* 16 (1924), 587-9.

_____. *Lulu*. Opera in three acts after the tragedies *Erdgeist* and *Büchse der Pandora* by Frank Wedekind. Text, Alban Berg, piano reduction, Erwin Stein. Orchestration of Act III completed by Friedrich Cerha. Vienna: Universal, 1978.

_____. *Wozzeck*. Opera in three acts (fifteen scenes). Text, Alban Berg, piano reduction, Fritz Heinrich Klein. Vienna: Universal, 1931.

Brand, Juliane, Christopher Hailey and Donald Harris, eds. *The Berg-Schoenberg Correspondence: Selected Letters*. New York: Norton, 1987.

Brecht, Bertolt. "Two Essays." *The Score* 23 (1958), 14–26.

Buchanan, Herbert. "A Key to Schoenberg's *Erwartung*." *Journal of the American Musicological Society* 20 (1967), 434–49.

Büchner, Georg. *Gesammelte Schriften*. Ed. Paul Landau. 2 vols. Berlin: Paul Cassirer, 1909.

Burney, Charles. *An Eighteenth-Century Musical Tour in Central Europe and the Netherlands*. Ed. Percy A. Scholes. London: Oxford University Press, 1959.

Busoni, Ferruccio. *Arlecchino*. Theatrical caprice in one act. Text, Ferruccio Busoni. English trans. Edward J. Dent. Piano reduction, Philipp Jarnach. Wiesbaden: Breitkopf & Härtel, 1968.

_____. *Die Brautwahl*. Fantastic musical comedy after E. T. A. Hoffmann. Text, Ferruccio Busoni. Piano reduction, Egon Petri. Berlin: Harmonie, 1912.

_____. *Doktor Faust*. Poem for music. Text, Ferruccio Busoni. Ed. and completed by Philipp Jarnach. Piano reduction, Egon Petri and Michael von Zadora. Leipzig: Breitkopf & Härtel, 1926.

_____. *Entwurf einer neuen Aesthetik der Tonkunst*. Trieste: C. Schmidl, 1907. Second, enlarged edn. Leipzig: Insel Bücherei Nr. 202, 1916.

_____. *Ferruccio Busoni: Selected Letters*. Ed., trans. and foreword, Antony Beaumont. New York: Columbia University Press, 1987.

_____. *Turandot*. Chinese fable after Gozzi in two acts. Text, Ferruccio Busoni. Piano reduction, Philipp Jarnach. Leipzig: Breitkopf & Härtel, 1918.

_____. *Über die Möglichkeiten der Oper und über die Partitur des "Doktor Faust"*. Leipzig: Breitkopf & Härtel, 1926.

_____. *Von der Einheit der Musik, verstreute Aufzeichnungen*. Berlin: Hesse, 1922.

_____. *Wesen und Einheit der Musik*. Berlin: Hesse, 1956.

Carley, Lionel. *Delius: A Life in Letters, 1862–1908*. London: Scolar, 1983.

_____ and Robert Threlfall. *Delius, a Life in Pictures*. London: Oxford University Press, 1977.

Carner, Mosco. *Alban Berg: The Man and the Work*. London: Duckworth, 1975.

Conrad, Peter. *Romantic Opera and Literary Form*. Berkeley: University of California Press, 1977.

Cooke, Deryck. "Delius's Operatic Masterpiece." *Opera* 13 (1962), 226–32.

_____. "Schoenberg's Representation of the Divine in *Moses und Aron*." *Journal of the Arnold Schoenberg Institute* 9 (1986), 210–16.

Crawford, John. "*Die glückliche Hand*: Schoenberg's *Gesamtkunstwerk*." *The Musical Quarterly* 60 (1974), 583–601.

Delius, Frederick. *Romeo und Julia auf dem Dorfe*. Lyric drama in six scenes after Gottfried Keller. Text, Frederick Delius. Piano reduction, Otto Lindemann. Vienna: Universal, 1910.

Dent, Edward J. "Busoni and his Operas." *Opera* 5 (1954), 391–7.

_____. "Busoni's *Doktor Faust*." *Music and Letters* 7 (1926), 196–208.

_____. *Ferruccio Busoni: A Biography*. 2nd ed. London: Oxford University Press, 1984.

_____. "The Return of Busoni." *The Athenaeum*. (December 17, 1920), 844–5.

Donnington, Robert. *The Opera*. New York: Harcourt, Brace, Jovanovich, 1978.

_____. *Wagner's "Ring" and Its Symbols*. 3rd edn. London: Faber & Faber, 1974.

Drew, David. "Brecht versus Opera." *The Score* 23 (1958), 7–10.

Drummond, John D. *Opera in Perspective*. Minneapolis: University of Minnesota Press, 1980.

Friedell, Egon. *A Cultural History of the Modern Age*. Trans. Charles Francis Atkinson. 3 vols. New York: Knopf, 1954.

Garlington, Aubrey S., Jr. "E. T. A. Hoffmann's 'Der Dichter und der Komponist' and the Creation of the German Romantic Opera." *The Musical Quarterly* 65 (1979), 22–47.

Gatti, Guido M. "The Stage Works of Ferruccio Busoni." *The Musical Quarterly* 20 (1934), 267–77.

Geissler, H. W. *Gestaltungen des Faust. Die bedeutendsten Werke der Faustdichtung seit 1587*. 3 vols. Munich: Parcus, 1927.

Goethes Faust. Kommentiert von Erich Trunz. Hamburg: Wegner, 1963.

Goldman, Albert and Evert Sprinchorn, eds. *Wagner on Music and Drama*. New York: Dutton, 1964.

Gradenwitz, Peter. "The Religious Works of Arnold Schoenberg." *The Music Review* 21 (1960), 19–29.

Grout, Donald Jay, with Hermine Weigel Williams. *A Short History of Opera*. 3rd edn. New York: Columbia University Press, 1988.

Haggin, B. H. "The Transformation of Literature in Opera." *The Sewanee Review* 86 (1978), 428–34.

Henderson, Robert. "Schoenberg and 'Expressionism'." *The Music Review* 19 (1958), 125–9.

Hill, Richard S. "Schoenberg's Tone Rows and the Tonal System of the Future." *The Musical Quarterly* 22 (1936), 14–37.

Hutchings, Arthur. *Delius*. London: Macmillan, 1969.

Janik, Allan and Stephen Toulmin. *Wittgenstein's Vienna*. New York: Simon & Schuster, 1973.

Jarman, Douglas. *Alban Berg: "Lulu."* Cambridge: Cambridge University Press, 1991.

_____. *Alban Berg: "Wozzeck."* Cambridge: Cambridge University Press, 1989.

_____. ed. *The Berg Companion*. London: Macmillan, 1989.

_____. *The Music of Alban Berg*. Berkeley: University of California Press, 1979.

Jefferson, Alan. *Delius*. London: Dent, 1972.

Kant, Immanuel. *Werke*. Ed. Ernst Cassirer. 11 vols. Berlin: Bruno Cassirer, 1922–3.

Keller, Gottfried. *Sämtliche Werke*. Ed. Jonas Fränkel. 8 vols. Zurich: Rentsch, 1926–38.

Keller, Hans. "Moses, Freud and Schoenberg." *Monthly Musical Review* 88 (1958), 12, 63.

_____. "Schoenberg and the First Sacred Opera." *Essays on Music: An Anthology from 'The Listener.'* Ed. F. Aprahamian. London: Cassell, 1967, 213–7.

_____. "Schoenberg's Comic Opera [*Von Heute auf Morgen*]." *The Score* 23 (1958), 27–36.

_____. "Schoenberg's *Moses und Aron.*" *The Score* 21 (1957), 30–45.

_____. "The Eclecticism of *Wozzeck.*" *The Music Review* 12 (1951), 309–15.

Kelly, James William. "The Faust Legend in Music." *Detroit Reprints in Music* (1976), 112–21.

Kerman, Joseph. *Opera as Drama.* New and rev. edn. London: Faber & Faber, 1989.

_____. "Terror and Self-Pity: Alban Berg's *Wozzeck.*" *The Hudson Review* 5 (1952–3), 408–19.

_____. "Wagner: Thoughts in Season." *The Hudson Review* 13 (1960), 329–49.

Klein, John W. "Delius as a Musical Dramatist." *The Music Review* 22 (1961), 294–301.

_____. "*Wozzeck*—a Summing-up." *Music and Letters* 44 (1963), 132–39.

Kraus, Karl. *Ausgewählte Werke.* Ed. Dietrich Simon. 3 vols. Munich: Langen Müller, 1971.

Krenek, Ernst. "Busoni—Then and Now." *Modern Music* 19 (1942), 88–91.

Langer, Susanne K. *Feeling and Form: A Theory of Art.* New York: Scribner's, 1953.

Leibowitz, René. *Schoenberg and his School.* Trans. Dika Newlin. New York: Da Capo, 1975.

Leichtentritt, Hugo. "Ferruccio Busoni." *The Music Review* 6 (1945), 206–19.

Lessem, Alan Philip. "Schoenberg, Stravinsky and Neo-Classicism: The Issues Reexamined." *The Musical Quarterly* 68 (1982), 527–42.

Lewin, David. "*Moses und Aron*: Some General Remarks and Analytic Notes for Act I, scene 1." Ed. Benjamin Boretz and Edward T. Cone in *Perspectives on Schoenberg and Stravinsky.* Princeton: Princeton University Press, 1968, 61–77.

Lindenberger, Herbert. *Opera, the Extravagant Art.* Ithaca: Cornell University Press, 1984.

MacDonald, Malcolm. *Schoenberg.* London: Dent, 1976.

McKeon, Richard. "Literary Criticism and the Concept of Imitation in Antiquity." *Modern Philology* 34 (1936), 1–35.

Medieval Legends No. 1: Dr. Johannes Faustus. Puppet Play. London: David Nutt in the Strand, 1893.

Mellers, W. H. "The Problem of Busoni." *Music and Letters* 18 (1937), 240–7.

Mitchell, Donald. "The Character of Lulu: Wedekind's and Berg's Conceptions Compared." *The Music Review* 15 (1954), 268–74.

Monson, Karen. *Alban Berg.* Boston: Houghton Mifflin, 1979.

Mordden, Ethan. *Opera in the Twentieth Century: Sacred, Profane, Godot.* New York: Oxford University Press, 1978.

Neighbour, Oliver. "Moses." *The Musical Times* 106 (1965), 422–5.

Neumann, Karl. "Wedekind's and Berg's *Lulu*." *The Musical Review* 35 (1974), 47–57.

Newlin, Dika. *Schoenberg Remembered: Diaries and Recollections.* New York: Pendagron, 1980.

_____. "The Role of the Chorus in *Moses und Aron*." *American Choral Review* 9 (1966), 1–4, 18.

_____. "Why is Schoenberg's Biography so Difficult to Write?" *Perspectives of New Music* 12 (1973–4), 40–2.

Palmer, Christopher. *Delius: Portrait of a Cosmopolitan.* London: Duckworth, 1976.

Palmer, Philip Mason and Robert Pattison More. *The Scources of the Faust Tradition from Simon Magus to Lessing.* New York: Oxford University Press, 1936.

Perle, George. *Serial Composition and Atonality: An Introduction to the Music of Schoenberg, Berg and Webern.* 4th ed. Berkeley: University of California Press, 1977.

_____. "The Character of Lulu: a Sequel." *The Music Review* 25 (1964), 311–19.

_____. *The Operas of Alban Berg: "Lulu."* Berkeley: University of California Press, 1985.

_____. *The Operas of Alban Berg: "Wozzeck."* Berkeley: University of California Press, 1980.

_____. "*Woyzeck* and *Wozzeck*." *The Musical Quarterly* 53 (1967), 206–19.

Pirrotta, Nino. "*Commedia dell' arte* and Opera." *The Musical Quarterly* 41 (1955), 305–24.

Pisk, Paul A. "Schoenberg's Twelve-Tone Opera." *Modern Music* 7 (1930), 18–21.

Porter, Andrew. "*Stiffelio*—an Introduction." *Opera* 44 (1993), 15–19.

Proctor-Gregg, Humphrey. "Busoni, Pianist and Composer." *The Sackbut* (July, 1920), 101–4.

Radice, Mark A. "The Anatomy of a Libretto: The Music Inherent in Büchner's *Woyzeck*." *The Music Review* 41 (1980), 223–33.

Redlich, Hans F. *Alban Berg: Versuch einer Würdigung.* Vienna: Universal, 1957.

_____. "Schoenberg's Religious Testament." *Opera* 16 (1965), 401–7.

Redwood, Christopher. *A Delius Companion.* London: Calder, 1976.

Reich, Willi. "A Guide to *Wozzeck*." *The Musical Quarterly* 38 (1952), 1–21.

_____. *Alban Berg. Mit Bergs eignen Schriften und Beiträgen von Theodor Wiesengrund-Adorno und Ernst Krenek.* Vienna: Reichner, 1937.

_____. *Schoenberg: A Critical Biograpy.* Trans. Leo Black. London: Longman, 1971.

Ringer, Alexander. "Arnold Schoenberg and the Politics of Jewish Survival." *Journal of the Arnold Schoenberg Institute* 3 (1979), 11–48.

_____. "Arnold Schoenberg and the Prophetic Image in Music." *Journal of the Arnold Schoenberg Institute* 1 (1976), 26–38.

_____. *Arnold Schoenberg: The Composer as Jew.* Oxford: Clarendon Press, 1990.

_____. "Faith and Symbol: On Arnold Schoenberg's Last Musical Utterance." *Journal of the Arnold Schoenberg Institute* 6 (1982), 80–95.

_____. "Schoenbergiana in Jerusalem." *The Musical Quarterly* 59 (1973), 1–14.

_____. "Schoenberg, Weill and Epic Theater." *Journal of the Arnold Schoenberg Institute* 4 (1980), 77–98.

Rubsamen, Walter H. "Schoenberg in America." *The Musical Quarterly* 37 (1951), 469–89.

Rufer, Josef. *Composition with Twelve Notes Related Only One to Another.* Trans. Humphrey Searle. London: Rockliff, 1954.

_____. "Schoenberg—Yesterday, Today and Tomorrow." *Perspectives of New Music* 16 (1977), 125–38.

_____. *The Works of Arnold Schoenberg: A Catalogue of His Compositions, Writings and Paintings.* Trans. Dika Newlin. London: Faber & Faber, 1962.

Schmalfeldt, Janet. *Berg's "Wozzeck": Harmonic Language and Dramatic Design.* New Haven: Yale University Press, 1983.

Schmidgall, Gary. *Literature as Opera.* New York: Oxford University Press, 1977.

Schoenberg, Arnold. *Briefe.* Sel. and ed. Erwin Stein. Mainz: Schotts, 1958.

_____. *Die glückliche Hand.* Drama with music. Text, Arnold Schoenberg. Piano reduction, four hands, Eduard Steuermann. Vienna: Universal, 1923.

_____. *Erwartung.* Monodrama. Text, Marie Pappenheim. Piano reduction, Eduard Steuermann. Vienna: Universal, 1922.

_____. *Harmonierlehre.* 3rd edn. Vienna: Universal, 1922.

_____. *Moses und Aron.* Opera in three acts. Text, Arnold Schoenberg. Trans. Allen Forte. Piano reduction, Winfried Zillig. Mainz: Schotts, 1957.

_____. *Pierrot Lunaire.* Song cycle on poems of Albert Giraud. Trans. Otto Erich Hartleben. Piano reduction, Erwin Stein. Vienna: Universal, 1923.

_____. *Style and Idea.* Ed., Leonard Stein. Trans. Leo Black. London: Faber & Faber, 1975.

_____. *Von Heute auf Morgen.* Opera in one act. Text, Max Blonda. Trans. Eric Smith. Mainz: Schotts, 1961.

Schorske, Carl E. *Fin-de-Siècle Vienna: Politics and Culture.* New York: Knopf, 1980.

Searle, Humphrey. "Busoni's *Doktor Faust.*" *The Monthly Musical Record* (March-April, 1936), 54–6.

Simrock, Karl. *Puppenspiel.* (See Geissler, H. W.)

Skelton, Geoffrey. "Schoenberg's *Moses und Aron*." *The Musical Times* 95 (1954), 304–5.

Slonimsky, Nicolas. *Music Since 1900*. 4th edn. New York: Scribner's, 1971.

Smith, Joan Allen. *Schoenberg and His Circle: A Viennese Portrait*. New York: Schirmer, 1986.

Smith, Patrick J. *The Tenth Muse: A Historical Study of the Opera Libretto*. New York: Knopf, 1970.

Stefan, Paul. "Schoenberg's Operas." *Modern Music* 2 (1925), 12–15.

_____. "Schoenberg's Operas." *Modern Music* 7 (1929-30), 24–28.

Stein, Jack. "From *Woyzeck* to *Wozzeck*: Alban Berg's Adaptation of Büchner." *The German Review* 47 (1972), 168–80.

Stein, Leonard. "Schoenberg's Jewish Identity (A Chronology of Source Material)." *Journal of the Arnold Schoenberg Institute* 3 (1979), 3–10.

Steiner, George. *The Death of Tragedy*. New York: Knopf, 1961.

Stevenson, Ronald. "Busoni—the Legend of a Prodigal." *The Score* 21 (1956), 15–30.

Strunk, Oliver, ed. *Source Readings in Music History*. New York: Norton, 1950.

Stuckenschmidt, Hans H. *Ferruccio Busoni: Chronicle of a European*. Trans. Sandra Morris. London: Calder & Boyars, 1970.

_____. "Introduction to *Moses und Aron*." *Paul Pisk: Essays in His Honor*. Austin: University of Texas Press, 1966.

_____. *Schoenberg: His Life, World and Work*. Trans. Humphrey Searle. London: Calder, 1977.

Vlad, Roman. "Busoni's Destiny." *The Score* 17 (1952), 3–10.

Vogel, Vladimir. "Impressions of Ferruccio Busoni." *Perspectives of New Music* (Spring-Summer, 1968), 167–73.

Wagner, Richard. *Gesammelte Schriften und Dichtungen*. 2nd edn. 10 vols. Leipzig: Fritsch, 1887–8.

Walker, Alan. "Schoenberg's Classical Background." *The Music Review* 19 (1958), 283–9.

Warlock, Peter, pseud. [Philip Heseltine]. *Frederick Delius*. With additions by Hubert Foss. New York: Oxford University Press, 1952.

Wedekind, Frank. *Stücke*. Munich: Langen Müller, 1970.

Weisstein, Ulrich, ed. *The Essence of Opera*. New York: Norton, 1969.

Wellesz, Egon. *Arnold Schoenberg*. Trans. W. H. Kerridge. London: Dent, 1925.

Werfel, Alma Mahler. *And the Bridge is Love*. New York: Harcourt, Brace, 1958.

_____. *Gustave Mahler: Memories and Letters*. Ed. Donald Mitchell, trans. Basil Creighton. London: Murray, 1968.

White, Pamela C. "Schoenberg and Schopenhauer." *Journal of the Arnold Schoenberg Institute* 8 (1984), 39–57.

_____. *Schoenberg and the God-Idea: The Opera "Moses und Aron"*. Ann Arbor: UMI Research, 1985.

      . "The Genesis of *Moses und Aron*." *Journal of the Arnold Schoenberg Institute* 6 (1982), 8–55.

Wörner, Karl H. "Arnold Schoenberg and the Theater." *The Musical Quarterly* 48 (1962), 444–60.

      . "Schoenberg's Biblical Opera *Moses und Aron*." *The Musical Quarterly* 40 (1954), 403–12.

      . *Schoenberg's "Moses und Aron"*. Trans. Paul Hamburger. London: Faber & Faber, 1963.

Youngren, William H. "Berg's *Lulu*." *The Atlantic Monthly* 260–3 (1987), 93–6.

Index

Opera has long been considered a form of music, but in his book *Opera as Dramatic Poetry* Wallace Dace suggests that our perception of this richly complex art form is changing. Although music remains the primary means of expression, modern operas seem more closely related to the drama than to the symphony. Part of the reason for this may be the tendency of many composers since Wagner to write their own librettos, then set them to music. In this way, the composer maintains control over all the elements of his opera: plot, characters, lines, stage movement, scenery, and lighting, as well as the music. Following this line of thought, Dace examines the major operas of four modern composers who created their own texts—Frederick Delius, Ferrucio Busoni, Arnold Schoenberg, and Alban Berg. And in his concluding chapter, he formulates a definition of opera derived from Aristotle's *Poetics*.

Cover photo: Günter Reich as Jack the Ripper and Karan Armstrong as Lulu in the final scene of Alban Berg's *Lulu* in a production conducted by Jesus Lopez Cobos, directed by Götz Friedrich, and designed by Andreas Reinhardt at the Deutsche Oper Berlin, 1982.